Afghanistan's Endless War

Afghanistan's Endless War

State Failure, Regional Politics,
and the Rise of the Taliban

LARRY P. GOODSON

UNIVERSITY OF WASHINGTON PRESS

Seattle and London

For the Afghan people,
in hopes that they soon know peace again

Library of Congress Cataloging-in-Publication Data
Goodson, Larry P.
Afghanistan's endless war : state failure, regional politics,
and the rise of the Taliban /
Larry P. Goodson.
p. cm.
Includes bibliographical references and index.
ISBN 0-295-98050-8 (alk. paper)
1. Afghanistan—History—1989-
2. Afghanistan—Social conditions.
I. Title.
DS371.3 .G66 2001
958.1—dc21
00-060701

Contents

Maps and Tables

Preface

I first saw Afghanistan in 1986, from high in the Khyber Pass. I was standing at an outpost of the Khyber Rifles, the Pakistani military unit that has guarded that section of the frontier since the colonial days of the British Raj. As the Pakistani briefing officer explained the positions of Soviet and Afghan army units on the other side of the border, I saw hazy mountains in the distance. Behind those somewhat sinister hills lay the hidden land of Afghanistan, crossroads of Asia. I was hooked. My childhood fascination with the "mysterious East" had finally brought me to this barren outcropping, near where the regimental crests of British units that had served and bled in the area were proudly maintained by the Khyber Rifles, current masters of the terrain. On the other side of the border, Soviet troops were serving and bleeding in Afghanistan. Would their regimental crests be accorded the same respect one day in Afghanistan? I didn't think so.

I was in Pakistan in 1986–1987 on a fellowship from the American Institute of Pakistan Studies to collect data for my doctoral dissertation on the relationship between the Afghan refugees, Afghan fighters, and Pakistani support for both. I lived in Peshawar, capital of the North-West Frontier Province of Pakistan, during that year. Peshawar was then, as it had often been before in its history, an Afghan town. Always the gateway to Central Asia, Peshawar was then teeming with Afghans, de facto headquarters of both a massive refugee relief effort and a grim resistance campaign against the Soviet occupation. Only the war correspondents know for sure, I suppose, but places like Peshawar in the mid-1980s must be rare. Everyone there was connected to the war, or so it seemed. The place reeked of intrigue (and also reeked literally, owing to the open sewers in the old city). Assassination and murder were commonplace as Soviet agents slipped across the border to destabilize Pakistan's support for the Afghans. Peshawar was actually the "car bomb capital of the world" that year, although Beirut received all the press coverage for such activity, and there was never a night when tracers did not arc over the city, always fired by persons unknown for reasons unknown.

I probably should not have been surprised, then, that so many people thought I was an agent of the US Central Intelligence Agency (CIA). I mean, there I was, driving around in an old jalopy that looked like the perfect candidate for a car bomb, dressed and groomed (long beard and everything) and to the best of my limited ability speaking like an Afghan, and people were supposed to believe I was a student? Right! With a flimsy cover story like that, and with so many real intelligence agents running around, it is little wonder that people thought I was one, too. I often wondered what the real CIA agents thought about my inadvertent impersonation.

Fortunately for the intelligence community, I really was only a student engaged in research, and I learned early on that some important things were happening in forgotten, distant Afghanistan. For example, as 1986 began, it was not entirely certain that the Soviet Union would not continue south through Pakistan to the Arabian Sea. By the time I left in 1987, it was obvious that the Soviet Union was going to lose in Afghanistan. Perhaps the full implications of that loss were not yet clear—that the defeat in Afghanistan would bring about the crumbling of the Soviet empire, although this happened with startling suddenness less than two years later when the withdrawal of Soviet troops from Afghanistan signaled to Eastern European intellectuals that the Brezhnev Doctrine was dead.

Another major lesson I learned was that Afghanistan was not going to return to its prewar peaceful stability once the Soviets were gone. I remember some of the expatriates at the American Club and the Red Cross–run Bamboo Bar (about the only places in town where you could get a drink) in 1987 running a betting pool on how long it would take the *mujahideen*—the Afghan rebels—to sweep into Kabul after the Soviet troops pulled out. Optimists were guessing days and weeks; pessimists thought the Najibullah regime would hang on longer than that, perhaps a few months. I never bet, and more's the pity, because

I had come to realize that the war had deepened some powerful centrifugal forces within Afghan society even as it had discredited and destroyed the country's governmental institutions. Nonetheless, so long as the Soviets supported the communist regime in Kabul, even if from a distance, it would be impossible for the fractious mujahideen to win. The seeds of Afghanistan's state failure had been well planted by then—the deepening of ethnic tensions, the rising of Islamist ideology, and the entrenching of a narcotics economy were all becoming the defining characteristics of the country. Virtually overnight, Afghanistan changed from the West's valiant ally, waging a frontline war against communist expansion, to a rogue state, home to drug traffickers, Islamist terrorists, and bloody warlords. I wish I had placed a bet, but even I, the most pessimistic man in Peshawar in 1987, could not have predicted that fourteen years later Afghanistan would still be wracked by a seemingly interminable civil war and that all the features that were emerging as problems during the 1980s would cause the collapse of the country in the 1990s.

In early 1992, shortly after the Soviet Union passed into the history books, the Najibullah regime fell, and groups of squabbling, cantankerous mujahideen descended on Kabul, which they almost immediately began to destroy as they fought among themselves over who would run the city and country. I went back to Afghanistan to see for myself the new rulers in action. One evening in August I found myself walking with several foreign journalists after curfew, trying to get back to my dwelling in the Wazir Akbar Khan section of Kabul from the UN compound, where I had had dinner. Suddenly, a couple of overloaded jeeps came roaring down the street and skidded to a stop next to us. Our momentary terror changed to relief when it turned out that the young soldiers of the new government merely wanted to offer us a ride. We clambered in. I sat in the back, wedged up tight against the Kalashnikov rifle of a soldier who was probably no more than fifteen or sixteen. As we bounced along, I realized that this boy-man represented a whole generation of Afghans who knew nothing but war. He smiled, happy at the prospect of the looming conflict, which in fact broke out a couple of days later, just after I had left Kabul to return to Pakistan. That the fight would be with rival Afghan factions divided increasingly along ethnic lines—not a holy war against foreign invaders—seemed not to trouble my young friend. On my way back to Peshawar, over a rutted road destroyed by war and lack of maintenance, my bus passed through nineteen checkpoints, all representing different groups that controlled different sections of the road. Afghanistan was clearly a failing state whose political institutions did not function and where loyalties were being expressed on very local levels.

I returned to Afghanistan yet again in 1997, this time to see the country under the rule of the Taliban, a group of former mujahideen turned religious students from the southwest of the country who had taken control of Kabul in September 1996 and were making inroads into the northern part of the country in 1997. Again, the evidence of state failure was everywhere, from the still-unrepaired roads (although the local checkpoints had been cleaned out) and the absence of public utilities (Herat, for example, had only generators for its electricity) to the desultory quiet in virtually every government office I ventured into. But the Taliban presence was apparent and sometimes ominous, especially in the fear that hung around women like the *burqas* (head-to-toe shrouds) the Taliban made them wear. For the first time in Afghanistan I was approached by women on the street, forced into begging or worse by harsh Taliban social policies that took away their livelihoods. Also for the first time I found that the "hassle factor" had increased to an annoying level as teenage Taliban on the streets restricted my movements, my ability to take photographs, what I wore and carried in my bag, and so on. In the past I had always been happy to be on an adventure in Afghanistan. This time I was happy to leave, for Afghanistan had become a place of petty, narrow-minded intolerance. As the war ground relentlessly on, the failure of the state and civil society caused the intolerance to degenerate into increasingly virulent ethnic hatred and cleansing.

Yet as a scholar, I cannot leave Afghanistan behind, for its importance to the international system continues. Its role as the catalyst to the end of the Cold War is over, but now it has become the archetype of a failed state and a perfect example of how nonstate actors move into the vacuum created when a state fails. That this phenomenon is occurring in a volatile region amid other struggling states just makes more compelling our need to understand Afghanistan today.

In order to understand Afghanistan and the region it anchors, we must focus attention on six critical factors, which are analyzed in the pages that follow. These factors are Afghanistan's ethnic-linguistic cleavages, its social structures, its religious ideology, its long and devastating conflict, its geopolitical position, and its limited economic development. The relative weight of each factor in understanding Afghanistan shifts with time, making it impossible and invalid to suggest that one or several of them are sufficient to explain the situation there. Thus, much of the recent scholarship on Afghanistan's modern period, which focuses on one or a few factors at a time, falls short in helping us to understand Afghanistan.

For example, Olivier Roy's excellent work on Afghanistan, including his *Islam and Resistance in Afghanistan* (1986, 1990), has concentrated most heavily on the rise and role of political Islam in the struggle for the soul of modern Afghanistan. As Islamism became transformed into neo-fundamentalism in Afghanistan, Roy's disillusionment with what he came to perceive as an intellectually barren ideology led to *The Failure of Political Islam* (1994a) and *From Holy War to Civil War* (1995). In the latter book, Roy suggested that the ideological failure of political Islam in Afghanistan has contributed to a resurgence of ethnicity as the chief determinant of identity, a theme that has appeared in other of his recent writings.[1] Roy tends to downplay the role of outside actors in Afghanistan, however, especially in relation to economic development there.

Other recent work on the impact of ideology, religion, and ethnicity in Afghanistan also tends to overlook or dismiss the geopolitical role of outside actors, ignore the geoeconomic position of Afghanistan, and perceive the recent military struggle in that unhappy country as an outcome of these more enduring forces, rather than as an important independent variable in its own right.[2] For example, in his *Heroes of the Age* (1996), David Edwards argues that "Afghanistan's troubles derive less from divisions between groups or from the ambitious strivings of particular individuals than they do from the moral incoherence of Afghanistan itself" (p. 3). His concern about the failure of the Afghan state to make itself both legitimate and necessary is echoed in recent work by Nazif Shahrani, who contends that the Western inspired imperial state fits Afghanistan's realities rather poorly.[3]

Barnett Rubin's work best exemplifies the political economy approach to understanding Afghanistan.[4] Through his numerous writings he explains much of Afghanistan's modern social and political developments in terms of the rentier state model of its economic foundations.[5] Where Roy sees new elite formation and power as products of the transformative effects of war and the traditional ties of ethnicity,[6] Rubin understands the transformation of Afghanistan's social order in terms of how the state acquired and distributed resources.[7] Afghanistan's economy, both before and during the war, was based primarily on agriculture and pastoralism, neither of which generated large amounts of revenue. Moreover, for most of the twentieth century Afghan rulers concluded that they "could not effect global social transformations in Afghanistan but should instead establish and expand a nation-state enclave insulated as much as possible from the traditional society.... Instead, while compromising with the traditional forces that had brought them to power, they forged links with the international state system and market that enabled them gradually to enlarge a state-dominated export enclave centered in Kabul."[8] Again, though, this analysis only tells part of the story.

There is also a growing body of scholarship that explores the military, humanitarian, and diplomatic role of outside actors in Afghanistan. Perhaps inevitably, most of the literature on the recent military struggle in Afghanistan grew out of the Soviet-Afghan period of the war.[9] Many of the Afghan War books of the 1980s were written by journalists and provide anecdotal accounts of their little corners of the war, mixing a modicum of analysis into their tales of the perils and rigors of reporting from the Hindu Kush.[10] None of these works explores in detail what happened in Afghanistan after the Soviets left in 1989 or the Najibullah regime fell in 1992, and there has been no comprehensive effort by independent scholars to document the destruction of Afghanistan caused by two decades of high-intensity warfare and to integrate an understanding of that destruction with the other factors that have been so influential in modern Afghanistan.

A small but useful literature on the humanitarian and diplomatic activities of outside actors in Afghanistan helps to highlight the more benign forms of foreign involvement there.[11] The growing awareness of Afghanistan's war as a regional problem that both threatens to spill over into neighboring countries and simultaneously proves to be an irresistible lure to the neighbors' desires to meddle in Afghanistan is just beginning to make its mark in published works.[12]

To date, no single work has analyzed both the comprehensive impact of the war on those factors that have historically been most influential in Afghanistan (ethnicity, state-versus-society struggles, Islamic ideology, economy) and the way in which Afghanistan today influences a dramatically changed region (geopolitics). My purpose in this book is to fill that gap and to provide readers with a comprehensive understanding of how various factors intersect and combine to shape Afghanistan today. Moreover, it is my contention that Afghanistan has a singular importance in the regions it touches and that it must also be understood in terms of how it influences its neighbors and other international actors. In this latter sense, Afghanistan provides a useful point of departure for understanding how failed and failing states, through the very ills that are brought about or exacerbated by their weakness, can have such disproportionate influence in regional and international politics in the new millennium.

To understand Afghanistan today, we must integrate the major themes in the recent scholarly literature on that country, for Afghanistan is explained partially by the significant cleavages that divide its population (ethnic, linguistic, regional, sectarian, racial, and tribal, often overlapping); partially by the ideological struggle between traditional, modern, and Islamist forces there;[13] partially by the gulf between state and society that has both led to and been exacerbated by the state's reliance on economic rents for development and consumption; and partially by the varied and multifarious web of influences wielded by outside actors in the country. Above all, we must understand the depth and range of transformations that more than two decades of enormously destructive war have produced in Afghanistan.

In this book I attempt to provide an integrated framework for understanding Afghanistan today by exploring the six factors that are most influential there, each in turn. To begin with, I show how Afghanistan's setting, especially its ethnic, religious, social, and geographic characteristics, has always limited the development of a strong Afghan state and has acquired renewed importance in the wake of the state's demise during the 1980s and early 1990s. This important framework for understanding Afghanistan, which explores two of the six factors in some depth (ethnic-linguistic cleavages and social structures), is introduced in chapter 1. Second, I examine Afghanistan's early history of inadequate state building and tepid nationalism and how these factors left a weak state poised on the eve of its descent into the hell of modern war in 1978. Chapter 2 is devoted to an exploration of the historical factors that, in combination with Afghanistan's ethnolinguistic, religious, social, and geographical setting, explain its failure to develop into a strong state by the modern era. This chapter's analysis helps provide an understanding of how geopolitics and economic development prior to 1978 brought Afghanistan to the point it has reached today.

Chapter 3 provides a history of how high-technology, protracted war affected low-technology, traditional Afghanistan and made it into a collapsed state and fragmented society that threatens regional stability and development. This chapter analyzes the war as having so far passed through a series of eight stages of increasing, then decreasing, intensity.

The remainder of the book shows how Afghanistan has been transformed by modern war, how its tenuous claim to statehood has been undercut by the vast changes imposed by the events of the last twenty years, and how its present disarray bodes ill for the region it anchors. Chapter 4 documents the widespread destruction of Afghanistan's physical infrastructure and human resources, as well as the profound alteration of its ethnic-religious balance, socioeconomic system, and sociocultural framework. This chapter gives special attention to the ideological struggle within Afghanistan that has given rise to the present Taliban movement there. This leads into chapter 5, which explores how Afghanistan fits into the changing regional environments of Central, South, and Southwest Asia, the three regions in which its presence and influence are felt. Especially important in this chapter is an analysis of how outside actors continue to affect Afghanistan, and I devote considerable attention to the complexity of relationships within Afghanistan's sphere of influence. It is here that I explore how the emerging regional powers contest with one another both within and through Afghanistan for geopolitical and geoeconomic reasons.

The book concludes with an analysis of the future of Afghanistan, examining several scenarios in terms not only of their likelihood but also of their effects on Afghanistan's neighbors. In chapter 6 I also return to a consideration of what state failure means both for failed states themselves and for the stability of the regions in which they are located, assessed in light of empirical evidence from the Afghanistan case study.

This book would never have been written without the support of numerous friends and scholars around the world. The field research on which it is based was made possible by grants from the American Institute of Pakistan Studies, the American University in Cairo, Campbell University, and the Federalist Research Institute. During my research trips to Afghanistan and Pakistan in 1986, 1987, 1992, and 1997, hundreds of people, including Afghan mujahideen leaders and soldiers, allowed me to interview them or observe their living conditions in Afghanistan and the refugee camps of Pakistan. Most of these people must go unnamed here for their own safety, but their contribution to my understanding of the Afghan tragedy is gratefully acknowledged. I also interviewed or corresponded with many US, Afghan, and Pakistan government officials, UN officials, journalists, analysts, and specialists on Afghanistan. Altogether, those who can be acknowledged include Anwar-ul-Haq Ahady, Herbert Bodman, David Champagne, William Coughlin, John Dixon, Brad Hanson, Edward Haynes, Anil Hira, John

Kelly, Charles H. Kennedy, Steve Masty, Theodore Mataxis, Sean Naylor, Adeeb Popolzai, Rasul Baksh Rais, Olivier Roy, Barnett Rubin, Robert Rupen, Saeed Tahirkheli, Marvin Weinbaum, James White, Ahmed Zeb, and the staff of the US Educational Foundation in Pakistan. Although he passed away in 1989, the great scholar of Afghanistan Louis Dupree had a profound effect on my approach to understanding the Afghans. To his widow, Nancy Hatch Dupree, still working in Peshawar on behalf of the Afghans, I would say that I hope Louis would be proud of this effort.

I also wish to thank the anonymous readers of the manuscript and my excellent editors, Michael Duckworth and Jane Kepp, for their efforts to improve this book. Last, I thank my wife and partner, Tomasa Rodriguez Goodson, and our children, Alexandra and Jonathan, for enduring the time I spent away from them, both in body and in mind, as I explored this tragic subject over many years. To all of those named above I offer my heartfelt thanks and my assurances that any errors that remain in this work are mine alone.

Afghanistan's Endless War

1 / Afghanistan in the Post–Cold War World

Although it is little noted today, one of the world's most famous border crossings lies between Afghanistan and Pakistan at a tiny town called Torkham. It is there that the fabled Khyber Pass cuts through Pushtun Afridi tribal territory to take the traveler out of the high mountains of Central Asia to the plains of India. These days there are a lot of people on the street in Torkham because under the Taliban, the most recent rulers in Kabul, long-haul buses no longer cross the border. Instead, passengers get out and walk the last few hundred meters and submit to a desultory inspection by a teenage Taliban soldier before passing into Pakistan's Khyber Agency. Actually, the little stroll out of Afghanistan is quite refreshing, for before it occurs the traveler will have bounced for hours (three if from Jalalabad, ten if from Kabul) over roads that no longer deserve that name and through country that is largely barren of life. To get out and walk at the end of such a journey brings an almost visceral sense of separation, of leaving it behind, that many travelers desperately need when departing Afghanistan today.

Not that many travelers find their way to Afghanistan at the beginning of the twenty-first century. Since the rabidly puritanical Taliban movement swept into Kabul in September 1996, Afghanistan has been cut off from most of the rest of the world. Only Pakistan, Saudi Arabia, and the United Arab Emirates have recognized the Taliban as the legitimate government of Afghanistan; the rest of the world either recognizes the ousted government of Burhanuddin Rabbani, now clinging desperately for survival to a small northern stronghold, or ignores Afghanistan altogether. Taliban policies that degrade and harm women have raised the ire of Western human rights and feminist organizations, while Taliban sanctuary for suspected terrorists and the blossoming of the opium-heroin trade under Taliban patronage has prompted Western nations, led by the United States, to adamantly withhold recognition for their regime, despite its de facto control of nearly 90 percent of the country by late 2000.

Prior to the Taliban, years of war and lawlessness had destroyed much of the country, driven millions of its people into exile, and brought its economy to a standstill. The "Hippie Trail" that brought thousands of travelers through Afghanistan to India in the 1960s and 1970s no longer exists, and virtually no business organizations have been willing to invest in such a troubled country. Only a handful of outsiders venture into Afghanistan today—aid workers, journalists, intelligence agents—not counting the thousands of Islamists who have come to join the Taliban on their holy crusade to conquer Afghanistan, establish an Islamic state and society there, and then ... what? Poised between Central Asia, the Middle East, and South Asia, is Afghanistan the headquarters of a new global movement of Islamist militancy that blends anti-Western adherents from all over the Islamic world? Or is Afghanistan today merely the shattered remnant of a country destroyed by two decades of horrible war, whose society is now struggling to re-create itself?

Certainly Afghanistan today is one of the poorest and most troubled countries in the world. No longer isolated in the mountain fastnesses of central Asia, it finds itself a critical geographic crossroads once again—as it has been through the ages. It began the twentieth century as the buffer state that separated the British and Russian empires; it ends the century as the linchpin to trade and political development in Central Asia. Afghanistan will be the key to peace and stability, economic development and growth, and social change and human development in this region of the world. Thus it comes as no surprise that all of Afghanistan's neighbors are deeply involved in manipulating its internal affairs. Pakistan and Iran, Russia and India, Uzbekistan and Tajikistan, Turkmenistan and Saudi Arabia, even Turkey and China: all have significant interests in Afghanistan and most have supported at least one of the many parties contesting for power in that country's interminable and devastating civil war.

Afghanistan is a country shaped and molded by its experience with more than two decades of war. The Afghan War has been one of the deadliest and most persistent conflicts of the second half of the twentieth century. Nearly 2 million Afghans have been killed so far (as well as at least 15,000 Soviet soldiers during the 1980s), and 600,000 to 2 million wounded.[1] More than 6 million Afghans fled to Pakistan and Iran, producing the world's largest single refugee population since 1981, while at least 2 million more Afghans were internally displaced.[2] Thus, more than 50 percent of Afghanistan's indigenous population (estimated at 15 to 17 million persons at the war's beginning, now estimated to be as many as 22 million) became casualties—killed, wounded, or made homeless by the war.

Every region of Afghanistan has been touched by the war. Even residents of the government-held urban centers in the 1980s were not safe. The countryside was ravaged, with widespread destruction of villages, fields, orchards, and irrigation systems. The Soviet army in Afghanistan and the Afghan communist government planted an estimated thirty million mines throughout the country, most of them completely unmarked and unmapped.[3] Afghanistan's natural resources, particularly the natural gas reserves near Shiberghan, flowed north to the Soviet Union during the 1980s, and Afghanistan's economy collapsed. Today Afghanistan's chief export is opium, in which it surpassed Burma in 1998 to become the world's leading producer. Otherwise, its economy is still in complete disarray. The education system and other modernizing sectors of Afghan society were completely disrupted,[4] and the struggle for control of the central government delays efforts to improve the situation. Afghanistan, a desperately underdeveloped country attempting to modernize throughout the twentieth century, finally caught up to the modern world—in high-technology warfare. The result has been the ruin of the country and society and very nearly the destruction of the people and their culture.

That such an impoverished and war-torn country should have such an important role to play in its neighbors' futures is not unusual, nor is the sad reality that there has been little effort to end its long war or rebuild its shattered infrastructure. The changed context of international affairs in the wake of the Cold War, which Afghanistan played a pivotal role in bringing to an end, now endows Afghanistan's role with greater importance while simultaneously making it harder to understand that role or predict its dynamics exactly. Nonetheless, in this book I attempt to forecast Afghanistan's future and how that future will affect the region in which Afghanistan is so centrally located. In a broader context, I adopt the thesis that Afghanistan's situation is illustrative of a significant problem facing the post–Cold War world. It is useful to understand what is happening in Afghanistan not just because its continued turmoil has such a great influence on the region but also because of what it reveals about the transforming nature of the international system today.

THE STATE IN THE POST–COLD WAR ERA

For the past 350 years, the international system has been constructed of states, although most of the more than 190 states that exist at the beginning of the new millennium are less than 50 years old. A *state* is a political entity that has a recognized territory, a population that sees itself as belonging to the state, and institutions of government that are sovereign within that territory. Although the word *nation* is often used synonymously with state, *nation* refers more to the shared identity, often centered on a common language, religion, history, or other cultural trait, that a group of people sometimes feels. Psychological attachment to a nation, or *nationalism*, has often been central to state formation in the modern era. The relationship between state formation, which involves the creation of coercive, extractive, and regulatory institutions of governance, and nation building, which is often centered on the use of symbols and the selective interpretation of history to create the psychological bonding characteristic of nationalism, differs from one country to another. Indeed, not all states possess strong nationalism, for they may be multinational or have national groups that straddle their borders with other countries. Nor do all national groups possess states. Owing in part to the strength of its nation building, but also to other factors discussed in greater detail later, a state may be relatively weak or strong in relation to both its own society and other states in the international system.

The end of the Cold War has altered the environment in which the state exists, presenting different states with a range of both challenges and opportunities. How well a given state does in this altered environment depends on its position in the international and regional systems in which it exists, its internal stability and strength, and its regional conditions. So far, however, there have been some obvious winners and losers. The United States, the major Cold War victor, today finds itself the world's sole superpower, with the military power, robust economy, and political voice to lead the international order. Russia, the major

Cold War loser, has become but a weakened component of the now-dissolved Soviet Union, and despite possessing a large nuclear arsenal and substantial regional weight, its depressed economy and political instability make even its claim of great power status a tenuous one.

The impact of the end of the Cold War on other states has been just as mixed. On the one hand, it released the middle and regional powers in the international system from the constraints imposed by a bipolar world. In the 1990s regional powers found they could once again engage in foreign policy-making independent of Washington or Moscow, and geopolitical maneuvering began in numerous capitals throughout the world. Although the post–Cold War international order may well be unipolar on one level, the lack of clear hegemonic behavior by the United States has contributed to the development of a robust multi-polarity.[5] Not only China, Russia, and the European powers but also numerous Third World countries have engaged in power projection, arms acquisition, and other such activities vis-à-vis neighboring countries, especially as it has become increasingly obvious that neither the United States nor the United Nations has established clear standards for intervention in regional conflicts.[6]

On the other hand, the elimination of Cold War constraints has not only provided opportunities for second- and third-tier powers but also posed problems for weak states. No longer important to the major powers for strategic reasons, these states, predominantly found among the poorer developing countries, face challenges to their continued existence from a variety of threats. Indeed, for these states, the end of the Cold War era has revealed an international system that is flawed and troubled.

For the weaker states, the system itself and the concept of the state are under attack from below and above. Both the forces of "tribalism" (nationalism, religious fundamentalism, political dogmatism) and "globalism" (integration, transnational regimes, multinational corporations) threaten the existence of the weak state today, and even the continuation of a world system organized around states.[7] To Europeans and North Americans, who live in healthy, mature states and for whom this international system feels natural on the basis of their long experience with both its founding and its domination, its potential collapse threatens to destabilize the foundations of their world. Most of the world's population, however (about 80 percent), lives in the developing world, and many of these people reside in states whose political structures, boundaries, and even very existence are highly artificial, often mere legacies of a now-repudiated colonial history whose passing was never lamented. The surge of state building that accompanied the decolonization of the European empires in the twentieth century did not always produce strong, vibrant states with loyal, nationalistic populations.[8] Thus, it is not uncommon in many Third World countries for national loyalty to be quite weak and for the institutions of the state (governmental, financial, social) to suffer from a crisis of legitimacy. Yet in some fashion or another, these states basically held together for most of the period following the decline of the colonial empires.[9]

That is, they held together until the glue holding the international system in place—the Cold War and the bipolar structure that characterized it—finally weakened with age. With the end of the Cold War, the weaker states in the international system began to fall apart, no longer buttressed by client-patron relationships with the major powers. The communist countries of the Second World began to unravel first, but they were followed quickly by weak Third World states such as Ethiopia, Somalia, Sudan, and Zaire (now Congo). Although these countries had never developed into strong states, Cold War bipolarity in the international system had imposed on them a constraining rigidity that assured their continued existence. After the Cold War ended, these states began to change, to be transformed, and in some cases, ultimately to dissolve. It was always assumed in the West that with the end of the Cold War would come the fundamental alteration—even the end—of the Eastern European states. It was less well understood that the end of the Cold War could also sound the death knell for many weak Third World states.

Afghanistan is such a state: a weak and fragmented country on the verge of collapse and perhaps even disintegration, brought to this condition by the Cold War struggle of the superpowers and their post–Cold War disinterest in its fate. Afghanistan's state structures persist largely because of neighboring countries' maneuvering for geopolitical and economic advantages in the post–Cold War power vacuum in the region. A distant and uninterested United States and a weakened Russia exert limited influence in Afghanistan's part of the world at the moment, allowing resurgent or newly emergent regional powers such as Iran, Pakistan, Turkey, and Uzbekistan to jockey for position.

Afghanistan sits astride three major regions—the Middle East with its Islamic civilization, South Asia with its Hindic civilization, and Central Asia with its Orthodox Christian and Confucian/Sinic civilizations—and it guards the southern access to the oil and mineral wealth of Central Asia.[10] The geopolitical and economic stakes are high for

Afghanistan's neighbors, which leads them all to play proxy games in Afghanistan's seemingly endless civil war. Thus it is that Afghanistan, a country whose central government and formal economy have essentially ceased to exist, can influence several major regions of the international system. Indeed, the situation in Afghanistan today reveals many of the dynamics affecting the entire international system as it undergoes a great transition. It demonstrates what happens when weak states come under enormous internal and external pressures to survive, and it illustrates how regional powers compete for influence in the absence of superpower leadership.

THE PROCESS AND IMPACT OF STATE FAILURE

Both nation building and state consolidation in certain transitional (formerly Second and Third World) states have been delayed or even arrested by factors both domestic and international. Domestically, societal cleavages between competing ethnic, linguistic, religious, and economic groups frequently cause or exacerbate fragmentation, undercutting the concept of the nation. (By fragmentation, I mean the weakening of a central government's control over its periphery, which may or may not lead to state disintegration.) Economic underdevelopment, coupled with poor political institutionalization, further fractures society between modernizing and traditional elites, leaving peasants and the urban underclass alienated and largely outside the struggle for domestic power.[11] Even geographical and topographical factors, such as vestigial colonial boundaries, strategic location or isolation, and absence or possession of critical resources, may undermine the creation of strong states in the developing world.[12]

International factors also have delayed nation and state building in the Second and Third Worlds. The existence of the Cold War for most of the post–World War II period created an essentially bipolar international system that often affected developing states. Superpower competition quickly moved beyond the frozen frontiers imposed by the Iron Curtain in Europe to the more fluid developing areas and was frequently manifested in efforts to manipulate struggles for power within Third World countries.[13] Regional conflicts of the 1980s in Afghanistan, Angola, Central America, Cambodia, and the Horn of Africa were the logical extension of a pattern of superpower involvement in Third World conflicts that had assumed even more blatant proportions a generation earlier, especially in Southeast Asia. Motivated by different ideologies and worldviews, each superpower saw the other as engaged in dangerous expansion (US perception of the USSR) or unwarranted containment (USSR view of the US) and sought allies and clients in the developing world. The two superpowers were drawn into ideologically tinged anticolonial struggles, the USSR supporting fledgling leftist revolutionaries while the US sought to maintain pro-Western regimes through counterrevolutionary tactics. The development of an international economic framework that was biased structurally against the single-commodity-based economies of many developing states further limited their ability to mitigate internal unrest brought on by scarce resources that often were distributed inequitably.[14]

The combination of these factors frequently led to unrest, rebellion, revolution, and civil war in the developing countries. These forms of political violence can hasten or delay the process of nation building, serving either to eliminate cleavages and resolve power struggles or to deepen existing divisions and harden attitudes. Similarly, political violence may allow the coercive arm of the state, its military and security forces, to penetrate society more completely, thus advancing state building, or it may lead to the destruction of existing state institutions, undermining state building. There is no clear prescription for the role of violence in nation and state building. For example, whereas revolution may have some value for restoring a lost sense of nationhood and cultural heritage to colonial peoples, post-independence violence that continues as part of the internal struggle to shape national agendas is generally destructive of national unity and state political institutions. If the nation being destroyed, however, is replaced by a new nation or nations whose foundations run along more viable ethnic-linguistic-religious or economic lines (e.g., Eritrea), or if improved state institutions are created out of the rubble of those institutions that are destroyed, then the violence may have served a useful purpose after all.[15]

With the end of the Cold War, Third World states that have labored to develop politically and economically no longer face many of the constraints mentioned earlier. Especially critical is the sudden absence of an organized power system in international politics as the major powers turn inward to reorient resources once committed to the continuation of the Cold War and as the second-order powers of Europe concern themselves with further integration of the European Union. In this power vacuum the continued existence of states that have had only marginal success at political institutionalization and have been saddled with internal problems appears no longer significant to the international power balance. Thus, in the face of challenges to their continued existence, many weak states are failing, either through the collapse of their governing institutions, through internal fragmentation, or even through political disintegration. Although this phenomenon has been most obvious so far in the former Soviet Union, former Yugoslavia, and former Czechoslovakia, all of which have disintegrated, it is appearing in virulent form in Somalia, Sudan, India, Pakistan, Sri Lanka, sub-Saharan Africa, and Afghanistan. More ominously, the collapse of one state may have profound implications for regional stability, as is the case in Afghanistan.

The post–Cold War world is on the verge of profound change, as Robert Kaplan suggested in his provocative article "The Coming Anarchy": "Most people believe that the political earth since 1989 has undergone immense change. But it is minor compared with what is yet to come. The breaking apart and remaking of the atlas is only now beginning. The crack-up of the Soviet empire and the coming end of Arab-Israeli military confrontation are merely prologues to the really big changes that lie ahead."[16] Some of this "remaking of the atlas" will occur in the developed world, and some of it will involve the integration of economies, polities, and even societies (e.g., in the integrating states of the European Union, Germany, Yemen, and possibly Korea and China). But the bigger and more threatening changes will occur in the developing world and will involve state failure. Weak states will be especially prone to this malady and may well infect their surrounding regions with the violence and instability that generally accompany state failure.

Weak states have distinctive political, social, economic, demographic, and even geographic characteristics. Among these characteristics are limited political institutionalization and penetration in society, strong ethnic, linguistic, and/or religious divisions, and slow economic and social development. Some other characteristics may also be present, such as rapid population growth and/or resource problems, the interference of neighboring countries and/or big powers, and even geostrategic location. Weak states have poor capabilities "to *penetrate* society, *regulate* social relationships, *extract* resources, and *appropriate* or use resources in determined ways (author's emphasis)."[17] In the Cold War years, many weak states managed to maintain their territorial integrity because of the relative rigidity of the international system. In the more fluid post–Cold War era, an age of both globalist and localist pressures, weak states appear to be more likely to fail. That in itself is a phenomenon worthy of our attention, but its importance is compounded when we consider the impact that weak state dysfunction, collapse, fragmentation, and ultimately disintegration can have on regional and even international stability.

Afghanistan provides us an excellent case with which to explore this *weak state syndrome* that is such a threat to the international order in the new millennium. Four specific features of the Afghan case make it especially worthy of analysis in relation to weak state syndrome. First, it is an extremely weak state, almost the archetype of one, made all the weaker by two full decades of highly destructive war. Second, Afghanistan is the axle on which several regions swivel, one of which, Central Asia, is composed of newly emergent states, relatively weak themselves, that regional powers wish to influence. Third, Afghanistan also borders on or is influenced by several regional powers, all of which have begun to attempt to project their power in the wake of the Cold War. These include Russia, China, India, Pakistan, and Iran (the first four are nuclear powers), with Saudi Arabia and Turkey also having an interest. Finally, Afghanistan has been the on-again, off-again recipient of superpower and international attention and manipulation, which has contributed to its weakening yet holds out the greatest hope for shaping a viable future for the country.

UNDERSTANDING AFGHANISTAN:
THE PULL OF CENTRIFUGAL FORCES ON THE STATE

In order to have a foundation for understanding Afghanistan's present collapse and problematic future, it is necessary to have a bit of background on some important contextual features that shape Afghan politics. Several relatively unchanging factors made the emergence of a strong state in Afghanistan quite difficult and challenge the existence and eventual rebuilding of the Afghan nation and state today. I look closely at four factors here. First, Afghanistan's population is characterized by deep and multifaceted cleavages. People are divided foremost along ethnic and linguistic lines, but sectarian, tribal, and racial divisions also exist, and all of these are reinforced by a spatial pattern of population distribution into different regions of the country. Second, Afghanistan's religious framework is based on a syncretic blend of various interpretations of Islamic doctrine with local customs, making the country simultaneously unified by one faith and divided by hundreds of variations on its practice. Third, in a country where tribal social groupings still exist, the social system is based on communal loyalties and emphasizes the local over higher-order identity formations. Fourth, the rugged topographical features and geographical position of Afghanistan, coupled with its lack of economic development, isolate it internationally and magnify the distance of its people from the government (map 1.1).[18] Often these factors combine to reinforce each other, and at other times they overlap each other, but collectively they create a rigid, if complex, foundation for modern Afghan politics. All of them hampered the emergence of a strong state in Afghanistan, and it is hardly surprising that after two decades of warfare they should be prominent once again.

A fifth factor of great importance is modern Afghan history, for the process of Afghan state building has also provided a framework within which current politics must occur. Afghanistan's location between and history of meddlesome neighbors have been especially significant among the historical factors that I explore in the next chapter. The rest of this chapter offers a look at the first four contextual factors.

Although Afghanistan became formally independent from British control after the Third Anglo-Afghan War in 1919, it had been a largely

MAP 1.1 Afghanistan and its immediate neighbors in 1997. Source: ReliefWeb.

independent entity, albeit rarely unified or occupying its present borders, since the mid-eighteenth century. With the rise of the Durrani Pushtun tribe in western Afghanistan in 1747, nation building began, but such unity as did come about was always fragile, and a wide gulf existed between state and society.[19]

Afghanistan has never been a homogeneous nation but rather a collection of disparate groups divided along ethnic, linguistic, religious, and racial lines and forced together by the vagaries of geopolitics. Ethnicity is the most important contextual factor shaping Afghanistan today, as it has been throughout Afghanistan's history. Based on language and self-identity, there are around twenty-five distinct groups in Afghanistan, but perhaps only half as many of any size and really only five that concern us here. These are the Pushtun, Tajik, Uzbek, Hazara, and Aimaq (also known as Chahar Aimaq) people (see map 1.2).

The Pushtuns are the dominant ethnic group in Afghanistan today (indeed, they have dominated Afghan society since the mid-eighteenth century) and the largest remaining tribal society in the world.[20] Approximately seventeen million Pushtuns straddle the Afghan-Pakistani border, living primarily in the south, southwest, center, and east of Afghanistan and in the Federally Administered Tribal Agencies (or Areas), North-West Frontier Province, and northern districts of Baluchistan Province of Pakistan. Pushtuns comprise about 45 percent of Afghanistan's population (now estimated at around 22 million), speak Pushtu, and are overwhelmingly Hanafi Sunni Muslims. Caucasoid in racial type, Pushtuns have been the source of the traditional leaders of the country. They are divided into three major groups. The Durrani tribe, which ruled Afghanistan from 1749 to 1978 (through the Barakzai clan of the Mohammadzai subtribe), is primarily from north and west of Kandahar. The Ghilzai tribe, which the Durranis defeated in their quest for power, is located more in the east and in pockets in the north, especially in the Zabul and Ghazni provinces of Afghanistan. And a catch-all group of the remaining tribes, the "true" Pukhtuns, lives to the north and east of the Durranis and Ghilzai in both Pakistan and Afghanistan and include prominent tribes such as the Afridi, Wazir, Mohmand, Mahsud, Jaji, Mangal, Zadran, Kakar, Khatak, Orakzai, and Shinwari. These tribes are the largest permanent political and social units in Afghanistan, but they are further divided into lineages or subtribes, known as *khels*, and still further subdivided into extended family groups or clans, called *khol* or *kor*.[21] The allegiance of the individual almost never goes beyond the tribal unit. These relationships were outlined more clearly after the Durrani Pushtuns acquired power in Afghanistan.

With the rise of the Pushtuns to prominence, their tribal code (known as the Pushtunwali) took the place of a legal system in the settling of disputes. Although the Pushtunwali is a conglomerate of local tribal codes, certain primary themes have emerged. These include *melmastia* and *mehrmapalineh* (both concerning hospitality to guests), *nanawati* (the right of asylum), *badal* (blood revenge), *tureh* (bravery),

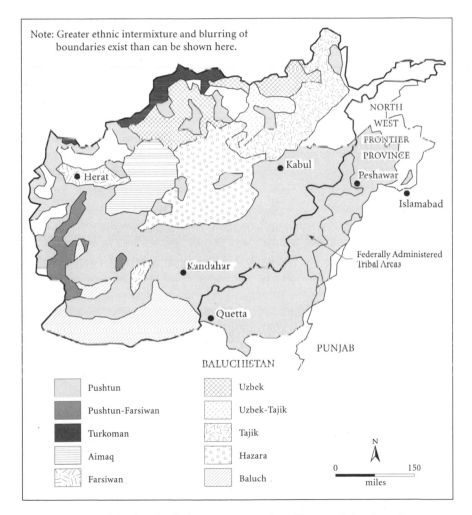

MAP 1.2 Afghanistan's ethnic groups. Reproduced by permission from Asta Olesen, *Islam and Politics in Afghanistan,* 1995.

meranah (manhood), *'isteqamat* (persistence), *sabat* (steadfastness), *imandari* (righteousness), *ghayrat* (defense of property and honor), and *namus* (defense of the honor of women).[22] As the Pushtunwali provided a code of behavior for the Afghan tribes, so the *jirga* (tribal assembly) provided a form of government. Syed Abdul Quddus captured the essence of this form of decision making when he stated, "The jirga, or assembly, by which most community business, both public and private, is settled ... is probably the closest approach to Athenian democracy that has existed since the original."[23] Membership is informal, and though jirgas are sometimes composed of just several reputable men, they frequently include all the men of a tribe. Although the creation of the jirga system has been attributed to the Khan of Kalat in the early 1760s, it certainly existed in some form earlier than that.[24] It is still the method for decision making in Afghanistan's rural Pushtun areas and Pakistan's Tribal Areas today, and in both areas it has proved to be an important intermediary mechanism between tribe and government.[25]

Despite the traditional dominance of the Pushtuns, there are significant minorities in Afghanistan, who generally resent the Pushtun ascendancy. These are largely nontribal minorities who speak Indo-European or Ural-Altaic languages and combine Western with Central Asian physical traits. They include Dari-speaking Tajiks, mainly Hanafi Sunni (some Ismaili Shia), who comprise 25 percent of the population and overlap into Tajikistan from northern Afghanistan (they are also traditionally found in Kabul). Turkic-speaking Uzbeks with Mongoloid features make up almost 10 percent of the population and, with the Turkomans, sit astride the border with the former Soviet Central Asian republics of Uzbekistan and Turkmenistan. These groups are primarily Hanafi Sunni. Afghanistan's largest Shia Muslim group (primarily Jafari Shia but also some Ismaili) is the Hazara people, who occupy the center of the country (known as the Hazarajat) and form perhaps 10 percent of the population. The Aimaq also make up perhaps 10 percent of the population and are found in western Afghanistan. The remainder of the population includes smaller ethnic groups such as the Dari-speaking Farsiwan and Qizilbash (who are, with the Hazara, primarily Jafari Shia) and the Baluch, Brahui, Moghol, and Nuristani (all Hanafi Sunni).[26]

None of these groups is entirely indigenous; that is, all of Afghanistan's major ethnic groups except for the Hazara overlap the international borders into neighboring countries, especially the Pushtuns (overlapping with northwestern Pakistan), the Tajiks (with Tajikistan), the Uzbeks (with Uzbekistan), and the Turkomans (with Turkmenistan and Uzbekistan). Moreover, the Hazara, Aimaq, and Farsiwan are thought to be ethnic cousins of the eastern Iranian Berberi.[27] Because all of Afghanistan's major ethnic groups either straddle the border with neighboring countries or have ethnolinguistic-religious ties to groups in neighboring countries, all of those countries have built-in incentives for meddling in Afghanistan's internal affairs.

Afghanistan's ethnic mixture has traditionally known a high propensity for violence, often between ethnic groups, subtribes, and even cousins. Only outside threats seem to unite the Afghans, and those alliances are temporary and limited. When the threat is eliminated or sufficiently reduced, people return to regular patterns of traditional warfare.

The second major factor that serves both to support the separation of Afghan society from the state and to foster divisions within society is religion, although the state successfully co-opted the religious hierarchy in the late nineteenth and early twentieth centuries in order to aid its rise over society.[28] Afghanistan is a Muslim country, with about 85 percent of the population Hanafi Sunni and the remainder Jafari (Twelver) Shia or Ismaili (Sevener) Shia. Prior to 1978, there were tiny populations of Hindus, Jews, and Sikhs in Afghanistan as well. The Hazara are Shia, as are some Tajiks, Farsiwan, Qizilbash, and Pushtuns. Afghanistan's Islam is basically a nonliterate, village Islam—a syncretic blending of basic Islamic beliefs with local practices such as those found in the Pushtunwali.[29] Several Sufi *tariqas* (brotherhoods) are still vibrant in Afghanistan, especially the Chishtiyya, Naqshbandiyya, and Qadiriyya orders.[30]

Islam has played different roles and is understood on different levels in Afghanistan, and Afghans have a complex and often contradictory attitude toward their sources of religious authority. Afghanistan hosts a mélange of Islam, perhaps influenced by the eclectic blend of religions found in nearby South Asia. In addition to the *'ulama* (religious scholars), co-opted as elsewhere by the state in the twentieth century, there are the *sayyids* (descendants of the Prophet Mohammed), Sufi *pirs* (holy men), and ordinary *mullahs* (preachers). And although the Prophet's cloak may be venerated in Kandahar, 'ulama may counsel kings, and the heads of Sufi orders may be patrons to thousands of devoted followers, for the average Afghan the religious authority figure is the village mullah, whose ignorance and low status are best symbolized in jokes about the greedy Mullah Nasruddin. Throughout Afghanistan local authority has traditionally been exercised by the landowning *khan*s (landed elites) and village/tribal *malik*s (headmen), not by the lowly mullahs.[31]

Despite the development of a violent and unremitting *jihad* (religious or holy war) and the rise of political Islam during the 1980s in Afghanistan, and despite legends concerning the early and widespread conversion of the Afghan people to Islam, religion has only recently been of great importance there.[32] The conversion process was not nearly as rapid or complete as it has traditionally been portrayed, and even now there is a blending of early animist beliefs with mainstream Islamic thought in more remote areas of Afghanistan (among the Pamiri and Wakhi people of the rugged northeast, for example, or among the Nuristanis who were forcibly converted in the 1890s). Basic Islamic beliefs are widely understood, but as Louis Dupree noted, "the Islam practiced in Afghan villages, nomad camps, and most urban areas (the ninety to ninety-five percent non-literates) would be almost unrecognizable to a sophisticated Muslim scholar. Aside from faith in Allah and in Mohammad as the Messenger of Allah, most beliefs relate to localized, pre-Muslim customs."[33] The vast majority of the people believe but are not particularly religious. Islam and the Pushtunwali in concert do govern daily life, but they are so pervasive that they are generally taken for granted, a luxury found only in societies with a homogeneous religion. That is how the Taliban can simultaneously emerge from traditional elements of Afghan society and yet be so alien to many parts of that society.

The major way in which Islam has traditionally acquired a more active role in Afghan society is by providing the ideology and driving force behind a jihad—then it can weld the tribes together into an intractable force against alien infidels. The Afghan-Soviet War of 1979–1989 is only the latest in a number of jihads in which Afghans have risen during the last 250 years; the next most recent was the Kashmir *lashkar* (war party) of 1947–1948.[34] Although the post-Soviet struggle in Afghanistan is a war among factions, all of whom are composed of Muslims, the Taliban have consistently presented their fight against fellow Afghans as a jihad in order to unify and embolden their followers.

Thus, both the Pushtunwali and Islam as understood in Afghanistan provide substantial normative justification for the existence of violence. The recent emergence of political Islam, or Islamism, in Afghanistan deviates from tradition and is at least in part a reflection of twentieth-century forces sweeping through the Islamic world.[35] As Olivier Roy noted, these forces affected Afghanistan by producing "a new brand of fundamentalism, which was mainly a blend of traditional Sunni fundamentalism with strong anti-Western cultural and political bias, inherited from the Islamist movements."[36] This neo-fundamentalism is exemplified by the Taliban movement and some of the mujahideen organizations that were its predecessors, and it is considered in more detail in chapter 4.

A third major factor that fosters divisions within Afghanistan is its traditional social system. Afghanistan's ethnic groups emphasize loyalty to the local social group, which may be defined in several ways, rather than to the state. The core of the social system is the *qawm*, which may be any communal group, including village, extended family, tribe, or ethnic group.[37] In rural Afghan society virtually all meaningful social relations occur within the qawm, which is typically governed by the jirga or *shura* (which also means a council or assembly of elder males).[38] If the government attempts to impose laws alien to the social codes of the qawm, especially if the religious hierarchy also objects, then there is a strong likelihood of violence in response.[39]

To mediate with the state, qawm elders select from among their ranks maliks or *arbabs* (local leaders) to serve as intermediaries.[40] Other significant local actors are the khans, who are large landowners with local or regional power aside from their relationship to the state. In traditional Afghanistan the larger khans were often the most powerful people in society. Their power was tenuous, however, because it was tied directly to their ongoing patronage efforts.[41] The government established strong relations with the khans, whose power grew with the growth of the state. Nonetheless, the khan's position ultimately depended on the support of the qawm jirga.[42]

The resulting socioeconomic structure, exacerbated by deep ethnolinguistic and tribal cleavages, clearly divided state from society.[43] Loyalty of the individual was to or within the qawm, which was governed by the jirga. The only force that could bring together people from different qawms was an outside threat, and the unity produced was always short-lived.

The fourth factor limiting national unity is Afghanistan's rugged topography, including some of the world's most forbidding terrain. The Hindu Kush mountains descend from the Wakhan Corridor and the high Pamirs to bisect Afghanistan. These mountains average 4,500 to 6,000 meters in height (14,769–19,692 feet) in the zone around Kabul, with some peaks as high as 7,500 meters (24,615 feet) farther northeast.[44] In the center of the country the Hindu Kush broadens out into the high Hazarajat plateau, which descends and disappears into the western deserts on the Iranian border (Registan, Dasht-i-Margo, Dasht-i-Lut). Although passes through the Hindu Kush and Hazarajat make movement between different regions possible, harsh winters and high altitudes have made interregional mobility difficult (only the completion of the Salang Tunnel in 1964 made overland traffic between Kabul and northern Afghanistan possible during winter months). Many remote valleys exist that are virtually inaccessible to the outside world (map 1.3).

Despite the development of railroads in the bordering countries, Afghanistan itself has no railroad, except for a few miles of track laid by the Soviets after the 1979 invasion to expedite the transfer of gas from the fields in Shiberghan near the Uzbekistan border. Afghanistan also has only one major road, the "Ring Road" that begins in the northwest at Torghundi and runs south through Herat to Kandahar. Skirting the impenetrable Hazarajat, the road turns northeast to Kabul and then cuts the Hindu Kush at the Salang Pass and continues to Mazar-i-Sharif and the Uzbekistan border at Termez. Supposedly, the road also links

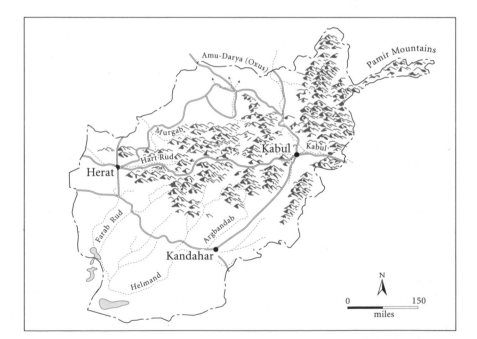

MAP 1.3 Afghanistan's physical characteristics. Reproduced by permission from Olivier Roy, *Afghanistan: From Holy War to Civil War*, 1995.

Mazar-i-Sharif and Herat, but this section was never much more than unfinished jeep track. The road from Kabul to Peshawar, Pakistan, that runs through Jalalabad and the Khyber Pass is also part of this system. After many years of war and virtually no funding for reconstruction, most of this road now consists of broken pavement or merely dirt and gravel, and travel is arduous and uncomfortable. I traveled it most recently in July 1997, taking twelve hours to go from Kabul to Peshawar. My bus suffered two tire punctures en route. There was no evidence of any serious reconstruction effort under way.

The four factors just described have all undermined state building throughout Afghanistan's history, and they are resurgent today. Nonetheless, despite the obstacles to building a strong central government, during the nineteenth and twentieth centuries Kabul was able to extend its control over much of the territory that is present-day Afghanistan.[45] Through the creation of a bureaucracy and national army, economic modernization and urbanization, construction of a transportation network, forced internal migration, the rise of the 'ulama, co-optation of the khans, and various other developments, Afghanistan witnessed the rise of state over traditional society. These subjects are explored in greater detail in chapter 2.

. The Afghan War has erased the position of the Afghan state by eliminating or severely damaging most of these institutions. As traditional elites such as the 'ulama and khans were destroyed and state structures collapsed, Afghanistan saw the rise of an unstable mixture of resurgent traditional society and nascent political elites that have contributed to the national political fragmentation. The emergence and empowerment of the Taliban could not have occurred but for the failure of the Afghan state, and the persistence of the movement despite some unsavory elements of its dogma, such as ethnic cleansing of northern minority groups and a harsh social policy toward females (dubbed "gender apartheid" by its opponents), illustrate the dangers state failure poses for a society. An analysis of how the war introduced or made unnaturally strong the factors that weakened the Afghan state and ruptured its ties to Afghan society will command our attention in chapters 3 and 4.

With the end of the Cold War and the collapse of the Soviet Union, Afghanistan finds its geostrategic position still important, but for different reasons. No longer merely a buffer state, Afghanistan is now a crossroads between states that want and need trade, as both Iran and Pakistan engage in a struggle for access to Central Asia's mineral wealth and markets. Thus, as in the days of the "Great Game" in the previous century—the competition between the Russian and British empires for control over Central Asia—Afghanistan finds itself once again a strategically significant country. Moreover, the growing "Talibanization" of Pakistan (that is, the application of Taliban social policies and interpretations of Islamic law) and the increasing Islamization of Central Asia highlight the way in which state failure in one country can infect its neighbors.[46] Afghanistan's transformed regional position and its interactions with neighboring states are explored in greater depth in chapter 5.

But before analyzing the changes wrought by war and national destruction on Afghanistan, I want to consider the last important contextual factor shaping the framework in which those changes occurred—Afghanistan's history. Some themes from Afghanistan's pre-1978 history are particularly relevant to our understanding of Afghanistan today, especially those that constrained the construction of the Afghan state and shaped the development of its national political culture. It is to that history that I now turn.

2 / Historical Factors
Shaping Modern Afghanistan

Afghanistan as a modern nation-state dates back only to 1919, but the same people have for millennia occupied the land it now claims.[1] From the earliest periods of Afghan and Central Asian history come lessons that are extremely applicable to the current situation there. This chapter explores four themes of Afghan and regional history that have had special relevance in shaping Afghanistan today. The first theme is that owing to its geographical location, Afghanistan has been subjected to countless invasions and incursions whose indelible imprint on the landscape has been matched by the social and demographic transformations they have wrought. Second, despite its location, or perhaps because of it, Afghanistan's people have exhibited fierce independence and martial skill throughout recorded history, making neither their military performance against the Soviet Union in the 1980s nor their continued civil war especially remarkable. Third, when Afghanistan did embark on state building in the eighteenth and nineteenth centuries, it did so despite the effects of the first two themes and of the centrifugal forces in Afghan society covered in the previous chapter. Fourth, when Afghanistan finally became a modern nation-state, it was forced to exist in the shadow of a powerful neighbor with expansionist tendencies that throughout the twentieth century came to dominate Afghanistan's affairs.

Evidence of human presence in Afghanistan and Central Asia exists from at least as early as the Middle Paleolithic period (Middle Stone

Age) at several sites in northern Afghanistan and Uzbekistan.[2] Although the thriving blade industry of this period suggests a prehistoric people sufficiently armed to be capable of warfare, firm historical evidence of a continuous cycle of invasion and conflict does not appear until the Early Bronze Age (c. 3000 BCE).[3] Thereafter, it is difficult to find a moment in Afghan history when some part of that country was not caught in the throes of some invasion, rebellion, or local war. Certainly since the rise of Zoroastrianism in the seventh century BCE, Afghanistan has suffered wave after wave of foreign nomadic invasions.[4] The unique and strategic position of Afghanistan in the ancient world aroused the interest of external rulers in controlling this territory.

History vividly recalls Alexander's Bactrian campaigns and his fabled marriage to Roxanne in his quest for "One World," but he was preceded in Central Asia by Darius the Great and the Achaemenids.[5] In the two millennia after Alexander (who is still recalled in Afghanistan today as "Iskander"), dynasties and empires would rise and fall in Persia, Central Asia, and the Indian subcontinent, many holding sway over only a portion of the land now known as Afghanistan. These included the Seleucid, Greco-Bactrian, Indo-Greek, Mauryan, Parthian, Saca, Yüeh-Chih, Kushan, Sassanian, Hepthalite, Hindu-Shahi, early Muslim Arab, Abbasid, Tahirid, Samanid, Saffarid, Ilek Khan Turk, Ghaznavid, Turkish Ghorid, Seljuk Turk, Turkish Khwarazm Shah, Delhi Sultans, Mongol, Kart, Timurid, Shaybani, Safavid, and Moghul.[6] In addition to Darius, Alexander, and Kanishka in ancient times, Genghis Khan, Tamerlane, and Babur all fought their way through Afghanistan in the second millennium CE, leaving scars on the landscape that still remain.

In the course of their campaigns in Central Asia, all these great rulers and conquerors were bedeviled by the ferocious tenacity of the indigenous hill tribes and steppe nomads who engaged them. The ancient literature available to us reveals several themes of Central Asian warfare that the Soviet Union should have noted prior to its 1979 invasion of Afghanistan. Underlying all else is the desire for independent decision making exhibited repeatedly by the Afghan and Central Asian tribes throughout history. Frank Holt identified this independent spirit in his study of Alexander's Bactrian campaigns: "Nominal control of the region the inhabitants were willing to concede to the new king, but any direct interference in local affairs was likely to arouse immediate opposition. It was Alexander's disruption of regional socioeconomic patterns on a permanent basis that suddenly made the presence of his army unacceptable to the inhabitants of the area."[7] After an earlier campaign against the Ariaspians (perhaps forerunners of present-day Baluch or Pushtun tribes), Alexander was so impressed by their tribal assembly method of governance that he allowed them to retain substantial autonomy.[8] This assembly, the jirga, remains the customary manner in which decisions are reached in Afghan tribal society today.

Although the Afghan love of independence is the most important lesson today's outside actors might have learned from early Afghan history, it is not the only one. In defense of their independence, the ancient inhabitants of the territory now known as Afghanistan were fiercely uncompromising warriors who excelled at political duplicity and guerrilla warfare. They mastered mobile hit-and-run and ambush tactics and understood the strategic importance of seasonal warfare and tribal alliances against a common enemy. They were comfortable fighting on the rugged terrain that was their home turf, and they were well aware how difficult it was for an invading army far from its home territory to effectively prosecute a protracted guerrilla war. The mountain and steppe peoples of Central Asia were formidable opponents, even for history's most fearsome conquerors; these were not people who could be pacified and then left to be cowed by garrison troops. In 329 BCE, Alexander found that he could not rely on his mercenary Greek troops—just as Leonid Brezhnev found that he could not depend on his second-line Central Asian troops in 1980 CE.[9] In short, even in ancient times the Afghans demonstrated tactical sophistication, an understanding of the strategic importance of political alliance, and a daunting combination of ferocity and tenacity that were all born out of their deep desire for independence. Later would-be conquerors should have taken heed.

If Afghanistan has been marked by a history of invasion and conquest, no less has it suffered from almost continuous internal strife among the native peoples living in its remote mountain valleys. Although this conflict has occurred throughout Afghan history, it was always most pronounced during periods of respite from foreign intrusion. Indeed, in the face of invasion Afghans frequently set aside bitter, long-standing grievances and united to meet the common enemy. The Abdali (later called Durrani) and Ghilzai Pushtuns did just that in 1731 to meet the Persian threat from Nadir Khan. As Dupree noted: "The two Pushtun tribes might fight each other to the death for control of Herat, Farah, and Qandahar, but any external invader welded them together in a common cause."[10] This theme is repeated again and again in Afghan history, although the opposite also occurred with great frequency—tribes would join with an invader, either through military defeat or through political capitulation/alliance, and assist him in his Central Asian campaigns.[11] Although the Afghan reputation for political duplicity is well founded, the tendency was more to play a new invader off against an old invader, rather than against the traditional tribal foe.[12] The most prevalent pattern throughout Afghan history, however, is one of short-term alliances between even traditional enemies in the face of a common external threat. These temporary political bonds do not necessarily apply to other areas of Afghan tribal society (for example, trade and intermarriage do not necessarily begin or increase). When the threat is eliminated or sufficiently reduced, there is a return to regular patterns of traditional warfare (fighting between rival Afghan groups does not always stop completely anyway; it may just be curtailed).

Since the advent of Islam, Afghanistan has epitomized the classic "inward-looking" peasant society.[13] Its terrain and wide ethnic diversity combine to reinforce a powerful sense of isolation and "separateness" of often small and discrete groups. Strict tribal mores, the competition for limited resources, and efforts at power projection also lead to clashes. Nothing in Afghan history illustrates this penchant for internecine warfare better than the well-documented post-Moghul period of four decades that preceded the formation of modern Afghanistan. After the decline of the Timurid empire of Central Asia at the beginning of the sixteenth century, the Muslim Indian Moghul dynasty and the Persian Safavid dynasty battled for control of Afghanistan. Their struggle lasted until the beginning of the eighteenth century, when the Moghul empire finally collapsed (usually dated to 1707, when Aurangzeb died).[14] Although "most of the northern and eastern Afghan tribes remained independent or gained independence as the Moghul empire deteriorated," a major rivalry developed in southern and western Afghanistan between the two major Pushtun tribes—the Abdali (Durrani) and the Ghilzai.[15] Their power struggle provides an excellent example of the cardinal rule of Afghan politics: "No Pushtun likes to be ruled by another, particularly someone from another tribe, subtribe, or section."[16] Forty years of scheming, warfare, and slaughter ultimately ended with the ascent of Ahmed Shah Durrani to power, which began a period of almost unbroken Durrani rule over most of what is present-day Afghanistan until the communist regime of 1978.

Even after Ahmed Shah Durrani brought the Durrani tribe into power in 1749, Afghanistan continued to suffer from foreign encroachment and internal upheaval. Although the Persian empire declined after the Safavid period, throughout the nineteenth and early twentieth centuries both the Russian and British empires pushed in on Afghanistan in their quest for territorial expansion.[17] This was possible because Afghanistan, like much of the rest of Central Asia and northern India, was a mishmash of independent khanates and tiny city-states with distinct tribal or ethnic power bases.[18] Only after the resolution of the Third Anglo-Afghan War in 1919 did Afghanistan become a completely sovereign nation-state. One century before that red-letter date, however, the European competition between the British and Russian empires that followed their defeat of Napoleon spilled over into the Asian arena. Inevitably, Afghanistan was caught in the middle of the British-Russian rivalry that Rudyard Kipling, in his novel *Kim* (1919), immortalized as the "Great Game."

AFGHANISTAN BECOMES A NATION-STATE

During the years of the Great Game in Central Asia—while Russia and Great Britain pushed their colonial frontiers forward as far as possible—Afghanistan became a modern nation-state. This process began in 1749, when Ahmed Shah brought his Durrani tribe into power, and culminated in 1919, when Amir Amanullah acquired independence for Afghanistan from British control as part of the settlement of the Third Anglo-Afghan War. Three important sociopolitical developments occurred during the nineteenth and twentieth centuries that have particular relevance for the current situation in Afghanistan. Socially, a broader ethnic consciousness grew gradually out of the internal anarchy and warfare that prevailed following the rise of Ahmed Shah Durrani. This was not nationalism, for identity was still manifested primarily at the qawm level, but the groundwork for nationalism was being laid. Politically, the dual pressures of growing internal cohesion and external encroachment from imperial Russia and Great Britain led to war, political manipulation, the forging of national boundaries, and ultimately the independence of Afghanistan. Militarily, refinement of ancient Afghan tactics following the widespread dissemination of gunpowder and firearms made possible the "internal imperialism" of Abdur Rahman that led to the formation of Afghanistan while Pushtun tribesmen and Turkic warriors held the foreign powers at bay.

When Kipling married a tale of childhood adventure to trenchant political commentary in his classic *Kim*, he also popularized a phrase that came to describe the imperial politics of a century. Momentous decisions made in the comfort of salons and drawing rooms in London and St. Petersburg, however, had to be implemented by young men in the uncertain and physically challenging environment of the Central Asian and North Indian frontier. Afghanistan was undergoing tremendous geopolitical change at the time. As the Uzbek, Moghul, and Safavid empires that had battled over Afghanistan in the sixteenth and seventeenth centuries passed into the pages of history (map 2.1), not only did the Russian and British empires step forward to take their places but the Afghans themselves embarked on a process of nation building that continues today. The 345 distinct tribal units in Afghanistan battled

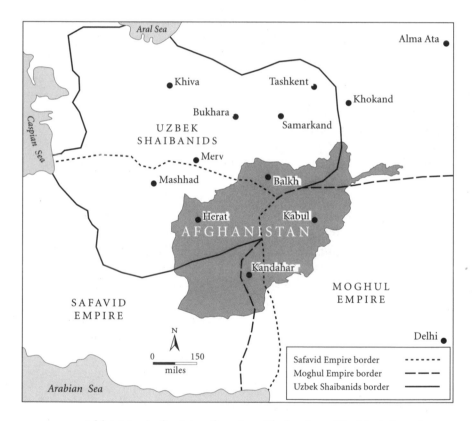

MAP 2.1 Afghanistan in the sixteenth century. The borders of the Moghul empire are indicated by a crosshatched line, the borders of the Safavid empire by a hatched line, and the borders of the Uzbek Shaibanids by a heavy solid line. The light solid line marks Afghanistan's present-day border. Reproduced with permission from Asta Olesen, *Islam and Politics in Afghanistan*, 1995, p. 20.

against but (to some extent) ultimately acquiesced to the gradual development of a stronger central government, all of which occurred in the face of the Anglo-Russian competition of the day.[19] This period has been exhaustively chronicled, often in the romantic terms of colonizing empire builders and particularly from the British perspective.[20] Thus, it is possible to reconstruct much of significance that was happening in Afghan society during this time.

The Growth of Ethnic Consciousness

The creation and transformation of ethnic consciousness are rarely assignable to discrete causes or specific dates, for groups constantly re-examine and redefine themselves. Certainly the major ethnic groups of Afghanistan today existed there in some form centuries earlier, and group membership was critical even then.[21] So why consider the nineteenth century the period that witnessed the rise of ethnic consciousness?

Foreign invasions, especially the devastating Mongol and Timurid campaigns, altered the indigenous population profile both by inflicting heavy native casualties and by infusing new blood into the region.[22] As Quddus noted: "But from 1st century BC to 5th century AD, during a span of 600 years, this area witnessed three immigrations from Central Asia of such gigantic magnitude—those of the Sakas, Kushans, Huns and Gujjars—that everything was swept before them, overwhelmed by them and submerged in them.... [I]t is impossible that these areas should have remained uncolonised and the blood of their inhabitants unsullied."[23]

After the Durrani ascendancy in the mid-eighteenth century, however, there would be no substantial long-term foreign presence in Afghanistan until the Soviet invasion of 1979. It was during this time that the Pushtun tribes finally emerged as the dominant ethnic group in Afghanistan, and with the creation of national borders Afghanistan's permanent minority groups were also delineated.[24] At the beginning of the Afghan-Soviet War in late 1979 there were significant populations of Tajiks, Uzbeks, Hazara, Aimaq, and Farsiwan in Afghanistan, as well as smaller numbers of Baluch, Brahui, Gujar, Kirghiz, Kohistani, Moghul, Nuristani, Pamiri, Qizilbash, Turkoman, Wakhi, and other peoples.[25] Many of these ethnic groups are divided by international borders.

The rise of the Pushtuns in Afghan history occurred during a period

of great anarchy; the absence of a central government or even any political institutions beyond the jirga provided a conducive environment for
this situation. The nineteenth century in Afghanistan witnessed a vast
struggle for power between various clans and families of the Durrani
tribe, and no central authority exerted control over the tribes in their
mountain strongholds. Dupree described the situation in a nutshell:

> [T]wo themes dominated the Afghan scene: internal disorder and exter-
> nal invasions and pressures. The final dismemberment of the Durrani
> empire occurred. Punjab, Sind, Kashmir, and most of Baluchistan were
> irrevocably lost, as the Mohhamadzai (Barakzai) and Saddozai princes
> (both Durrani Pushtun) fought for regional control.... They contested
> for four major areas, Kabul, Qandahar, Herat, and the northern Uzbak
> Khanates.... For brief periods, the three important khanates of Kabul,
> Qandahar, and Herat were united. Many smaller independent or semi-
> independent Pushtun units rose and fell, among them, Ghazni, Farah,
> Jalalabad, Girishk, Kalat-i-Ghilzai. Non-Pushtun areas (such as the Haz-
> arajat, Kafiristan, Badakhshan, Baluchistan) usually maintained their
> independent tribal integrity. During these unstable times, the Amir of
> Bokhara often made claims to territory south of the Amu Darya, or
> supported or assisted revolts against Pushtun control.[26]

Although by the twentieth century nascent political institutions were
developing in Afghanistan, a strong central government was never
achieved.[27] Tribal rebellion regularly threatened to destabilize or topple
the government in Kabul and continually menaced the British North-
West Frontier of India (now Pakistan).

Various means were employed to reduce this threat, including the
forced internal migration of dissident tribal factions to minority areas,[28]
which both served to bind the recalcitrant Pushtuns to the regime
and strengthened government control over the minority groups. Tribes
were also bribed to cooperate with the government, and in the British
areas political agents acted as intermediaries between the tribal maliks
and the Crown.[29]

Thus, from the nineteenth-century period of anarchy in Afghanistan
there developed an increased ethnic consciousness—although not an
ideology of nationalism—that laid the foundation for ethnic relationships in Afghanistan today. These social changes did not occur in a
vacuum, however, for there were tremendous political pressures from
external sources as well.

The "Great Game"

The Anglo-Russian competition in Central Asia ultimately fostered the creation of the modern state of Afghanistan, caused the demarcation of its ethnically divisive borders, and began the process that has culminated in the current Afghan War. The combination of nineteenth-century foreign encroachment and simultaneous internal anarchy created a state structure without the concomitant development of an Afghan nation.[30]

Many analysts have argued that the Soviet invasion in 1979 was motivated by the Soviet Union's desire for warm-water ports. There is some truth to this theory; it is one of a conglomerate of reasons for the Soviet adventure.[31] Dupree reflected on early Russian expansionist tendencies: "Since the time of Peter the Great (1682–1725), Russia coveted warm water ports to the south, either on the Dardanelles, in the Persian Gulf, or in the Indian Ocean. The Russian drive to the east began in 1734 with movements in Kazakhstan, and ended only when the great Asian empire of Russia reached the shores of the Pacific, and went on to Alaska and California."[32] The rise of the United States and its westward expansion beginning in the early 1800s ultimately thwarted Russian moves to the east, and by the end of the nineteenth century the emerging powers had drawn the line. The US acquired California and Alaska and dropped its Siberian claims, so Russia stayed in Asia while the US kept largely to North America. Pushing south across steppes, deserts, and mountains, however, the Russians collided not only with decaying Persian and Turkish empires but also with Great Britain in the golden age of its colonial period (map 2.2).[33]

In 1837, the Great Game reached what is now Afghanistan. In that year a Russian-aided Persian attempt to annex Herat was initiated. The siege was lifted in 1838, owing to British diplomatic pressure, the strong defense of the city, and the military activities of tribes from nearby Badghis.[34] Nonetheless, it was but "the first of many confrontations between Britain and Russia in the region during the nineteenth century."[35] To fully recount the convoluted tale of imperial geopolitics in nineteenth-century Central Asia far exceeds the scope of this chapter. Suffice it to say that both powers operated from an expansionist perspective and always with an eye on the actions of the other. The following excerpt from a memorandum by Prince Gorchakov in 1864 aptly summarizes the Russian view of the peoples of Central Asia (and is characteristic of the similar British view of the peoples of India):

The position of Russia in Central Asia is that of all civilized states which come into contact with half-savage, wandering tribes possessing no fixed social organization. It invariably happens in such cases that the interests of security on the frontier, and of commercial relations, compel the more civilized state to exercise a certain ascendancy over neighbors whose turbulence and nomad instincts render them difficult to live with.... The greatest difficulty is in knowing where to stop.[36]

Apart from its quest for warm-water ports, Russia's expansion was motivated by a desire to weaken British power, both in India and, by extension, in Europe.[37] Although neither power held Afghanistan during this time, its role as a buffer between them grew throughout the 1800s and led to repeated clashes on its fringes between indigenous and imperial forces. Russia was primarily concerned during this period

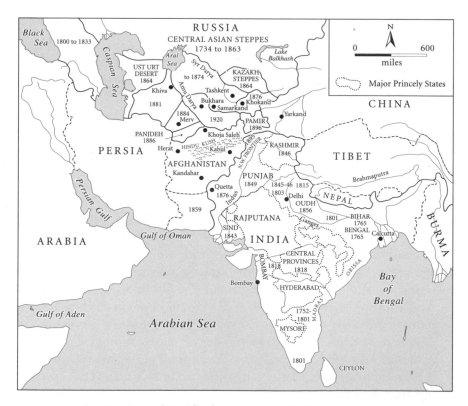

MAP 2.2 Russian and British advances toward Afghanistan, 1734 to 1920.
Reproduced with permission from Louis Dupree, *Afghanistan*, 1973, p. 342.

with winning control of the Central Asian khanates to the north of Afghanistan, whereas British attention was focused on annexing and pacifying the myriad princely states of India. Nonetheless, they inevitably encroached on Afghan territory, exploited local rivalries, and ultimately planted the seeds of war.

The British fought three wars in Afghanistan in eighty years, as well as numerous campaigns along the North-West Frontier against the recalcitrant Pushtun tribes. The First Anglo-Afghan War (1838–1842) was fought because of British concern over Russia's long-term interests in Afghanistan and points south. This conflict grew out of British apprehension over Russian involvement in Persia's siege of Herat during 1837–1838. When the Persians lifted the siege and retired from the battlefield in September 1838, Governor-General Lord Auckland nonetheless implemented the blatantly imperialist Simla Manifesto, which called for the invasion of Afghanistan and the restoration of the previous ruler, Shah Shuja (who at that time was living under British patronage in India). Being placed as a pro-British puppet on the throne in Kabul by force of arms automatically discredited him, whatever his previous position or current standing in Pushtun tribal politics might have been—a lesson apparently lost on the Soviet Union, which tried exactly the same maneuver in 1979 (with Babrak Karmal) and 1986 (with Najibullah).

The First Anglo-Afghan War is famous for the crushing of the British Army of the Indus on its ill-fated retreat from Kabul during January 1842 by, primarily, Ghilzai Pushtuns.[38] Out of sixteen thousand soldiers and camp followers, only one Englishman on an exhausted horse made it to Jalalabad alive (although a few Indian soldiers and camp followers also survived, and 105 prisoners were eventually rescued). This slaughter represented the most humiliating defeat of a British army in that country's colonial history and was characteristic of the ferocity of the Afghan fighting men. Although a subsequent British army exacted a painful retribution on Kabul in September 1842 (indeed, it was called the Army of Retribution), it retired to India less than a month later. As Dupree summarized it, "the realistic results of the First Anglo-Afghan War can be stated simply: after four years of disaster, both in honor, material, and personnel, the British left Afghanistan as they found it, in tribal chaos and with Dost Mohammad Khan returned to the throne of Kabul."[39]

The Anglo-Russian competition in Asia heated up after the First Anglo-Afghan War. Both states began to seriously push the limits of their power. The British gobbled up the princely states of India throughout the 1840s and into the 1850s (until the Indian Rebellion of 1857) while the Russians did the same to the khanates of Central Asia, through either military conquest or economic vassalage. Russian armies conquered vast areas of Central Asia by 1864, Tashkent and Samarkand by 1874, Khokand by 1876, Khiva and Merv by 1884, and Panjdeh and the Pamir Knot by the turn of the century (see map 2.2). Only the Bukhara area held out into the twentieth century, to be finally subdued in the bloody Basmachi campaign of the 1920s. Throughout this period the British attempted to extend their influence into Afghanistan, an area they did not control, in order to counter the threat of Russian expansion.[40] The Treaty of Peshawar in 1855 and its supplement of 1857 pledged Anglo-Afghan friendship and provided for mutual military obligations.[41] Meanwhile, the Afghan *amir*, Dost Mohammad, regained control of both Kandahar and territories to the north of Kabul but was unable to reacquire Herat. Throughout the 1850s and 1860s the British "vacillated between two policies ... to occupy Herat and Kabul, i.e., to annex the Afghan area into the British Indian Empire, or to retreat to the Indus River and leave Afghanistan strictly alone."[42]

With the ascension of Benjamin Disraeli and the Conservative Party to power (1874–1880; Disraeli's first period as prime minister during part of 1868 was very brief), Britain shifted in the 1870s to the "Forward Policy" vis-à-vis Afghanistan.[43] The British occupied Quetta in 1876 and began to press Amir Sher Ali for a British mission in Kabul. In response to this change in policy the Russians sent an unsolicited diplomatic mission to Kabul. The British then attempted to force their own diplomatic mission on Kabul and, when it was refused, invaded Afghanistan. Thus, the Second Anglo-Afghan War (1878–1880) began as the first did, over British concerns about Russian intrigues in Afghanistan.[44] Also like the first war, this conflict saw the murder of a British envoy in Kabul (in 1879) and the defeat of a British army (in 1880). Two developments of importance came out of it: the Treaty of Gandamak (1879), which, among other concessions, ceded strategic border areas to the British (notably the Khyber Pass) and provided for British control of Afghanistan's foreign affairs, and the rise to power of Abdur Rahman Khan in Kabul.

Amir Abdur Rahman Khan ruled Afghanistan for the last two decades of the nineteenth century, and with no way to expend his imperialistic energies externally (blocked by the British to the south and southeast, the Russians to the north and northeast, and the Persians to the west), he engaged in "internal imperialism" instead. In the process he forged the administrative machinery of the modern Afghan nation-state and solidified its international borders.[45] When he came to power, Abdur Rahman controlled only Kabul and its surrounding areas, but by almost unbroken fighting he achieved at least indirect control over almost all of present-day Afghanistan by the time of his death in 1901.[46] Not only did he defeat rival Durranis, Ghilzai, and other Pushtuns (Shinwaris, Mangal-Zarmats, Safis), but Abdur Rahman also conquered the Uzbek, Turkmen, and Tajik regions north of Kabul, the central Hazarajat, and eastern Nuristan (Kafiristan). He viewed the process as putting "in order all those hundreds of petty chiefs, plunderers, robbers, and cutthroats.... This necessitated breaking down the feudal and tribal system and substituting one grand community under one law and one rule."[47]

Although prior rulers had employed forced migration to rid themselves of their enemies, Abdur Rahman raised the technique to a new level by shifting thousands of Ghilzai and others from their traditional tribal base southwest of Kabul to areas north of the Hindu Kush. This was a brilliant policy because, as Dupree wrote, "by moving large numbers of his enemies, Abdur Rahman accomplished two immediate aims: he removed dissidents from areas which they might again infect with the germs of revolt, and he created a force loyal to himself, for, although the Ghilzai (Pushtun) might be anti-Durrani (Pushtun) while living in their own tribal zones, they were pro-Pushtun in the northern non-Pushtun (Tajik, Uzbak, Hazara, Turkoman) areas."[48] Abdur Rahman also abolished the tax on non-Pushtuns, created a provincial government system that eroded the power of the tribes, created a national government (including a civil administration and general assembly), and strengthened the army, his ultimate source of power.[49]

Meanwhile, Britain and Russia almost went to war over the Panjdeh Crisis of 1885, which led the two powers to form a number of boundary commissions to demarcate Afghanistan's borders. In 1887, 1891, and 1896 commissions decided Afghanistan's northern boundaries, and in 1893 the Durand Line separating Afghanistan from British North-West India was delineated. Although there is substantial evidence that this latter boundary, at least, was not thought by the amir to be a permanent border, it became one nonetheless, despite the fact that it divided traditional Pushtun territory.[50] Some tribal areas lost to British India in the last quarter of the 1800s that are now part of Pakistan include Chitral, Dir, Swat, Bajaur, Khyber, Kurram, Waziristan, Zhob, Loralai, Pishin,

Quetta, and Nushki.[51] Finally, the Persian-Afghan boundary was settled in 1905.

From 1901 to 1919 Abdur Rahman's son, Habibullah, ruled as amir. Although he refused to ratify the Anglo-Russian Convention of 1907, which defined the Asian spheres of influence of these two powers, their tacit agreement to consider the convention valid established the principle of future Afghan neutrality. After maintaining that neutrality through World War I, Habibullah was murdered in 1919, and his son, Amanullah, seized power. British reluctance to fully recognize the new amir or reward Afghanistan's neutrality with complete independence led the staunch nationalist Amanullah to begin the Third Anglo-Afghan War within two months of taking the throne. This war lasted for only one month (May–June 1919), but it led to the Treaty of Rawalpindi, which finally freed Afghanistan to conduct its own foreign affairs.[52] Thus, in 1919 Afghanistan became a fully independent state.

Military Adaptation

Although the pressure of foreign encroachment and internal civil conflict combined with a growing ethnic (especially Pushtun) consciousness to give birth to a nascent Afghanistan, none of it would have been possible without the fighting ability of the Afghan tribesmen. Their continued martial capability in the face of significant changes in military tactics and weapons ensured the survival of Afghanistan. This is the third important nineteenth-century development in Afghanistan that has particular relevance for the present situation there.

Throughout the Great Game, one constant was the willingness of the Afghan tribesmen to fight (primarily Pushtuns against the British and Turkic peoples against the Russians), not only against foreign invaders and neighbors but among themselves as well. Since the earliest mentions of Afghans in recorded history they have been known as fiercely capable fighters. Nothing that occurred in the nineteenth century besmirched that proud reputation. The entire century in Afghanistan was a mosaic of warfare, with different conflicts so overlapping that it is almost impossible to tell where one began or ended.

The Afghans—the Pushtuns especially—have become "almost genetically expert at guerrilla warfare after centuries of resisting all comers and fighting among themselves when no comers were available."[53] Certainly, their tactical sophistication can be considerable; they have always specialized in hit-and-run attacks, ambushes, and similar tactics imposed by the terrain. The intractability of the Pushtuns, made even stronger by aspects of the Pushtunwali such as its emphasis on revenge killings and appeasing honor, both justifies and enhances the doggedness that makes them such daunting warriors. As specialists in guerrilla warfare, the Afghans have always been capable of protracting a conflict, although the self-interest of the individual sometimes leads to a dissolution of tribal forces hastily brought together for some less-than-compelling reason. As the British eventually learned, good strategy frequently meant to wait the tribesmen out, and they often used this knowledge against the Pushtuns in their interminable skirmishes with them, by striking against the tribes when their ardor had cooled. The British presence among the Pushtuns was always minimal, even in Peshawar, and confined to the fringe of Pushtun territory (the British never actually controlled many of the tribal areas they claimed, nor do the Pakistanis today). Thus, the British used this tactic with some success. As partisans, however, fighting against a foreign invader on their own territory, the Afghans were relentless. Even in defeat they were never broken, and inevitably small war parties (*lashkars*) would continue the fight from the high mountains.[54]

The key to the development of this guerrilla expertise is the extremely rugged terrain of Afghanistan and the Tribal Areas of the North-West Frontier Province of Pakistan. Not only did harsh living conditions make tough survivors of those inhabitants who reached adulthood, but more specifically the high mountains and barren deserts limited the opportunities for conventional military engagements. Only certain routes and passes through the mountains were possible—an ideal setting for ambush, sniping, hit-and-run, and other preferred tactics of the guerrilla fighter. Furthermore, the strong individuality of the Afghans made it difficult for them to achieve the kind of rigid discipline necessary to a professional army. Like the Boer farmers of South Africa in the 1890s, the Pushtuns were natural guerrillas.

The Hindu Kush and its various spurs not only limited Afghanistan's enemies in their offensive tactics but also provided almost unassailable bases from which tribal guerrillas could operate. Unlike in the Mau Mau Emergency in Kenya in the 1950s, when British forces were ultimately able to penetrate the White Mountains strongholds of the insurgents to crush the rebellion, neither the British nor anyone else has been able to penetrate the tribal strongholds of the Afghans.[55] Although the British were always able to take Afghan cities and towns and almost always able to defeat Afghans on the battlefield (exceptions being the

British retreat from Kabul in 1842 and defeat at Maiwand in 1880), they were never able to drive the attack home and crush the Afghans' high mountain bases. Instead, British expeditionary forces settled for punitive destruction of villages in the rebellious areas, sometimes including the inhabitants, a tactic that inevitably guaranteed hatred and future rebellion.[56] This pattern has been evident more recently, on both sides of the Durand Line. In Afghanistan, the Soviet and Kabul forces mounted more than a dozen major offensives into the Panjshir Valley in the 1980s in an effort to destroy the resistance leader Ahmed Shah Massoud and his mujahideen; every effort failed, leaving them with little to do except destroy the villages that provided support for the rebels.[57] More recently, in 1996–2000, the Taliban suffered the same difficulty north of Kabul in their confrontation with Massoud. In Pakistan during the 1980s, although the army periodically made an effort to clean out the heroin laboratories in the Tribal Agencies, it never really succeeded (although conditions in Afghanistan in the 1990s became comparatively safer for laboratories there, so most of them were moved across the border).[58]

Because of the difficulties in subjugating, controlling, or even influencing the Afghans, Pushtun tribes bordering the so-called Settled Districts were frequently paid for their quiescence. That is to say, they were bribed to maintain peaceful behavior.[59] This was the carrot in British imperial policy toward the Afghans (the British certainly used the stick as well). Payments were made to certain tribes not only so that they would remain peaceful but specifically so that they would allow traffic to pass on the roads through their areas. Certain tribes, such as the Afridi who controlled the Khyber Pass, were especially able to benefit from this policy. Of course, eventually this led to more violence, for the temptation to extort more money was always strong. Also, the situation inevitably elicited jealousy and often led to intertribal violence with other, strategically less well-placed tribes or clans.[60]

One important trait of the Afghans has been their flexibility in adapting to new military technology and tactics. This probably stems from their repeated exposure to invasion by the leading practitioners of warfare throughout history. They have used gunpowder since at least Moghul times; indeed, Babur introduced firearms to the Indian subcontinent.[61] The Pushtuns are famous for their ability to make weapons, and in gunsmiths' shops in towns like Darra Adam Khel in Pakistan's Tribal Areas you could buy good copies of the Soviet Kalashnikov in the 1980s, just as you could have bought a copy of the British Lee Enfield there at the turn of the century.[62] Although many of the older tribesmen began the current Afghan conflict relying on these bolt-action weapons of a bygone era, their successful transition to Stinger missiles and multibarreled rocket launchers (also for sale in the Tribal Areas) demonstrated once again their flexibility, at least in military matters.[63] Even drug smugglers and families engaging in traditional feuding have beefed up their arsenals with modern weapons.[64]

Although the Afghans adopted modern military technology quickly, developing a modern army took longer. Part of the reason for this was that the image of manhood promoted by the Pushtunwali emphasized the independence of the individual—the ideal man combined the virtues of both warrior and poet, as did the Afghan hero Khushal Khan Khattak.[65] Thus, cooperation and acceptance of authority has been limited, even in important military operations. As Richard Nyrop and Donald Seekins quoted an anonymous observer: "[T]ribal wars have been characterized by their blitzkrieg nature, by their swift irresistible penetration and by the rapid, inevitable disintegration of the *lashkar* (tribal war party). Often the Pushtun warrior will simply pack up and leave after a hard day's fighting without coordination with, or command from, the *lashkar*."[66] Numerous observers have explained this phenomenon, at least partially, as attributable to the seasonality of traditional warfare in Afghanistan.[67] Fighting seasons were circumscribed traditionally by harvest time and the onset of winter. Prior to the fall harvests, men were too busy to fight, and the long, harsh winters made physical conditions for fighting impossible. In any event, the Pushtun tribesmen enjoyed great success against the British through the use of guerrilla methods, forcing political settlements on the imperial power during the nineteenth century, just as in 1989 the Afghans' protracted guerrilla war forced the USSR to a military withdrawal and political settlement.

Efforts to develop a modern Afghan army began in the mid-eighteenth century under Shah Shuja and continued into the modern era. Foreign advisers were employed, European methods and weapons were introduced, and cash payments were implemented in place of booty. These changes, however, were not enough to replace the non-hierarchical tribal system. Even the reforms instituted under Abdur Rahman, such as the disciplinary system and the *hasht nafari* (in which one man in every eight was selected for military service on a rotating basis), did not completely eradicate the vestiges of tribalism that still limited the army's performance. After Abdur Rahman, subsequent amirs and kings relied on foreign military missions for training (especially those of the Turks and Germans) and on foreign aid for weapons and equipment (especially aid from the British, Germans, French, and, ultimately, Soviets).[68] By the second half of the twentieth century, great strides had been made with the Afghan Army, although the tribally based mujahideen defeated it, finally achieving victory in 1992 following the collapse of the Soviet Union and its support for the Afghan communist government.

By 1919 Afghanistan was completely independent, albeit extremely poor and underdeveloped. The next three decades saw important developments for the future of the fledgling country, not only in Afghanistan itself but also in the larger region of Central and South Asia. To the north the emerging Soviet state consolidated its control over the Central Asian khanates, while to the south and east a growing independence movement in India finally led Britain to divest itself of all of its South Asian colonies. What did all these events mean for Afghanistan?

AFGHANISTAN AND THE SOVIET UNION IN CENTRAL ASIA

In the period between the two world wars, tremendous changes occurred in the Indian subcontinent and the USSR that had important implications for the development of the fledgling nation-state of Afghanistan. British exhaustion at the end of World War I contributed substantially to both Afghanistan's independence and the rise of the movement for independence in India.[69] The situation in the new Marxist state of the Soviet Union was more complex. The Russian Revolution led to the early withdrawal of Soviet forces from World War I, while the domestic scramble for power led to widespread civil war in south Russia, the Ukraine, and Siberia until 1920.[70] In Central Asia during this time the indigenous Muslim peoples rebelled against Russian rule, and their suppression demonstrates remarkable parallels to the Soviet effort in Afghanistan during the 1980s.[71]

The betrayal of the Muslim nationalist movement by the new Soviet ideology was not entirely unexpected in Afghanistan and the larger Muslim world, though it still produced great resentment. The Soviet leaders, determined to conquer Turkestan (Central Asia), used four interrelated tools to accomplish their goal. First, diplomatic pressure was exerted against Afghanistan to prevent it from openly supporting the so-called Basmachi movement in an attempt to form a Central Asian confederation. Second, economic penetration of the region, begun when the tsars first conquered the Central Asian khanates, made possible the use of blockades, famines, and similar tactics to undermine support for the nationalist movement. Third, political manipulation of cleavages along lines of ethnicity (Turkomans, Uzbeks, Tajiks, Kirghiz, Kazakhs), religion (Qadimists vs. Jadidists), politics (Muslim nationalists vs. Emirate/White forces), and socioeconomic status (poor peasants vs. kulaks/bourgeoisie) allowed the co-opting of certain groups (notably the Young Khivans and Young Bukharans) and the weakening of the resistance. Fourth, military force was used throughout Central Asia, especially during the Basmachi period of 1917–1931, following the model provided by the conquest of the Turkestan khanates by tsarist forces in the nineteenth century. In this section I consider each of these methods in turn, for after World War II the Soviet Union would begin using the same tools to conquer Afghanistan.

By the late 1800s Russia had conquered almost all of the Muslim khanates of Central Asia. The two emirates of Khiva and Bukhara, however, maintained a modicum of autonomy as protectorates. In 1917, a potent nationalist Muslim movement under various names swept both the annexed and "independent" areas and linked with Russian revolutionaries in common antigovernment agitation.[72]

The Russian Revolution aroused the aspirations of the Central Asian Muslims, who believed they would finally be free. Both the general ideology and specific public statements of the new Soviet government called for "national self-determination." In November 1917 Vladimir Lenin proclaimed to the Central Asian Muslims, "Your beliefs and customs, your national and cultural institutions, are henceforth free and not to be violated. You may freely and without hindrance organize your national life."[73] Likewise, the USSR supported Afghanistan against Great Britain and was the first country to recognize newly independent Afghanistan in 1919. The Soviet-Afghan friendship treaty of 1921 noted that Khiva and Bukhara were independent emirates.[74]

In November 1917 Khokand and the Ferghana region, part of the annexed area of tsarist Russia, were declared independent by a Muslim Central Council.[75] By February 1918 Khokand had been captured by pro-Soviet forces, who slaughtered its population and looted the city.[76] During this same period both Khiva and Bukhara declared full independence and engaged Soviet forces in battle. Through political manipulation of certain elements of the Muslim nationalist movement, the Soviets were able to defeat the Khivan and Bukharan forces and place co-opted elements ("Young Khivans" and "Young Bukharans") in power. By 1921 the Soviets had gained control of both former protectorates, and although each was called independent, in neither case did the Soviets withdraw their troops. In 1924 the USSR annexed both "independent" emirates. Thereafter, the native languages—variations of Turkish and Persian—were suppressed, as was the Islamic religion. Throughout the 1920s and even the 1930s Muslim rebels known as the Basmachis (bandits) fought a fierce guerrilla war in Central Asia. Almost all were eventually defeated and executed or escaped to Afghanistan and Iran. As for the Young Khivans and Young Bukharans, they were executed during Stalin's purges and "replaced by young bureaucrats trained in new Soviet schools."[77]

During the Soviet conquest (or reconquest) of Central Asia,[78] only Afghanistan was in a position to offer meaningful support to the Muslim nationalists (although there was limited Turkish, British, and US support, primarily diplomatic).[79] There was a very real possibility that this support would be forthcoming, for Amanullah viewed himself as a leader of the pan-Islamist movement. The subsequent collapse of that movement, as well as the similar Khilafat movement in India and the pan-Turanist movement out of Turkey, limited his ability to act. Amanullah's dreams of leading a great Central Asian Muslim confederation, perhaps even seating the caliphate in Afghanistan, died with the short-lived Khivan and Bukharan emirates.[80]

The new Soviet government proved its capability and resilience in Turkestan in the face of substantial Afghan concern. Soviet strategy was simple: profess support for the independence of Khiva and Bukhara to defuse international concern while dividing and crushing the independence movements there. An excellent example of Soviet diplomatic duplicity in this regard is a letter from the Soviet ambassador to Afghanistan in response to Afghan protests over Soviet occupation of Khiva and Bukhara. An excerpt from this letter of February 1922 reads as follows:

> The Government which I represent has always recognized and respected the independence of the two governments of Khiva and Bukhara. The presence of a limited contingent of troops belonging to my Government is due to temporary requirements expressed and made known to us by the Bukharan Government. This arrangement has been agreed to with the provision that whenever the Bukharan Government so requests, not a single Russian soldier will remain on Bukharan soil. The extension of our friendly assistance in no way constitutes an interference against the independence of the sovereign State of Bukhara. If the Government

of Bukhara should cease to formulate its request and should prove dissatisfied with the continuation of such brotherly assistance, then the Government I represent shall most immediately withdraw its troops.[81]

Not only did Soviet troops never leave these two emirates, but the letter provided a model for Soviet statements on Afghanistan sixty years later.

The final method enabling the Soviets to crush resistance in Turkestan derived from the earlier economic penetration of the region under the tsarist regimes. Since Russia had extended its hegemony to Central Asia in the nineteenth century there had been increasing emphasis on the intensive cultivation of cotton as a cash crop at the expense of local grain production. An early demand of the Muslim nationalists seeking Central Asian autonomy was for a return from cotton to grain production so that the local population could feed itself.[82] When the uprising in Ferghana occurred, civil war was raging throughout the USSR. White forces took Orenburg, which they held from September 1917 to September 1919, thereby cutting the railroad that connected European Russia to Central Asia. Although this did weaken the pro-Soviet government in Tashkent, it also caused widespread famine in Turkestan, which no longer grew enough grain to feed itself.[83] Thereafter, the Soviets used a two-sided economic policy vis-à-vis Central Asia. Economic relations were normalized with areas that had been pacified, whereas continued blockades were imposed and famines subsequently introduced in places where resistance continued.

If Afghanistan faced a Central Asia in upheaval during the 1920s and 1930s, its own domestic politics were also undergoing change. Amanullah, son of Habibullah, was king for most of this period (1919–1929). After his success in acquiring Afghanistan's independence in 1919, he centralized power at the expense of his brothers and changed his title to king in 1923. Determined to modernize Afghanistan rapidly, especially following a tour of India, Egypt, Persia, Turkey, and Europe in 1927–1928, he introduced dramatic reforms, such as requiring Western dress in Kabul and eliminating women's veils, that sparked rebellion among religious and tribal leaders.[84] Habibullah (also known disparagingly as Bacha Saqqao, "son of a water carrier"), the Tajik warlord of Kohistan, an area north of Kabul, drove Amanullah from the throne and ruled Kabul for just under a year.[85] Habibullah was defeated in October 1929 (and executed the following month) by a Pushtun tribal army led by the former commander of Amanullah's army, Mohammad Nadir Khan, and his brothers from the Musahiban family of the Mohammadzai

Durrani Pushtuns. Nadir Khan became king and founded the dynasty that ruled Afghanistan until 1973.

After the Soviet reconquest of Turkestan and the additional conquests of Khiva and Bukhara (1918–1922), Soviet forces fought an almost continuous guerrilla war against Basmachi nationalists until 1931.[86] Even after the last major Basmachi band was defeated, isolated guerrilla incidents still flared up for many years. Diplomatic pressure limited Afghan support for the Basmachis (although Afghan "volunteers" did participate),[87] who nonetheless frustrated Soviet aims toward Central Asia for over a decade. The Basmachi guerrilla campaign in the 1920s and 1930s displays striking similarities to the mujahideen war in Afghanistan in the 1980s. For example, because various components of the Basmachi movement differed ideologically, the Basmachis never achieved sufficient unity to successfully prosecute a conventional war against the larger, combat-hardened Soviet armies. This made possible a key facet of the Soviet model for the conquest of Central Asia—exploitation of ethnic, religious, and political cleavages among the resistance. Because the Basmachis were such a heterogeneous, broadly defined group, few general leaders ever emerged. Enver Pasha, the Young Turk with dreams of a renewed Turkish empire based in Turkestan, came closest to unifying the Basmachi movement.[88] After his death in combat against Soviet forces in 1922, Afghan support for the Basmachis all but disappeared. Rival leader Ibrahim Beg fought on until he was captured and executed in 1931, but the major challenge to the Soviets had passed by 1923. The Soviets also took advantage of famine and related epidemics in Central Asia in 1922–1923 to undermine support for the Basmachis. Food was imported primarily to towns; peasants could receive it only in exchange for growing cotton. The Basmachis were forced into banditry to survive, which damaged their prestige among the peasants.[89]

The warfare, famine, and disease combined to produce hundreds of thousands of refugees who crossed into northern Afghanistan. These people strengthened the minority populations already living there, as well as introducing the karakul sheep, which became a major new industry for Afghanistan. The refugees also provided a sanctuary and base of operations for the Basmachi rebels. As Dupree noted: "Ibrahim Beg waged a guerrilla war against the Soviets, using hit-and-run tactics, always falling back to sanctuary across the Afghan border. In June 1930, the exasperated Soviet army crossed the Amu Darya and followed Ibrahim Beg for about forty miles, 'in hot pursuit.' The troops failed to capture the *basmachi* leader, but succeeded in stunning the Afghans by this frontier violation."[90] Nadir Shah, the new king of Afghanistan, sent an army across the Hindu Kush into northern Afghanistan to drive Ibrahim Beg back into Turkestan, where he was captured and executed. In this manner relations between Afghanistan and the Soviet Union were normalized, and a treaty of neutrality and nonaggression between the two countries was signed in 1931 (an earlier treaty of nonaggression and neutrality in 1926 was also initiated by the Soviets to reduce Afghan support for the Basmachis).[91]

With Ibrahim Beg's death, the Soviets were finally able to consolidate their Central Asian possessions in the absence of major Basmachi-led resistance. The famine produced by Stalin's collectivization policy in the early 1930s, however, led to the rebirth of the Basmachi movement in the region, especially in Tajikistan, which made possible purges of the remaining co-opted national leaders in Central Asia.[92] Indeed, cross-border movements between Afghanistan and the USSR of both refugees and Muslim nationalist fighters continued into at least the mid-1950s;[93] they were paralleled by similar movements of mujahideen in the 1980s.[94]

By 1931 the USSR had consolidated its control over Central Asia, eradicated serious resistance to its regime as embodied in the Basmachi rebels, and normalized its relations with neighboring Afghanistan, the only possible source of support for any rebel movement. The early Soviet leadership had used four methods in order to accomplish its goal of controlling and pacifying its Central Asian republics: diplomatic pressure, economic penetration, military force, and political manipulation. The successful execution of the Soviet reconquest of Central Asia provides a model for subsequent Soviet relations with Afghanistan.

AFGHANISTAN UNDER THE SOVIET SHADOW

Scholars have examined the post-independence history of Afghanistan in several ways. Most, including Vartan Gregorian, Louis Dupree, Ludwig Adamec, and Richard Nyrop,[95] proceed in a chronological fashion, dividing their analyses by the periods of the different rulers. This conventional method allows readers to develop an understanding of both the continuity and changes in Afghan history in a meaningful political framework. Thus, it is possible to consider post-independence, pre-communist Afghanistan as having six historical periods (table 2.1). It is useful to keep these periods in mind, and indeed the remainder of this chapter roughly (but not entirely) follows this format. The analytical focus, however, centers on how the Soviet Union increased its influence in Afghanistan between 1919 and 1978.

After its conquest and consolidation of Turkestan, the USSR turned its attention to Afghanistan. By using essentially the same methods that worked in Turkestan, the Soviets were able to invade Afghanistan when the opportunity and need to do so presented itself in late 1979.

From the very beginning of Afghanistan's era of independence, the new Soviet government attempted to influence events there. This effort derived from the historical competition between Britain and Russia for Central Asia, the even older Russian drive south toward warm waters, and the still older animosity between Russians and Turkic Muslims. Within a few years of Afghanistan's independence the Soviets were in a position in Turkestan to focus their attention farther south. By employing the tools of international relations—diplomatic pressure, economic penetration, political manipulation, military assistance, and ultimately military force—the Soviet Union was able eventually to sweep Afghanistan into its orbit. Examination of the last method, the military force used in Afghanistan in the 1980s, is central to understanding subsequent developments in Afghanistan and is considered in detail in the next chapter. Here I examine modern Afghan history in terms of the Soviet use of the other four methods of influence and penetration.

The USSR began its quest for supremacy in Afghanistan by the patient use of diplomacy. The new government in Moscow under Lenin was the first to recognize Afghanistan's independence and establish diplomatic relations. In fact, an exchange of letters between Amanullah and Lenin relating to the establishment of relations between the countries preceded the Third Anglo-Afghan War that ensured Afghan independence.[96] This correspondence was begun by Amanullah, but the

TABLE 2.1. Afghan Periods and Rulers, 1919–1978

Period	Date	Ruler
1. Early independence	1919–1929	Amanullah
2. Civil war	1929	Bacha Saqqao
3. Nadir Shah interlude	1929–1933	Nadir Shah
4. Constitutional monarchy	1933–1963	Zahir Shah
5. Democratic experiment	1963–1973	Zahir Shah
6. Daoud republic	1973–1978	Mohammad Daoud

Soviets quickly followed up on the opening it provided. By October 1919 the two countries had exchanged missions to discuss Afghanistan's new independence in foreign affairs and the possibilities this created.[97] By August 1921 the two countries had signed and ratified a treaty of friendship (Afghanistan's first treaty since full independence and the Soviet government's first treaty) providing for the establishment of consulates in both countries, the provision of Soviet technical assistance, a Soviet annual subsidy of one million rubles, and the establishment of a telegraph line from Kabul to Soviet territory.[98] The Soviet Union established early consulates at Herat and Mazar-i-Sharif. This treaty served as a modest beginning for Soviet efforts to influence Afghanistan and was still cited in the early years of the current Afghan War as justification for Soviet involvement there.

Afghanistan and the USSR signed two more major treaties before World War II, both preceded by Soviet violations of Afghan territory. After a minor border incident over the Soviet occupation of an island in the Amu Darya in 1925, the two countries signed the Treaty of Nonaggression and Neutrality of 1926. This treaty also provided for the establishment of air service between Moscow and Kabul via Tashkent.[99] The last several years of Amanullah's rule were the apex of Soviet influence in Afghanistan until the 1950s. The Soviet Union had the largest foreign colony in Kabul and initiated various small aid projects throughout the country during this period.[100] The Soviet government also gave Amanullah thirteen military aircraft along with the necessary pilots and technicians.[101]

The swift pace of Amanullah's reforms and efforts at modernizing Afghanistan, however, ultimately produced a revolt in November 1928 that drove him from power. In an inept attempt to regain the throne for him, the Soviets sent 850 to 1,000 men into northern Afghanistan disguised as Afghans and under the nominal leadership of the Afghan ambassador. During April–June 1929 this force captured Mazar-i-Sharif and Tashkurghan and moved toward Kabul, but it was withdrawn in the face of international disapproval.[102] In June 1930 the Soviets again sent a force into Afghanistan, this time in "hot pursuit" of the Basmachi leader Ibrahim Beg. The resolution of this issue led to the signing of a second treaty, the Treaty of Neutrality and Nonaggression of 1931, between the Soviet Union and the government of the new Afghan king, Nadir Shah. Despite this new treaty, both Nadir Shah and Zahir Shah, the son who succeeded him in 1933, grew disenchanted with the Soviets and distanced Afghanistan from the USSR in the 1930s.

Although all the methods used by the Soviets to influence Afghanistan were tied at least indirectly to the diplomatic process, in the early years of Afghanistan's independence the USSR had to rely most heavily on diplomacy to achieve its ends. Until the British left the Indian subcontinent in 1947, Afghanistan, despite its independent status, was still caught between the British and the Soviets. Thus, Soviet efforts to swing Afghanistan into its orbit were modest and, even at that, frequently thwarted by the British.[103] Furthermore, throughout the 1920s and 1930s the USSR was busy combating internal unrest and famine, achieving international recognition, and espousing the spread of communism. It was only after World War II that the nascent superpower, somewhat stymied in Europe, took advantage of the power vacuum created in Central Asia by the withdrawal of the British to intensify its efforts in Afghanistan, as well as in Iran.[104]

Soviet economic penetration of Afghanistan developed in earnest in the 1950s, but early efforts accompanied the diplomatic initiatives of the 1920s and 1930s. Primarily these efforts consisted of the transportation and technical assistance already mentioned and agreements governing the barter of goods in the 1930s. By the early 1930s Afghanistan was exporting wool, carpets, and cotton to the USSR and in return importing oil, gasoline, sugar, and tea.[105] Although trade grew steadily between the two countries, Afghanistan still refused to accept Soviet trade missions in the 1930s, preferring to keep economic relations on the level of barter agreements.[106] Nadir Shah and his successors tried to walk a fine line between Great Britain, which provided military aid in 1931, and the USSR.[107] Afghanistan expanded its relations with Germany and, to a lesser extent, Italy and Japan during the 1930s; the Germans were the dominant foreign presence in Afghanistan by World War II. Still, as Bruce Amstutz noted, "the Soviet share of Afghanistan's foreign trade rose from 7 percent in 1924–25, to 17 percent in 1933–34, and to 24 percent by 1938–39."[108] During World War II, economic development in Afghanistan slowed down considerably as political and military events dominated the attention of the major powers.

Afghanistan remained neutral during World War II, despite its ties to both Allied and Axis powers. World War II so altered the balance of power in Central Asia, however, that the USSR was able to step up its program for acquiring influence in Afghanistan. In 1947 Great Britain, in response to the clamor in India for independence and in recognition of its own newly weakened position in international affairs, partitioned

India into two independent states, India and Pakistan (including Bangladesh, which became an independent nation in 1971). The Muslim state of Pakistan included the Pushtun tribal areas between Afghanistan and the North-West Frontier Province, which provided the basis for an irredentist Afghan claim to this territory that led to a simmering international dispute over the "Pushtunistan" issue until 1955.[109]

Meanwhile, as Great Britain and the other European powers faded from the prominence of international leadership, two new "superpowers" emerged from World War II to take their places: the United States and the Soviet Union. These two states quickly became rivals, Europe was divided into blocs, and by the end of the 1940s the Cold War was well under way. The US had emerged from its isolationism of the 1930s with a vengeance, determined to finance the reconstruction of Europe and develop foreign policy and economic interests all over the world. It could not replace the British presence in the Indian subcontinent, however, leaving the USSR without a real rival in its quest for hegemony over Afghanistan. By 1950 it appeared that the Great Game might finally be over.

During the 1950s the USSR overwhelmed a half-hearted US effort to compete for Afghanistan's friendship with a combination of diplomatic initiatives, economic and technical aid, and military assistance. As both Leon Poullada and Siddieq Noorzoy have argued,[110] Soviet efforts in Afghanistan have always been intentional elements of an overall plan rather than ad hoc or unintentional responses to poorly understood situations. In the late 1940s and early 1950s Afghanistan made repeated overtures to the United States for economic and military aid. For a combination of reasons, but primarily because of Pakistani concern over Afghan intentions, particularly during the Pushtunistan dispute, Washington consistently demurred.[111] Finally, in 1956 Afghanistan accepted military aid from the USSR. This opening, along with trade and transit disruptions by Pakistan during the Pushtunistan trouble, made it possible for the USSR to reestablish its economic relationship with Afghanistan. As Noorzoy pointed out:

> In addition to opening a major avenue of penetration and dependency via the military, this also opened an equally important avenue of penetration through bilateral economic relations.... By 1967, Soviet credits to Afghanistan totaled $570 million. By 1978, the total committed and uncommitted Soviet credit to Afghanistan had climbed to $1.265 billion. A comparison with US credit and grants, which started before 1955 but

totaled only $470 million by 1977, makes it clear that the Soviet strategy was to outperform US financial aid in the developmental process.[112]

Furthermore, the Soviets concentrated loans in certain economic sectors, rescheduled loan repayments, and increased the number of their advisers in Afghanistan until by 1978, "the Soviet economic presence and influence on the formulation of Afghan planning and policy became pervasive."[113]

This was quite intentional. A huge line of credit, low-interest and interest-free loans, transit and barter agreements, construction of the gas pipeline from Shiberghan—every aspect of Soviet economic aid policy increased Afghan reliance on the USSR.[114] That was not all. Soviet diplomacy and military assistance were also undertaken with the intention of drawing Afghanistan closer to the USSR. Poullada outlined the Soviet strategy as follows:

1. To gain maximum psychological advantage, certain project offers were timed to coincide with moments of maximum pressure and distress felt by Afghans in their quarrel with Pakistan....

2. Soviet programs (usually undertaken in Kabul, where they achieved maximum visibility) were devised to win the gratitude of the Afghan public and impress them with Soviet benevolence, so as to lull them into a false sense of security and overcome deep-rooted Afghan suspicion of the Russians....

3. Aid offers were aimed at increasing Soviet potential for political leverage....

4. Economic aid was designed to increase Afghan dependence on the USSR....

5. The Soviet program was designed to improve the long-term strategic value of Afghanistan if and when a Soviet occupation should take place....[115]

Consequently, Soviet aid focused on high-visibility, maximum-use projects (such as paving the streets of Kabul), as opposed to US aid, much of which was bogged down in the Helmand Valley dam and irrigation scheme in remote southwestern Afghanistan.[116] Soviet construction centered on northern Afghanistan, where the road sections from Termez to Kabul and from Kushka through Herat to Kandahar were built to military standards (the US built the Kandahar-to-Kabul section). Also, the Soviets built the Salang Tunnel through the Hindu

Kush, finally linking northern Afghanistan with the rest of the country, and major airfields were built or improved at Bagram, Shindand,
and Kabul (all of which facilitated the Soviet invasion in late 1979–
early 1980).

In addition to the friendly diplomatic posture and massive economic
aid, the Soviets parlayed their initial opening—the agreement on military assistance—into a carte blanche to modernize Afghanistan's armed
forces. Beginning with tanks, bombers, fighters, helicopters, and small
arms, the Afghans supplied their army and air force with Soviet and
Soviet-bloc weapons. Afghanistan first bought $3 million worth of
weapons from Czechoslovakia in 1955. In July 1956, a $32.4 million arms
deal with the Soviets was reached, and the "Sovietization" of the Afghan
armed forces began. By 1978, Soviet military assistance to Afghanistan
totaled $1.25 billion, almost equal to total Soviet economic aid. Fur-
thermore, during this period some 3,725 Afghan military personnel
were trained in the Soviet Union, and Soviet military advisers operated
in Afghanistan.[117] Training programs in the USSR provided the Soviet
intelligence services with an excellent opportunity to subvert and in-
doctrinate Afghan officers, who would later make possible the success
of the 1978 communist coup.

Thus, by 1978 the Afghan armed forces had been transformed, and
their capability was well known to the Soviets. Henry Bradsher stated:
"From armed forces of 44,000 men, plus 20,000 central police, with
almost antique weapons and fewer than twenty-five old piston-engine
warplanes in 1956, the Afghan armed forces had grown by the time of
the 1978 coup to an army of 100,000 men and an air force of 10,000,
both moderately well equipped with modern, but not the very latest,
Soviet weaponry, plus 30,000 paramilitary central police."[118]

By 1978, then, Soviet diplomatic initiatives, economic aid, and military assistance had combined to establish substantial Afghan depen-
dency on the USSR. Poullada summarized it this way:

> By 1978, the Soviets had completed seventy-one separate projects, of
> which fifty-two were still being operated by Soviet technicians. Sixty
> more projects had been agreed upon and the Soviet Union had invested
> more than 3 billion dollars in Afghanistan. By 1978 they had also trained
> 5,000 students in Soviet academic institutions and 1,600 in technical
> schools, plus 3,725 military personnel, of whom some had been coopted
> by the KGB. Long before they ever sent a soldier over the border, the
> Soviet presence in Afghanistan was already overpowering.[119]

In the 1960s, the Soviet Union intensified its efforts to penetrate Afghanistan even further by attempting to manipulate the Afghan political process. It was the use of this method that led to the 1978 coup and the ultimate Soviet invasion of Afghanistan.

The great expansion of Soviet involvement in Afghan society occurred under the first rule of Mohammad Daoud (1953–1963), first cousin to King Zahir Shah. As prime minister, Daoud, like Amanullah in the 1920s, courted the Soviets in part because of his difficulties with Pakistan to the south and the relative neglect of the United States. In 1963, under pressure from the king, Daoud resigned, primarily because of his intransigence over the Pushtunistan issue. He anticipated a return to power through elections mandated by a new constitution; the 1964 constitution, however, precluded royal family members from holding high political office. So he waited while, over the next ten years, Afghanistan embarked on a cautious democratic experiment. Unwillingness to fully embrace democracy (particularly the royal refusal to sanction political parties), combined with continued Western apathy and growing Soviet influence, led to the failure of this experiment.

In July 1973, while Zahir Shah was in Italy, Daoud declared himself president of the new Republic of Afghanistan. During his second period of rule, Daoud began to subtly distance Afghanistan from the USSR and seek more aid from the West and, especially, from Saudi Arabia.[120] In a substantial departure from his approach to ruling in the 1950s, this time Daoud eased the leftists who had supported his coup out of significant governmental positions and demonstrated a traditional nationalist approach to government. When Daoud ordered the arrest of communist party leaders in April 1978 after demonstrations in Kabul following the death of a communist leader, he precipitated the communist coup that toppled his government and brought about his death.[121]

The People's Democratic Party of Afghanistan (the communist party, known as the PDPA until 1990, when it was renamed the Watan, or Homeland, Party) was formed in January 1965 in Kabul.[122] Within two years it had split into two bitterly antagonistic factions—the Khalq (Masses) and the Parcham (Banner)—that never really reunited (except for a brief period in 1977 and 1978 prior to the coup). The PDPA was small (Khalq had about 2,500 members in 1978, Parcham between 1,000 and 1,500) and without real power in the 1970s.[123] However, because of Soviet penetration of the military (especially the officer corps among armored units and the air force) and government workers, key military elements were under communist control and able to attack Daoud in the 1978 coup.

Soviet involvement in Afghanistan, particularly since World War II, had been clearly designed to bring Afghanistan under Soviet hegemony. To achieve this goal, the USSR had used several methods interactively. Prior to World War II the focus was on purely diplomatic initiatives and economic aid, but after the war the Soviets expanded their approach to include military assistance and political manipulation. The success of these combined methods was manifested in the predominant position of the USSR in 1978; it was Afghanistan's biggest trade partner and source of economic aid, it had modernized Afghanistan's armed forces, and with its support Afghanistan's nascent communist party had overthrown the government and was running the country. In April 1978 it certainly appeared that the Soviet Union had finally won the Great Game and taken another step southward toward the Arabian Sea.

But one of the bloodiest and most destructive wars in Afghanistan's history was yet to come. The fledgling Afghan PDPA that overthrew the Daoud government soon faced a national rebellion. By late 1979 it was clear that the PDPA regime would fall without Soviet support, and so on Christmas Day, 1979, the first of some eighty thousand Soviet troops began entering Afghanistan.[124] The direct military intervention of the USSR transformed the Afghan War into a regional and even global geopolitical struggle with ramifications that far exceeded the ruin it brought on Afghanistan itself. It prompted the fall of the Soviet Union and communism in Eastern Europe and the resurgence of Islamism in the Sunni portion of the Muslim World. These events in turn revived and transformed the Great Game for control of and access to Central Asia, even as the nature of that game and some of its players changed. It was the devastating Afghan War that sparked those momentous changes.

3 / Modern War in Afghanistan
Destruction of a State

The dominant factor in Afghanistan's recent history is continuous war since 1978. This war has encompassed seven discrete stages roughly similar in length (an average of thirty-five months each) and is now in an eighth, perhaps final stage. Each stage has been marked by changes in political strategy and military tactics, and taken together they show a pattern of increasing intensity through stage four, followed by declining intensity through the subsequent stages. The transformation of the war through the first five stages represented the efforts of the Soviet Union and the Afghan communist regime to develop a strategy to defeat the mujahideen and then later their efforts to extricate themselves from the conflict. The ultimate failure of the Afghan government to do either, and hence the victory of the rebels, was due to at least four major factors: the nature of the insurgency, the support of the refugees for the insurgents, the involvement of outside actors in support of the insurgents, and the fall of the Soviet Union (and thus the loss of its support) in late 1991.[1] With the defeat of the Najibullah regime in April 1992, the conflict was transformed into a sixth stage, this time between rival mujahideen groups over control of Kabul and the countryside. The capture of Kandahar by the Taliban in November 1994 and their victory in Mazar-i-Sharif in August 1998 mark the beginning and end points of the seventh stage. The eighth stage of the war and predictions for its future conclude this chapter.

How did this terrible tragedy, Afghanistan's long nightmare, happen? The communist coup in April 1978 gave little indication that such a devastating war would ensue. The country's turbulent history had fostered the development of traditional and circumscribed patterns of violence that performed specific roles in society; there was no modern tradition for a war of great magnitude.[2] No one predicted that the local, low-intensity rebellions of late 1978 would evolve into a war of national destruction that would change the course of world history. Yet, as the sections that follow detail, that is exactly what happened.

STAGE ONE: FROM COUP D'ETAT TO SOVIET INVASION (1978–1979)

Three major events occurred during the first stage of the Afghan War. First, a coup d'etat in April 1978 overthrew Mohammad Daoud's nationalist regime and installed the fledgling communist party in power. Second, a rebellion, perhaps more reactionary than loyalist, broke out in the summer of 1978 in response to the coup and the new government's radical reform program. Third, the Soviets intervened in December 1979, in response to the deteriorating position of the Kabul government as the rebellion intensified and widened.

The Afghan War began with the communist coup d'etat by officers in the army and air force on April 27, 1978. This event, now known as the Saur Revolution, developed out of unrest on both sides of the political spectrum over Daoud's policies. Religious traditionalists were unhappy with his "modernization and centralization of authority, which threatened villagers' virtual autonomy."[3] The PDPA, whose bitterly antagonistic factions Khalq and Parcham had ended their ten-year split in a unification conference in July 1977, resented the steady erosion of its position that Daoud's distancing from the Soviet Union had caused.[4]

The new government enjoyed a honeymoon period that for most of the country lasted through the summer of 1978. The summer months were a busy time for the predominantly rural Afghans. Their traditional pattern of local rebellion to express displeasure with government began after the fall harvest. Also, the communists moved slowly in the beginning, focusing first on intraparty squabbles. In July 1978, after a rapprochement of one year, Khalq and Parcham split again. The first of a series of purges sent Babrak Karmal and other senior Parchamis abroad as ambassadors.[5] Open violence was kept to a minimum, however, and the independent-minded Afghan villagers ignored the promulgated reforms. No effort was made to suppress Islam; instead, government officials made a public effort to embrace it.

This moderate approach was somewhat successful, but in late October a series of sweeping reform policies wiped out all previous progress.

A disastrous symbolic move occurred with the introduction of the new national flag in October; the traditional Islamic green was replaced by communist red. It was quickly followed by new policies regarding land reform, credit reform, marriages, and mandatory education for both sexes. Young officials were sent to the countryside to implement these reforms. As Richard and Nancy Newell noted:

> Any one of these programs, tactlessly introduced, would almost certainly have aroused a bitter reaction among most segments of the population. When they were introduced together as a package under the red banner of communism, the effect was catastrophic.... Taken together, these re-forms virtually guaranteed opposition. Their enforcement ... was brought home by government servants who saw no virtue in using tact or diplo-macy. Incidents of protest quickly mushroomed into local armed revolts.[6]

These reforms struck at the very heart of the socioeconomic struc-ture of Afghanistan's rural society; indeed, their sudden nationwide introduction, with no preliminary pilot programs, suggests that this was their real purpose. The bases of authority in rural society were the family and the tribe or clan. Implementation of these reforms eroded the underpinnings of these bases of authority; consequently, it is hardly surprising that they were so fiercely resisted. When the Khalq regime signed a friendship treaty with the USSR in December 1978, it made clear under whose patronage the restructuring of Afghanistan would occur. Thereafter, the rebellion spread rapidly and unremittingly.

By early 1979, most of Afghanistan was in open revolt against the Khalq government. At least twenty-four of the (then) twenty-eight pro-vinces of Afghanistan had suffered outbreaks of violence.[7] The rebellion first developed in the Nuristan valleys of Kunar province in the summer of 1978. By the autumn of 1978, widespread resistance was occurring in the Tajik northeast and the central Hazarajat region. These pockets of earliest upheaval all appeared among oppressed minority populations whose resistance was motivated in part by traditional ethnic hostility toward the Pushtun-dominated government.

Although the initial outbreaks of violence took place among the minorities, antigovernment activity spread rapidly among the Push-tuns, from whom the major early mujahideen groups developed (for sketches of the major political actors in Afghanistan over the past two decades, see the appendix). Most of the leaders split off from Gulbuddin Hekmatyar's Hezb-i-Islami party and acquired the support of local fronts;[8] some of these parties were looser coalitions than others. Push-tun activism was motivated by anger at the reform policies, abhorrence of the new government's manifestly anti-Islamic ideology, and desire for national liberation. By the spring of 1979, nationwide resistance to the Khalq regime had developed. Without the preexisting ethnic tensions and ill-timed government reform policies it is questionable whether the rebellion would have begun so suddenly or spread so vigorously. That it did led inexorably to the Soviet invasion.

In the early spring of 1979, war came to the cities of Afghanistan. In mid-March there was a general uprising in Herat. More than one hundred Soviets reportedly were hunted down and killed in savage violence that claimed three thousand to five thousand lives.[9] Revolts and uprisings in other major cities quickly followed. In April, Afghan army units mutinied in Jalalabad, killing their Soviet advisers and refusing to fight the resistance.[10] Many of these soldiers went over to the mujahideen, equipment in hand. Desertion, unwillingness to serve, and attrition reduced the Afghan Army; by the end of 1980 it had been reduced from eighty thousand to thirty thousand men.[11]

The government in Kabul felt the pressure generated by the popular uprisings in the countryside, particularly the savage fighting in Herat and the defection of its troops in Jalalabad. In April Afghan government forces with Soviet advisers massacred 1,170 men and boys of Kerala village in Kunar, near the border with Pakistan.[12] This atrocity became one of the best known in a war replete with atrocities, and it marked a clear deviation from the stylized tribal violence common less than a year earlier.

Although the conflict spread rapidly throughout Afghanistan, the Herat uprising in particular was responsible for two major developments. First, as Henry Bradsher argued, "Herat was a warning unheeded" that should have led the government to slow the pace of reform and attempt to win popular support.[13] Instead, on March 27, 1979, the Khalq hard-liner Hafizullah Amin assumed the prime ministership and active control of the government, leaving Nur Mohammad Taraki as president and party leader but increasingly without power. The remaining Parchami elements in the government were purged as arrests and executions grew.

Second, the Soviets recognized that they must increase their level of involvement in Afghanistan if the PDPA government was to survive. Accordingly, more advisers and weapons poured into Kabul, some as early as March. The Soviets also began to prepare for a possible invasion.[14] Elite officers and units were sent to Afghanistan, although publicly both governments asserted that the Afghans could take care of their own problems. On September 14, 1979, Amin ousted Taraki, who was killed three weeks later on Amin's orders.[15] Meanwhile, the Soviets' invasion preparations intensified as their dissatisfaction with the performance of the Kabul regime grew.[16]

At the Politburo meeting of November 26, the Soviet leadership committed itself to the invasion of Afghanistan. On December 17 there was an assassination attempt on Amin's life, possibly with Soviet complicity. In response, Amin and some loyal troops moved to the Darulaman Palace on the outskirts of Kabul.[17] If the Soviets had hoped to install Babrak Karmal after assisting another internal coup and assassination, they were now forced to consider another option. Bradsher summarized the Soviet frustration:

> [I]t must have been clear to Soviet leaders that their efforts to control the situation in Afghanistan had failed yet again. They had been unable to direct Afghan policy ... in the summer of 1979, they had failed to get rid of Amin and use Taraki as a more amenable leader in September, they had failed to rein Amin in during the autumn, and now they had failed to destroy him in a quiet, plausible way.... [I]t was time to ... use brute force where diplomacy and conspiracy had failed.[18]

Shortly before midnight on December 24, Soviet troops started landing at the Kabul airport; they were followed by troop landings at the air bases at Bagram and Shindand and the airport at Kandahar. By Christmas morning of 1979 the Soviets were in Afghanistan. On December 27 the Soviet forces attacked Darulaman Palace. The citadel was overrun after a night of vicious fighting, including the use of poisonous gas to overcome the defenders, during which Amin was killed.[19] By January 1, 1980, the Soviets had nearly eighty-five thousand soldiers in Afghanistan. They controlled the cities and government, and their puppet Karmal was in power. The initial invasion of Afghanistan was a success. Stage one of the Afghan War was complete.

STAGE TWO: NATIONAL RESISTANCE AND SOVIET ENTRENCHMENT (1980–1983)

In the immediate aftermath of the Soviet invasion, great uncertainty gripped Afghanistan, during which the Soviets became firmly entrenched in the cities and large towns. International opinion was swift and negative, especially from the United States, but except for symbolic gestures (a grain embargo, a boycott of the Moscow Olympics, UN condemnations), little was done. The opportunity to quickly present a unified opposition to the invasion was lost. Once the Soviets were in Afghanistan they ignored international disapproval and concentrated on consolidating their gains. Meanwhile, the nationwide rebellion against the heavy-handed Khalqi regime was transformed into a national revolution against the Parchami puppet government and its Soviet supporters.

The second stage of the war was characterized more by patterns and trends that developed than by discrete events of importance.[20] Several of these trends warrant analysis. First, the war itself quickly widened and intensified. By the spring of 1980 the Soviets had more than one hundred thousand troops in Afghanistan, and throughout the year they engaged in heavy fighting in all parts of the country. Combat was particularly fierce around Kabul, Baghlan, and Jalalabad and in the Salang Tunnel area. Violent uprisings occurred in Kandahar, Herat, and Jalalabad that wrested those cities temporarily from government control. Typical insurgency activities took place elsewhere, although reports from the northern and central areas of the country were spotty. Soviet efforts to regain control in Nuristan and the Hazarajat were unsuccessful.

Second, a tactical pattern emerged that would characterize the next two stages of the war. The mujahideen mounted attacks from the mountains; the Soviets responded with combined arms offensives up the valleys to relieve pressure on the cities and major roads. The mujahideen gained control of parts of Herat, Kandahar, and the other cities, especially at night. In late August 1980 the Soviets launched the first of what was to become a series of large-scale offensives up the Panjshir Valley after the elusive rebel leader Ahmed Shah Massoud. When they withdrew, the mujahideen resumed control.

These patterns of conflict intensified over the next two years as Soviet–Democratic Republic of Afghanistan (DRA) outposts were established along the horseshoe-shaped main road of Afghanistan. Amstutz described this early phase of the war: "By the end of 1981 all 29 provinces of the country were experiencing guerrilla warfare. No province remained loyal to the Kabul government or welcomed the Soviet forces. Reports were frequent of ambushes on Soviet–DRA convoys and attacks on government administrative posts in the countryside. Security on the main highways markedly deteriorated; nighttime highway traffic became confined to insurgent-manned jeeps and trucks."[21]

From 1981 onward, rural Afghanistan (more than 75 percent of the country) was effectively under resistance control except during periods when the Soviet–DRA forces were directly contesting it. Thus, a traditional insurgency pattern developed. The regime held the cities and a string of military bases and outposts while the resistance controlled the countryside. The ability of the mujahideen to display their control openly was directly related to the strategic value of the area in question and the proximity of Soviet forces. Some remote areas, such as the Hazarajat, Nimruz, and Nuristan, were essentially independent from the central government.

By the beginning of 1983 the Soviets were finishing their process of building bases and stationing units in every province of Afghanistan; it would be completed by the end of the year. In the three years since the invasion the Soviets had concentrated on establishing their presence throughout the country—particularly in the northern provinces, along the main road, and in the major cities—while mounting periodic major operations into guerrilla strongholds. Especially targeted were the Panjshir (six major operations) and other strategic valleys and the areas around Herat and Mazar-i-Sharif. Soviet–DRA forces tended to rotate between combined arms search-and-destroy operations and garrison duty. During this period the resistance was politically divided and militarily weak. Few of the combat mujahideen were adept at anything beyond limited guerrilla tactics. They were poorly armed and trained, and in certain areas resistance was temporarily driven into quiescence.

The overwhelming firepower of the Soviet forces, coupled with their total air superiority, introduced the destructiveness of modern combat to Afghanistan. Villages and civilian populations were targets from the beginning of the conflict; as in all guerrilla wars, the inability to distinguish the fighters from the usually supportive noncombatants fostered an indiscriminate attitude by the Soviets. In addition to the atrocities and horrors this approach engendered, it created refugees.

Refugees had fled Afghanistan since the mid-1970s in small numbers; by the time of the invasion some four hundred thousand were already in Pakistan. The Soviets' "rubbleization" tactics, calculated to destroy villages and basic infrastructure, forced people to flee in even greater numbers.[22] By the end of stage two, there were nearly 3 million refugees in Pakistan and an unknown number (probably exceeding 1.5 million) in Iran. The big surge in refugees occurred in the first two years after the Soviet invasion, when more than 4 million fled to Pakistan and Iran while hundreds of thousands more became internally displaced. Since 1981 the Afghan refugee population has been the largest in the world (for example, by 1990, Pakistan was host to 4 million Afghans, Iran had 2.4 million refugees, and more than 2 million people were internally displaced in Afghanistan).[23] The strategy that produced these refugees was taken directly from the teachings of Mao Zedong and the old guerrilla masters. Dupree termed it "migratory genocide" in an effort to capture the impact this terrible dislocation—and the danger and death that produced it—had on the Afghan people and their culture.[24]

A number of political and economic developments of importance also occurred during this stage. A nascent political opposition with its headquarters in Peshawar, Pakistan, had formed by 1980, but it was characterized by factionalism throughout this period (and afterward). Western support developed slowly because of the widely held belief that the rebels had no chance. As it became clear that the war would be protracted, the US set up a Central Intelligence Agency (CIA) arms "pipeline" through Pakistan to funnel aid to the resistance. Pakistan's Inter-Services Intelligence Directorate (ISI) managed the aid to and training of the mujahideen groups. Some knowledgeable observers have even suggested that the ISI ran the war.[25] Under Pakistani pressure, the numerous fledgling resistance and refugee organizations based in Peshawar ultimately crystallized into seven Sunni exile parties, generally headed by survivors from the Kabul University Islamist movement of the 1960s. These parties were classified as either "fundamentalist" or "moderate" on the basis of factors such as their ideology, the background of their leaders, and their sources of support.

An early split of the Islamist movement had occurred in 1976–1977 when Burhanuddin Rabbani formed the Jamiat-i-Islami (Islamic Society), leaving Gulbuddin Hekmatyar and the Hezb-i-Islami (Islamic Party). This would become the most significant division among the Afghan mujahideen, culminating in their struggle for control of Kabul in the mid-1990s. These two parties became the largest of the resistance organizations, and until the emergence of the Taliban in 1994, Hekmatyar's party received the largest share of Pakistani aid. Hekmatyar's Hezb-i-Islami was 75 percent Pushtun, primarily from the Ghilzai and smaller tribes (Hekmatyar himself is a Kharruti Pushtun). Its strongest bases of support were in northeastern Afghanistan and among the Afghan refugee population in Pakistan.[26] Jamiat became the major organization of the northern minority groups—it was dominated by

Tajiks and other Persian speakers (Rabbani is a Badakhshani Tajik), but it also included some Pushtuns (primarily Ghilzai but also some Ali-kozai Durrani) and Uzbeks. Jamiat would be less rigid ideologically than Hekmatyar's party, and the Jamiat commanders enjoyed much greater autonomy. Perhaps for this reason, several rose to prominence, notably Ahmed Shah Massoud of the Panjshir Valley and Ismail Khan of Herat.

In 1979, Maulavi Yunus Khalis left Hekmatyar's Hezb-i-Islami and, with affiliated leaders such as the Jadran Pushtun tribal leader Mau-lavi Jallaluddin Haqani of Paktia and the Arsala brothers (Haji Din Mohammad; Nangarhar commander Abdul Qadir; and, most notably, Kabul commander Abdul Haq), formed his own Hezb-i-Islami. Khalis is a Khugiani Pushtun religious teacher. His small but militarily effective party, however, was overwhelmingly composed of Ghilzai and other east-ern Pushtun tribesmen.[27] The last major fundamentalist party, Ittehad-i Islami Bara-yi Azadi Afghanistan (Islamic Union for the Freedom of Afghanistan), was formed by Abdur Rasoul Sayyaf out of an ISI effort to create an alliance in early 1980. A Kharruti Pushtun like both Hekmat-yar and Hafizullah Amin, Sayyaf had strong ties to the Arab supporters of the mujahideen but very few Afghan mujahideen or commanders.

The three traditional political parties had also appeared as separate entities by 1980. Professor Sibghatullah Mojaddidi, imprisoned under Daoud, used his traditional family and Naqshbandiyya Sufi linkages to create the Jebha-i-Milli Nejat (National Liberation Front) by the end of 1978. Militarily the weakest of all the parties, Mojaddidi had the support of pockets of Pushtuns, including key Popolzai Durrani Push-tuns in Kandahar.[28] Similarly, Maulavi Mohammad Nabi Mohammadi turned the Harakat-i Inqilab-i Islami (Movement of the Islamic Revo-lution) coalition into his own party, which by all accounts was the strongest front early in the war.[29] Mohammadi is a Ghilzai Ahmadzai from Logar who had been a member of parliament in the 1960s. His party was based strongly on "the inward-looking, traditionalist, pro-vincial ulama" and, unsurprisingly, was the organization most affiliated with the rise of the Taliban in 1994.[30] The final party to form before the invasion was Pir Sayed Ahmed Gailani's Mahaz-i-Milli Islami-yi Afghanistan (National Islamic Front of Afghanistan, or NIFA) in late 1978–early 1979, based on family tribal ties and his Qadiriyya Sufi fol-lowers. Gailani not only had a religious title but also was married to a granddaughter of Amir Habibullah; he was thus the strongest propo-nent throughout the war of a return of the king to Afghanistan. His supporters included the leaders of the Barakzai Durrani Pushtuns in Kandahar.

In addition to the seven Sunni parties based in Pakistan, a number of smaller Shia parties emerged, primarily based in and supported by Iran. In the early days of the resistance, four Shia parties were important. The Shura-i-Inqilab-i Ittefaq-i Islami Afghanistan (Revolutionary Council of the Islamic Union of Afghanistan), headed by Hazara religious leader Sheikh Sayed Ali Beheshti, controlled the Hazarajat from 1979 to 1982. Isolated by the rugged topography of the nation's interior from the struggle against the Soviet Union, the Shia community conducted its own internal struggle among radicals, traditionalists, and Islamists. The other three groups were Sheikh Asif Mohseni's Harakat-i Islami (Islamic Movement), with support from both the Hazara and Qizilibash populations; Sazman-i Nasr-i Islam-yi Afghanistan (Islamic Victory Organization of Afghanistan), a strongly Khomeinist Hazara group; and Pazdaran-i Jihad-i Islami (Protectors of the Islamic Holy War), also a Khomeinist Hazara group.[31] More Shia groups would emerge later in the war,[32] and in 1989 Tehran forced them all into an umbrella organization known as Hezb-i-Wahdat (Unity Party).

Meanwhile, inside Afghanistan the Parchamis, having acquired power, engaged in a sometimes violent purge of their bitter rivals, the Khalqis. Arrests, torture, and executions of members of the general population increased, too. The Soviet Committee for State Security (KGB) particularly favored these methods in 1982–1983 after the lack of success by major military operations in 1980–1981.

The Soviets increasingly ran the government after the invasion. Numerous accounts exist of ministries and departments with figurehead Afghans unable to conduct even routine business without the approval of Soviet advisers, who totaled more than ten thousand by 1984.[33] Even Karmal had little room for independent decision making.[34] The Soviets also provided substantial economic aid ($350 million in 1980 alone), signed trade agreements providing Afghanistan with a market for its goods (primarily natural gas, which the USSR got at below market prices), and tripled their arms exports to Afghanistan ($683 million in 1980).[35]

Finally, a number of steps were taken to prepare Afghanistan for eventual integration into the Soviet sphere and perhaps ultimately into the union. More than ten thousand children were taken to the USSR for "education" programs, some to last as long as ten years.[36] The northern provinces bordering the Soviet Union underwent especially rigorous pacification campaigns. A "concentric circle" strategy was applied to the northern cities, whereby the Soviets tried gradually to take control of the areas around these cities, denying the resistance access and ultimately pacifying the resident population. The Soviets had even annexed the Wakhan Corridor by the fall of 1980. There were reports that Leonid Brezhnev wanted to annex the eight northern provinces, but the Afghan government, particularly the Khalqi faction, strongly resisted the proposal.[37] By the end of stage two, the "Sovietization" of Afghanistan was well under way.

In short, stage two was characterized by the widening of the war to every area of the country. The Soviet–DRA forces grew in strength while the mujahideen were weak and ineffective. Mujahideen successes were few, although Massoud blunted six major offensives in the Panjshir Valley during this period. Stage two demonstrated that the Soviet Union was preparing to stay in Afghanistan indefinitely. The Soviets had penetrated every department of the government, had reorganized their armed forces to meet the Afghan situation, were engaged in extensive weapons testing in the countryside, and appeared to be comfortable with winning the war gradually.

STAGE THREE: AIR WAR, INTERDICTION, AND DESTABILIZATION (1983–1986)

Stage three emerged in 1983 as the Soviets made a significant change in their military strategy. During the first years of occupation, Soviet priorities were to control the cities, protect the northern pipelines, keep the major roads open, and broaden the government's base of support. By 1983, the pipelines and roads were as secure as they would ever get, the Soviets controlled 15 to 20 percent of the country, primarily the cities and major military installations, and it was increasingly evident that the government's base of support could not easily be broadened. In late 1983 and early 1984 the Soviets stepped up their counterinsurgency campaign; the gradually improving mujahideen could not keep pace.

The other major change from stage two was that conditions in the arena of conflict had been transformed. Much of the population had fled or was disrupted by late 1983, the countryside had been ravaged, all parts of the country had seen warfare, and the major Soviet installations were well established. Thus, the next step for the Soviets was to intensify and widen the war and further weaken the support structure of the mujahideen. To that end they shifted to an air war in 1983, bombing villages and depopulating rural areas that provided vital support to the mujahideen.

Urban warfare was particularly fierce that year, notably in Herat, Kandahar, and Mazar-i-Sharif. More than three thousand Afghans reportedly died in the bombing of Herat in April, and Kandahar was also heavily bombed. Both of these bombing campaigns came in an effort to wrest control of large sections of these cities out of the hands of the resistance.[38] After six unsuccessful offensives in the Panjshir Valley, the Soviets negotiated a de facto truce with Massoud in March 1983. During the summer the mujahideen made two major attacks on Kabul. Mujahideen offensives in Paktia overran small DRA posts at Jaji and Khost, and the garrison at Urgun was besieged. In late December 1983–early January 1984, the Soviets relieved beleaguered Urgun.[39]

Although 1984 saw a continuation of the Soviet air war strategy, numerous large-scale offensives were also conducted. A guerrilla ambush in March near the Salang Pass prompted a concerted effort to crush the resistance in the Panjshir Valley. Panjshir offensive seven occurred during April–September 1984, followed by Panjshir offensive eight in October–November. The valley was largely depopulated, and DRA garrisons were left behind.[40]

Herat and Kandahar were the targets of multidivision offensives with heavy air support in June 1984; Herat also saw heavy fighting in July, August, and, with the other western provinces, November. The Soviets also tried to sweep the valleys around Kabul to reduce mujahideen pressure on the capital. They pushed up the Logar and Shomali valleys in July and August 1984 and destroyed the town of Paghman west of Kabul in late November 1984. Still, the introduction by the mujahideen of 107-mm and 122-mm rockets and SA-7 missiles allowed the resistance to keep the pressure on, with big rocket attacks on Kabul also in November 1984. Late in the year the Soviets made efforts to seal the border with Pakistan, particularly in Paktia.[41]

The emphasis on interdiction of mujahideen supply lines increased during 1985, and the Soviets augmented their air war strategy with increased use of artillery and rocket launchers to achieve "depopulation through firepower."[42] Nonetheless, the mujahideen, with improved arms and tactics, conducted several larger operations in 1985 and felt strong enough to stand and fight for the first time in the war.

In January–February 1985 the Soviets made an attempt to relieve their besieged garrison at Barikot, on the Pakistani border in Kunar. They were unsuccessful, but a concerted push in May–June 1985 succeeded.

Another Panjshir-based attack cut the Salang Pass highway between Kabul and Kunduz in March 1985 and led to the ninth unsuccessful Panjshir offensive later that summer. In an effort to isolate western Afghanistan from Iran, a June 1985 offensive in the Helmand Valley and a summer offensive in Herat were mounted. Also, late summer attacks on Khost by the rebels led to a Soviet offensive in Paktia during August–September 1985.[43] During 1985, conflict incidents for the first time averaged more than 200 per month: an average of 217 incidents took place in 24 of 29 provinces (Nimruz and the Hazarajat provinces were usually quiet).[44]

The war leaped in intensity in 1986 as it shifted into stage four. The first four months alone averaged 329 conflict incidents in 26 provinces.[45] There were many major engagements or other incidents throughout the country. Increased mujahideen activity was evident in all the northern provinces bordering the USSR, including an attack on the Faizabad air base in March 1986. In a major battle in early April 1986, a Soviet–DRA force attacked and destroyed an important mujahideen cave complex at Zhawar, Paktia. Rebel commander Jallaluddin Haqani led a spirited fight before ultimately being driven out. Although this was hailed as a Soviet victory, it came at a great cost in casualties and abated mujahideen pressure in the region only temporarily.[46]

To summarize, two important military trends occurred during this third stage of the war. First, the mujahideen finally began to jell into an effective fighting force. Although they were still disunited, even after the Peshawar parties formed a political alliance in June 1985, mujahideen combat operations improved. The Panjshir could not be wrested from Massoud, enabling him to operate against Salang and the Kunduz road. Support to the mujahideen took on meaningful proportions, including SA-7 and Blowpipe missiles and 107-mm and 122-mm rockets, and they had some success against Soviet air power. The Soviet press reported low morale and poor discipline among the troops.

Still, this stage belonged to the Soviets. Strategy shifted from consolidation of cities, highways, and the north to focus on the eastern provinces, although efforts were made to improve infrastructure in the north. "Rubbleization" of rural villages intensified the refugee crisis. Tactics changed; special operations and airborne units interdicted mujahideen supply lines. The ruthless use of air power was critical during this period because it increased the intensity of the war, caused widespread destruction, and provided a long-term advantage against the insurgency.

On the political front, repeated rounds of Geneva talks took place during this stage (April, June, and November 1983, August 1984, June 1985). Although little progress had been made since the talks had begun in 1982, major points of contention were gradually being hammered out during this period.[47] In 1985 Mikhail Gorbachev became the new Soviet general secretary. The Afghan resistance remained hopelessly divided and politically ineffective, unable to agree on anything, despite the creation of a unified front by the seven major Sunni parties in Peshawar on May 16, 1985.

Stage three lasted until the lack of progress in broadening support for the puppet regime led the Soviets to remove Karmal and replace him with former secret police (KhAD) chief Najibullah on May 4, 1986.[48] This act, coupled with another surge in war activity in 1986 and important strategic and tactical developments later in the year, marked the end of stage three and the beginning of stage four.

STAGE FOUR: RESISTANCE GAINS AND SOVIET WITHDRAWALS (1986–1989)

The political and military patterns of the previous two stages reached fruition in stage four. Not only was this period replete with important developments, but in intensity it was the climactic stage of the war. Throughout stage three, it was apparent that the mujahideen were slowly losing the war. The Soviet combination of refocusing strategic aims and refining new tactics (in particular the increased reliance on overwhelming air power) was effectively driving the mujahideen off the battlefield. The lengthy conflict, however, was also taking a toll on Soviet morale and political will to continue. A paradox emerged. Soviet military superiority, though still incomplete in light of mujahideen successes—most of them small-scale and minor, some spectacular and symbolic—nonetheless had driven rebels and civilians out of the countryside and onto the defensive. On the other hand, the resistance, which throughout the conflict was more capable militarily than politically, appeared to be winning the political competition for Afghanistan. The people of Afghanistan supported the resistance fighters overwhelmingly, and international opinion remained firmly on their side.[49]

The war in Afghanistan continued to intensify during stage four. Soviet strategy remained built around aerial bombardment of the rural areas that supported mujahideen operations. Nonetheless, many ground operations were conducted as well, particularly in the zone from

Kandahar to Bagram, in the provinces bordering Pakistan. There was also increased combat activity in the northern provinces, from Herat to Kunduz.[50] The positioning of small commando units to ambush supply routes continued to pose a formidable hazard to the mujahideen early in this period.

The most notable expansion of the war was the increased violation of Pakistani and Iranian territory by Soviet forces. The spillover into these countries—Pakistan especially—took several forms: air strikes, artillery attacks, terrorist explosions, assassinations, manipulation of politically disaffected tribes, and sabotage and disruption. These incidents tripled in 1986 and remained at this higher level of intensity until the Soviet withdrawal in 1989.[51] The Soviets deliberately widened the war in order to sow discontent among the local population and thus to pressure the Pakistani government. They also aimed to show the Afghan resistance fighters that their sanctuary was not safe.

During this fourth stage of the war the mujahideen improved militarily. Their operations became larger and more complex, including offensive operations bigger than ambushes.[52] Beginning in October 1986, certain resistance groups began to receive US-made Stinger missiles through the CIA arms pipeline. The gradual qualitative improvement in aid received by the mujahideen during the war (SA-7 and Blowpipe missiles, Oerlikon and 14.5-millimeter ZPU antiaircraft guns, multibarreled rocket launchers, long-range mortars, radios) culminated with the introduction of this advanced antiaircraft missile. The Stinger was the most important of the many new weapons used in the war; by the end of 1986 it provided the mujahideen with a credible air defense for the first time. Reports of incredible accuracy induced the Soviets to change their hitherto successful air war strategy.[53] They reduced the number of air missions, and pilots became reluctant to fly at low altitudes. The sense of impunity with which Soviet fighters, bombers, and expecially the terrifying helicopter gunships had previously operated were gone.

Statistics for the conflict during stage four demonstrate that the war had escalated to a fever pitch. Data indicate a monthly average of 346 incidents in 26 of 29 provinces in 1986, an increase of 61 percent over the monthly rate of the last 7 months of 1985.[54] The rate increased to 416 incidents for the first 10 months of 1987, again covering 26 provinces each month, an increase of 20 percent over the 1986 rate.[55] Quantitative evidence for 1988 and 1989 was unavailable to me, but accounts indicate that the conflict further increased in intensity, peaking in the months just prior to the Soviet withdrawal.[56]

After Gorbachev acquired power in March 1985, Soviet policy toward Afghanistan began to change. Increasing domestic discontent over the Afghan War found more open expression in the press and finally, with Gorbachev's February 1986 "bleeding wound" speech, received official countenance. Concerned with the state of the Soviet economy and overall relations with the West, Gorbachev pressured his generals and Afghan allies to bring the war to a resolution.

The May 1986 promotion of KhAD chief Najibullah to president was a calculated attempt by the Soviets to replace the discredited Karmal, whose ethnic background was unclear, with a Pushtun who might appeal to that traditionally dominant ethnic group (Najibullah was an Ahmadzai Ghilzai; his wife was descended from the Amanullah branch of the royal family).[57] Of course, the ruthless head of KhAD could hardly have been expected to be more acceptable to the Afghans; it is likely that he was also chosen for his hard-line attitude.

Najibullah quickly moved to broaden his government and buy time for the massive military option to bear fruit. He announced a unilateral ceasefire in January 1987, which both sides ignored from the beginning. This was followed by an attempt in May 1987 to form a "national reconciliation" government, which also failed. It was quickly apparent that Najibullah's government would be no more successful with the general population than was Karmal's regime. Still, during the years he remained in power, Najibullah took a number of steps to make the government more popular that collectively represented a retreat from the earlier communist ideology.[58]

Unfortunately for the mujahideen, the unified front of the Peshawar parties was also a failure. Internecine fighting among party factions in Afghanistan continued and, combined with policy differences and petty jealousies among the Peshawar politicos, undermined claims of unity by the resistance. Thus the mujahideen leaders were unable to take advantage of the eroding political position of the Kabul government.

In 1987, growing Soviet-American rapprochement increased pressure for a settlement on Afghanistan. The shuttle diplomacy of indirect talks by UN representative Diego Cordovez became more intense. Rounds six, seven, and eight of the Geneva talks were held in 1986, 1987, and 1988, respectively. The final set of talks in March 1988 ended in an agreement, signed on April 14, 1988, calling for a nine-month phased Soviet withdrawal from Afghanistan.[59] Although combat continued at high intensity in 1988, the withdrawal was completed on February 15, 1989. The withdrawal of Soviet combat troops marked the end of stage four.

STAGE FIVE: HIGH-INTENSITY CIVIL WAR (1989–1992)

The war did not end after the Soviet withdrawal but was transformed into a fifth stage of national civil war. Many observers expected the Kabul regime to fall rapidly, and heightened pressure by the mujahideen on Kandahar in the southwest and in Paktia, Kunar, and the eastern border provinces lent credence to these optimistic views. In March 1989, a joint mujahideen offensive was initiated to capture Jalalabad in order to put pressure on Kabul and provide the resistance leadership with an in-country base and symbolic capital. The Jalalabad offensive represented the mujahideen's mistaken move "from guerrilla to conventional warfare prematurely."[60] The inability of the mujahideen to coordinate their attacks, along with stiff resistance by government forces, led to the failure of the siege after three months. For the remainder of 1989 and into 1990 the war continued its high intensity despite the absence of Soviet combat forces.

Several important developments characterized this stage: continued covert Soviet involvement in the conflict and support for the Kabul regime, the resilience of the Najibullah government, continued disunity among the resistance, and the erosion of US support for the mujahideen. The critical question revolved around the possibility of Afghanistan's peaceful transition to legitimate national government given continued Soviet involvement and pressure.

In fact, the mujahideen were unable to defeat the Najibullah regime until April 1992 for two major reasons. First, the Soviets continued to provide extensive support to the regime in an airlift that rivaled the Berlin airlift of 1948–1949. Estimates of the monetary value of the assistance varied but fell within a range of $250 million to $300 million per month.[61] This assistance included the newly introduced FROG and SCUD missiles, which augmented the indirect fire capability of the Kabul government and nullified the impact of the Stinger missiles. Thousands of Soviet technicians and military advisers remained in Afghanistan after the withdrawal, and there were reports of Soviet soldiers masquerading in Afghan uniforms. There was also continued Soviet air support from bases in Soviet Central Asia.[62] During this stage, US aid to the mujahideen declined to an average of $40 million to $50 million per month.

After their withdrawal the Soviets also infused their standard policy of blaming the West for the Afghan conflict with new vigor. A major disinformation and propaganda campaign aimed at Western media and policymakers subtly altered perceptions. Ignoring or dismissing the awesome damage they had done to Afghanistan, the Soviets insisted that responsibility for continuation of the war rested with the mujahideen and their Western supporters. This view was coupled with a Soviet call for "negative symmetry," a mutual termination of military aid to their Afghan clients by both the US and the USSR, a position the Soviets had rejected during the negotiations for the Geneva accords (which had prompted the US to reserve the right to continue aiding the mujahideen, a practice known as "positive symmetry").[63] During the Geneva negotiations the mujahideen were well supplied, and a rough parity in armaments existed between mujahideen and DRA forces. As Western attention focused elsewhere following the Soviet withdrawal (notably on Eastern Europe and China in 1989) and as Western support for the mujahideen dried up, negative symmetry offered a clear advantage to the DRA regime.

Further, during the nine months of phased withdrawal of Soviet forces, combat operations were increased, mines were scattered around the countryside, and efforts to undermine Pakistani support for the mujahideen were intensified. The ammunition dump in Rawalpindi, Pakistan, exploded at the beginning of this period (April 1988), destroying a massive cache of CIA-supplied war materiel, and Pakistani President Zia ul-Haq was assassinated in August 1988, eliminating the major supporter of the mujahideen.

The second major reason for the continuation of the Afghan conflict was the inability of the Afghan resistance to mount a credible alternative. The Afghan Interim Government (AIG) formed in February 1989 was a failure, doomed by the perpetual bickering of the Peshawar party leaders who were its primary participants. The Shia minority was excluded from a role in the AIG, as were the major resistance commanders inside Afghanistan. The AIG split apart in late 1989, divided by internecine violence between the forces of Hekmatyar and Massoud.

In the absence of Zia and his most important generals, killed with him in August 1988, Pakistani support for the mujahideen became uncertain. Western aid was bottled up in the Pakistani pipeline, and more importantly, Pakistani pressure on the mujahideen for a victory mounted. It was this pressure that pushed the mujahideen into their ill-considered offensive against Jalalabad in March 1989. The mujahideen, masters of guerrilla warfare, lacked the cohesiveness essential to successful conventional warfare and thus were stymied by the new conditions of the fifth stage of the Afghan War.[64]

The relative strength of the Najibullah regime, bolstered by massive Soviet support, together with the fractiousness and uncertainty of the resistance, undermined by shifting Western and Pakistani support, made possible the survival of the Kabul government and the continuation of the Afghan War. Still, despite their usual failure to cooperate, the mujahideen mounted significant attacks on Khost, Herat, Kandahar, and Kabul during 1990.[65] A military stalemate existed throughout the year, with government forces in control of the strategic centers and able to use air power to stave off resistance attacks while the mujahideen struggled with their political discord and military inability to shift from guerrilla to conventional warfare.

In March 1990 Najibullah survived a coup attempt led by Defense Minister Shahnawaz Tanai, which demonstrated the continued division within the PDPA between the Parcham and Khalq factions (Tanai was Khalqi). Tanai subsequently joined Hekmatyar, who was caught in factional infighting of his own with the other resistance leaders during the year. This fighting culminated in a July 1990 ambush by Hekmatyar's forces of men loyal to Massoud and the subsequent execution of those responsible by Massoud's men in August 1990. Efforts to patch the rift that autumn achieved some success, but the inability of the resistance to unite led to growing disillusionment on the part of its Western supporters. Efforts to reach a diplomatic solution to the war, primarily between the US and the USSR, were rumored throughout the year, but none bore fruit.

Under pressure of the loss of Soviet support, Najibullah made conciliatory gestures throughout the year. He moved away from Marxism toward an Islamic nationalist identity by convening a *loya jirga* (national assembly), replacing key government ministers, and changing the name of the PDPA to Hezb-i-Watan (Homeland Party). He made numerous diplomatic trips abroad and floated several peace initiatives, but all of them included the proviso that he remain in or share power, and all were rejected by the resistance.

In 1991 the resistance made some gains. In March the long siege of Khost ended in victory for the mujahideen, and they immediately tightened their grip around Gardez. Division within the opposition ranks, however, continued to prevent the establishment of a unified alternative to Najibullah. The well-established rift between Islamist and traditionalist parties masked deeper ethnic-linguistic-religious differences and the demand of the Iranian-based resistance organizations and field commanders that they be represented in any political settlement. This situation provided an excellent arena for growing rivalry between Saudi Arabia, Iran, and Pakistan for control of Afghanistan's political future.[66]

Despite the Khost victory and the earlier Jalalabad campaign, this stage of the war was characterized more by events outside of Afghanistan—albeit inspired, at least in part, by the Soviet withdrawal from Afghanistan in 1989—than by the struggle for military supremacy on the ground. In May 1991 the United Nations produced a peace plan that finally offered the possibility of a transition away from fighting. More generally, 1989 brought the collapse of communism in Eastern Europe and 1990 the implementation of widespread economic and political reforms throughout that region and the Soviet Union. Despite the precipitous economic decline that occurred in the USSR during this period, Soviet weapons and economic assistance continued to pour into Kabul, averaging $300 million per month. It seemed that only the loss of Soviet patronage could bring Najibullah down.

The August 1991 Russian coup attempt against Mikhail Gorbachev marked the beginning of the end for the USSR—and for the Najibullah government. In September 1991 the two superpowers agreed to cut off military assistance to their respective clients in Afghanistan by the beginning of 1992. The Soviet Union also limited economic aid and tightened restrictions on such aid in late 1991. On December 25, 1991, Gorbachev resigned, and the Soviet Union broke apart. With its demise, the end of the communist government in Kabul was finally at hand.

STAGE SIX: FROM VICTORY TO FRAGMENTATION (1992–1994)

When Abdul Rashid Dostam's northern Uzbek militia rebelled against Najibullah's government in February 1992, the days of the regime were numbered. Najibullah agreed to step aside under the UN-sponsored plan that would replace him with a multiparty interim government. Determined not to be cheated out of victory after fourteen years of war, the mujahideen moved into Kabul in April 1992 in a surprisingly bloodless victory. An interim government was established on the basis of the April 1992 Peshawar accord; it was headed by Sibghatullah Mojaddidi of the Jebha-i-Milli Nijat but really was based on a fifty-man leadership shura with members from all the ten major parties then existing (seven Sunni and three Shia parties). This government held power in Kabul for two months, until late June 1992. Then Mojaddidi reluctantly but peacefully turned power over to Burhanuddin Rabbani, the leader of Jamiat-i-Islami, whose interim government was to rule for four months, or until October 1992. At that time, a mechanism to select a permanent government was to be implemented—either national elections or another shura.

Rabbani, however, refused to step aside in October and was elected president by an assembly dominated by his supporters in December 1992. His chief rival, Gulbuddin Hekmatyar, leader of one Pushtun-dominated Hezb-i-Islami party, rejected this government. In March 1993, eight major parties reached an agreement in Islamabad, Pakistan, to allow Rabbani to finish an eighteen-month term of office, but with Hekmatyar as prime minister. Also, elections for an assembly that would approve a new constitution were to be scheduled for within eight months.[67] Control of the defense ministry, held since the previous year by Ahmed Shah Massoud, Rabbani's chief supporter and Hekmatyar's major rival, was turned over to a sixteen-member council, with two members from each party. The northern Uzbek warlord Abdul Rashid Dostam was left out of the agreement entirely, as were the rulers of the western cities of Herat and Kandahar.

Despite the Islamabad accord, the rival mujahideen groups and militias could never settle on an acceptable power-sharing arrangement, and fighting flared repeatedly between groups who allied with each other in various and constantly shifting combinations. Indeed, ever since the collapse of the Najibullah regime there has been difficulty in making a national coalition government a reality. Continued violence between various resistance organizations, tribal militias, and former government forces, especially in and around Kabul, underscored the deep divisions between the groups vying for power. Although Hekmatyar and a cabinet were finally sworn in on June 17, 1993, Hekmatyar's own forces shelled the capital later that month, and he did not settle in the city or convene a full cabinet meeting. His status as a government official, like that of many others, was unclear for virtually all of stage six.[68]

The most obvious manifestation of the disunity of this and the next stage was the ugly internecine violence among former mujahideen rivals for power in Kabul. From almost the beginning of the post-Najibullah era, squabbling among contenders degenerated into violence. Because Massoud's Shura-i-Nazar (Council of the North), in conjunction with Dostam's militia, initially controlled most of Kabul, Hekmatyar's forces attacked the city numerous times from their bases south of the city in Charasyab. These attacks began in April 1992 and continued until Hekmatyar's forces fled in the face of the first Taliban advance on the city in early 1995. In one of the more ironic twists of the Afghan War, Kabul, which had survived the first five stages of the war relatively unscathed, became a major battleground. Perhaps as many as 50,000 people have been killed and 150,000 wounded there, and hundreds of thousands have fled the city, large areas of which have been reduced to rubble since 1992.[69] Despite these casualties, much of Afghanistan was peaceful during this stage, and the war's intensity slackened for the first time.

Control of various parts of Kabul and its environs, like control of various parts of Afghanistan, fell to competing groups. In 1992–1993, the northern minorities led by Massoud and Dostam controlled most of the city center and northeastern quarter, where many government buildings are located, while their Pushtun rivals occupied the high ground and suburbs south of the city. The Hezb-i-Wahdat controlled neighborhoods in the western quarter. This "Beirutization" of Kabul made the city into an armed camp, and the standard of living fell dramatically, with power and water supplies erratic and food stocks low. The battle for control of Kabul was a microcosm of what happened throughout Afghanistan during this stage—namely, the country's descent into ethnic violence and political fragmentation.[70]

Other actors held all the other major cities of Afghanistan during stage six. Kandahar was ruled by a regional council with a strong representation of supporters of Sayed Ahmed Gailani's Mahaz-i-Milli and Hekmatyar's Hezb-i-Islami. Jamiat commander Ismail Khan controlled Herat, but he did not come to Kabul and attempted to develop regional autonomy by relying upon support from Iran.[71] Mazar-i-Sharif was the de facto capital of the semiautonomous Uzbek and Turkic-speaking north-central area of Afghanistan and the home base for Dostam, while Jalalabad, on the road from Kabul to the Khyber Pass, was held by the other Hezb-i-Islami party, headed by Yunus Khalis and run by his lieutenant Haji Abdul Qadir and his brothers. Strategically located in the north, Kunduz was hotly contested by Massoud and Dostam. Of the major leaders during the Afghan War, only Nabi Mohammadi and his Harakat-i Inqilabi-i Islami were unable to take or vie for control of a key city or area, which perhaps helps explain their reemergence under the Taliban banner in 1994. Stage six was characterized by fragmentation and warlordism, although much of the fighting centered on Kabul and several other strategic towns. Coalitions of combatants were fluid, with the division between Hekmatyar and Rabbani-Massoud representing the only real constant.

In the summer and autumn of 1993, fighting in Kabul was primarily between the Iranian-backed Shia party Hezb-i-Wahdat and the

Saudi-supported fundamentalist Sunni party of Abdul Rasoul Sayyaf, Ittehad-i Islami. Much attention in Afghanistan was directed toward its northern border with Tajikistan, which had been crossed at that time by more than one hundred thousand Tajik refugees fleeing the civil war in their homeland in an eerie reprise to the Afghan exodus fifteen years earlier. There were repeated incidents of Russian forces shelling Afghan territory or attacking into Afghanistan from Tajikistan.[72]

Despite continual negotiations between representatives of various elements within Afghan society, there was little success in forming a national government during this stage. This was brought home most plainly on January 1, 1994, with the eruption of heavy fighting around Kabul yet again between the forces of Hekmatyar and Massoud. This time, Dostam's army sided with Hekmatyar in a coup attempt against Rabbani. Fighting, including air attacks, spread to Dostam's bases in Mazar-i-Sharif and continued at a level of intensity surpassing that of the combat in Kabul of August 1992. Temporary ceasefires in Kabul failed to hold. By March 1994 nearly one thousand people had died in the fighting since the beginning of the year, and more than one hundred thousand others had been made homeless. Pakistan's refusal since 1992 to accept Afghan refugees without visas forced most of the people displaced by this fighting to flee to Jalalabad or other locations within Afghanistan. Despite UN mediation efforts led by former Tunisian foreign minister Mahmoud Mestiri (who was replaced by German diplomat Norbert Holl in May 1996, who was followed by former Algerian foreign minister Lakhdar Brahimi in late 1997, who was followed by Spanish UN official Francesc Vendrell in January 2000), no political arrangement could be brokered that would satisfy all the claimants to power.[73]

The fragmentation deepened in 1994 and so did the frustration of regional power brokers, who simultaneously wanted Afghanistan to be peaceful yet were preoccupied with internal affairs. Afghanistan's continued violence especially frustrated Pakistan because it prevented that country from realizing its aspirations to trade and influence in Central Asia. Pakistani and Saudi Arabian fundamentalists began to support a new movement known as the Taliban (religious students) in the summer of 1994. The Taliban were Afghan refugees and war veterans based in rural Pakistani and Afghan *madrasahs*, or Islamic religious schools. Their arrival on the Afghan stage marked the end of the period of intra-mujahideen civil war and the beginning of stage seven in the Afghan War.

STAGE SEVEN: TALIBAN ASCENDANCE (1994–1998)

The Taliban first emerged in October 1994 when they initiated action between Kandahar and the city of Quetta in Pakistan to "rescue" a trade convoy bound from Pakistan to Central Asia through Kandahar and Herat. Presenting themselves simply as religious students who were fed up with the postcommunist struggle for Kabul and the lawlessness elsewhere in the country, the Taliban quickly found support in south-western Afghanistan. Headed by a council of largely unknown southern Pushtun religious scholars and students, the Taliban quickly made in-roads into central and eastern Afghanistan, disrupting the stalemate that had prevailed since 1992. The Taliban asked or paid drug kings, warlords, and militia commanders to surrender or leave, and many did so, perhaps unwilling to fight against religious students. The Taliban also fought some successful skirmishes throughout 1995. By a combina-tion of these methods they took Spin Buldak in October 1994, Kan-dahar in November 1994, and Lashkargah in January 1995. Then they drove toward Kabul and Herat.

By March 1995 the Taliban controlled about one-third of Afghan-istan and were on the outskirts of Kabul. They defeated the Shia Hezb-i-Wahdat and killed Wahdat leader Ali Mazari, reportedly committing atrocities against some of the Hezb-i-Wahdat soldiers they captured. Gulbuddin Hekmatyar evacuated his positions south of Kabul and fled east before the Taliban advance. But Massoud's government soldiers drove the Taliban back from the capital, and for the first time since early 1992 Kabul was no longer a city under siege. In April 1995 the Tal-iban advance toward Herat was stopped, and in May 1995 they clashed with Iranian troops in Nimruz. Resuming their drive north in late summer, the Taliban captured Herat in September 1995, forcing Ismail Khan to flee to Iran. That critical victory left them in control of more than 50 percent of Afghanistan. With Dostam powerfully positioned in the north and the Rabbani-Massoud government increasingly isolated in Kabul, the Taliban pushed on Kabul again. By November 1995 they had all but cut off the city, yet by the end of the year Massoud had driven them back from Kabul once again.[74]

Pressure on Rabbani to step down grew in early 1996, especially from a new alliance of Hekmatyar, Mojaddidi, Dostam, and Karim Khalili (the new leader of Hezb-i-Wahdat) called the Supreme Coordination Council. Moreover, because Hekmatyar's Pakistani support was increas-ingly flowing to the Taliban, he moderated his position early in the year, finally joining the government as prime minister in June 1996. An anti-Kabul alliance of the other major opposition leaders emerged briefly in the summer, but by August 1996 Hekmatyar and Dostam had reached a truce.

In September 1996, the Taliban suddenly took Kabul. They first struck to the east of the city, taking Jalalabad and then marching against Hekmatyar's forces in Sarobi (a small town fifty kilometers east of Kabul), which gave up with little fighting. Outflanked and uncertain of their support, Rabbani, Massoud, and Hekmatyar abandoned Kabul and fled north. Throughout the fall and winter of 1996 and early 1997 the front lines shifted back and forth twenty-five to seventy kilometers north of Kabul (the Kohistan-Shomali region) as Massoud, Dostam, and Khalili formed a somewhat shaky Northern Alliance.

Early 1997 saw the Taliban still south of the Salang Tunnel, the entrance to which had been dynamited by Massoud in order to prevent a Taliban breakthrough into the north. But in February 1997 the Taliban drove forward and captured key towns just south of the Salang Tunnel (Charikar, Ghorband), which allowed them to turn toward the center of the country, pushing back Khalili's forces in their advance through the Shibar Pass toward Bamiyan. During these months the Taliban were also pushing forward on their northwestern front in Badghis.

Suddenly, in May 1997, Dostam's lieutenant Abdul Malik revolted and took over Mazar-i-Sharif with the assistance of Taliban troops, forcing Dostam to flee abroad. Simultaneously the Taliban pushed forces through the now-open Salang Tunnel. After only four days, a popular uprising in Mazar-i-Sharif led to the massacre of the Taliban vanguard there (more than four thousand Taliban troops were eventually killed, most after having been captured) while Massoud suddenly cut the Salang Tunnel again, isolating their northeastern forces around Pul-i-Khumri. After briefly holding more than 90 percent of Afghanistan and being poised for final victory, the Taliban had suffered their most significant defeat of the war.

After the debacle in Mazar-i-Sharif, the Taliban garrison in Pul-i-Khumri retreated to Kunduz, where it took control of the airport long enough to be reinforced.[75] This force counterattacked west in October 1997, pushing into the edge of Mazar-i-Sharif before being driven back again in fierce fighting. Meanwhile, Massoud advanced toward Kabul in late July 1997, finally halting just outside of artillery range of the city, while Khalili's Hazara fighters pushed the Taliban out of the central highlands and encircled Kabul on the western side. By November 1997

Dostam had returned to control Mazar-i-Sharif, and Malik had in turn gone into exile, but Dostam could not regain the same level of strength he had held prior to the May 1997 coup. By the end of 1997 the Taliban controlled more territory than they had at the year's beginning, but after their losses of the summer and fall, their future appeared clouded. Throughout this period desultory UN efforts to negotiate peace via the "Six Plus Two" framework (Afghanistan's six contiguous neighbors plus the US and Russia) made no headway.

As 1998 dawned the Taliban increased their pressure on the Hazara population by restricting the supply of food aid to the starving people of central Afghanistan. By the summer of 1998 the Taliban had begun to probe cautiously eastward again from their western headquarters in Herat, through Faryab and Jowzjan provinces. Reportedly using funding supplied in part by the Saudi dissident financier Osama bin Laden to once again buy off local commanders, the Taliban intended their summer campaign to be their big push to bring the war to an end.

Some eight thousand Taliban troops, supported by tanks and armored personnel carriers, drove through Faryab in July and overran Dostum's headquarters at Shiberghan in early August. Mazar-i-Sharif fell a week later, followed by Bamiyan in September 1998. In both cases the Taliban closed the cities to outside observers, and atrocities occurred. More than eight thousand noncombatants had been reported killed in and around the two towns by the end of September 1998, and thousands more were reported to have been relocated as ethnic cleansing returned to Afghanistan. Also in August, Massoud pulled back from his headquarters town of Taloqan in the face of advancing Taliban troops out of Kunduz. With these victories leaving the Taliban in control of 90 percent of the country and Massoud their only major rival still able to field a significant military force by the autumn of 1998, it appeared that the Afghan War might finally be drawing to a close. Thus, the Taliban victories in Mazar-i-Sharif and Bamiyan marked the end of this stage of the war.

International attention was also focused on Afghanistan during this period, and it, too, peaked during the early fall of 1998. Taliban social policies, especially their interpretation of *sharia,* or Islamic law, as it pertains to the appropriate behavior and activities of women in society, led to the marginalization of the movement by most international actors. The UN and international aid organizations found it increasingly difficult to conduct their operations in Afghanistan during this stage and eventually withdrew from the country completely in July and

August 1998. The Taliban's repeated rejection of any framework for the creation of a broad-based government that included representatives of the northern minorities, as well as their tolerance of and even active participation in the increasingly lucrative opium growing and heroin production in Afghanistan, also served to isolate their regime. Western governments, especially the United States, also rejected the Taliban because of their willingness to provide safe haven and training facilities for Islamic militants, especially those under the patronage of Osama bin Laden, who was wanted for involvement in the June 1996 bombing of an American barracks in Khobar, Saudi Arabia. When bin Laden's men bombed US embassies in Kenya and Tanzania in early August 1998, the US retaliated later in the month with cruise missile strikes on suspected bin Laden training facilities near Khost, and US-Taliban relations dipped to their lowest point.

Indeed, although they have constituted the de facto government of Afghanistan since their capture of Kabul in September 1996, the Taliban have had virtually no positive presence in the wider world. Following their brief success in Mazar-i-Sharif in May 1997, the Taliban government was recognized by Pakistan, Saudi Arabia, and the United Arab Emirates, but the rest of the world has continued to recognize the Rabbani regime as the legitimate government of the country. During their second conquest of Mazar-i-Sharif in August 1998, Taliban forces invaded the Iranian consulate and killed the diplomats there. This action sparked the mobilization of nearly 250,000 Iranian regular army and Revolutionary Guards troops along Iran's border with Afghanistan, where they engaged in some minor border clashes later in the fall. Despite inflamed rhetoric, Iran did not invade Afghanistan, but the Iranian government has continued to supply Massoud and has maintained its enhanced military presence along the border. Other regional actors, especially Russia, India, Uzbekistan, and Tajikistan, have grown increasingly uneasy with the Taliban's continued success, for these countries view the Taliban as merely Pakistan's proxy. Indeed, Iran, Russia, Tajikistan, and Uzbekistan, along with the Rabbani government, all alleged that the recent Taliban victories in northern Afghanistan were due in part to direct Pakistani military involvement, including more than fifteen hundred troops and numerous combat sorties by the Pakistan air force in the 1998 Mazur-i-Sharif campaign.[76]

Despite the slaughter in Mazar-i-Sharif in both 1997 and 1998, combat in general continued to decrease in intensity during this stage, as most of the country was peaceful. Indeed, although this stage of the war was marked by some sharp engagements, especially around Kabul, it was also characterized by a tendency for battles to be avoided. The three major combatants all enjoyed outside support (Dostam by Uzbekistan, Rabbani-Massoud by Iran and Russia, the Taliban by Pakistan and Saudi Arabia), but their use of armor, artillery, and air power decreased. Thus, the intensity of the war in stage seven continued in the downward spiral that had begun after stage four.

The rise of the Taliban movement introduced significant changes to the political landscape of Afghanistan. Most importantly, the Taliban absorbed other major Pushtun players (for example, Mohammadi and Khalis) or drove them off the Afghan stage (for example, Hekmatyar and Sayyaf). Likewise, the near defeat of Rabbani-Massoud and Dostam, together with the killing of Mazari and atrocities against the Hazara, served to stiffen opposition to the Taliban along ethnic and sectarian lines. Many observers feared that the atrocities that accompanied the fall of Mazar-i-Sharif and Bamiyan presaged full scale Taliban efforts at ethnic cleansing of the Hazara population. Regional actors grew increasingly involved in supporting Afghan clients, usually in order to frustrate the aspirations of their regional rivals. The Taliban movement is under Pakistani patronage, and the nature of its weaponry, funding, and training suggested from almost the moment of its emergence that this was something other than a movement of religious students.[77] Thus Pakistan, with the financial support of Saudi Arabia and the earlier tacit approval of the United States, is responsible for the existence and maintenance of the Taliban.[78] Iran and India, both eager to frustrate Pakistani ambitions toward penetration of Central Asia, supported the Northern Alliance, especially the Tajik forces of Massoud and the Hazara forces of Khalili. Russia, Tajikistan, and Uzbekistan have also supported the Northern Alliance.[79]

STAGE EIGHT: ENDGAME? (1998–?)

The situation has become more fluid since the Taliban captured Mazar-i-Sharif in August 1998 and Bamiyan in September 1998, but by the beginning of 2001 the Taliban had gradually consolidated their position in Afghanistan's north. Taliban efforts in the fall of 1998 to defeat Massoud were unsuccessful, and he held his positions on the plains north of Kabul, recaptured Taloqan in October, and pushed into Kunduz province, where his troops dug in twenty to twenty-five kilometers north of the city.

After the usual quiet winter devoted to resupply, reinforcement, and training, small-scale combat resumed in the spring of 1999. Remnants of the Hezb-i-Wahdat forces managed to initiate some guerrilla activities in the Hazarajat region, culminating in their recapture of Bamiyan in April 1999. Although the Taliban retook Bamiyan several weeks later, in May, the situation remained fluid in the central highlands throughout 1999.

The ebb and flow of fighting on several fronts was relatively minor throughout the spring and summer, as both Massoud and the Taliban maneuvered carefully for battlefield advantage while peace negotiations took place in several foreign venues. In March 1999 the Taliban and the United Front (or Northern Alliance) opposition reached a tentative power-sharing agreement in Ashkhabad, Turkmenistan, but almost immediately returned to the battlefield as Taliban leader Mullah Omar Akhund issued pronouncements backing away from the deal. Efforts to revive the deal led to a meeting within the "Six Plus Two" framework at Tashkent in mid-July, even as the Taliban were gearing up for a long-expected summer offensive. After the failure of these negotiations, the Taliban launched a massive attack north of Kabul that pushed Massoud's forces back into the Panjshir Valley and out of Kunduz. In early August, however, the opposition forces boiled out of the Panjshir in a surprise counterattack that drove the Taliban back to their original lines and inflicted more than one thousand casualties. Later in August and throughout the fall, the Taliban carefully pushed north again, even as Massoud and other United Front commanders attacked them in other locations around the country, from Kunar in the east to Faryab in the northwest.

Despite the inconclusive results of the 1999 fighting, several important trends were clearly strengthened. First, the Taliban continued to exacerbate the ethnic divisions between themselves and the largely Tajik, Hazara, and Uzbek opposition, this time by deliberate scorched earth tactics designed to drive all of the minority population out of the Shomali plains north of Kabul.[80] Some 160,000 refugees fled the fighting, many into the Panjshir Valley, which had great difficulty supporting them adequately during Afghanistan's bitter winter. Another 70,000 were forcibly relocated into Kabul and points south.[81]

Second, the links between the Taliban and Pakistan's religious right wing and government became more obvious than ever. Pakistan accepted the principle of noninterference in Afghanistan's civil war at the July Tashkent talks, but reportedly some five thousand to eight thousand Pakistani "volunteers" participated in the Taliban's July 1999 offensive, operating in separate units. Leaders of the Northern Alliance alleged that Pakistani regular troops also took part in the fighting, "along with a 'brigade' of largely Arab militants under the command of fugitive Saudi terror tycoon Osama bin Laden."[82] After Massoud's crushing counterattack in early August, the Taliban issued a call for reinforcements from Pakistan's madrasahs, and several thousand more students poured into Afghanistan, forcing some of the seminaries to close.

Third, the international community (led by the US) strengthened its anti-Taliban posture, motivated not only by the ethnic cleansing during the fighting of stage eight but also by the reappearance of Osama bin Laden after he had disappeared from sight for most of 1999. Moreover, an unprecedented leap in opium production showed that the Taliban were making no serious inroads in curbing the narcotics traffic, and their reported training of Islamist fighters led to renewed fears of "Talibanization" of neighboring countries and territories such as Pakistan, Kashmir, Uzbekistan, and Chechnya.[83] In October 1999, the UN Security Council announced plans to impose sanctions on the Taliban if they did not turn Osama bin Laden over to the US for his alleged involvement in terrorist activities, and sanctions were duly imposed in November 1999, following Taliban noncompliance. UN mediator Lakhdar Brahimi resigned his post in October, citing the unwillingness of the Afghan belligerents, especially the Taliban, to pursue peace as an insurmountable obstacle to his job. Also in October the Pakistani military, headed by General Pervaiz Musharraf, ousted the Nawaz Sharif government. This action grew in part out of disagreements between Musharraf and Sharif over Pakistani policy toward Kashmir and Afghanistan, after Sharif tried to curb the religious right following bloody sectarian violence in early October, and after he attempted to sack Musharraf.[84]

The new Pakistani government almost immediately tightened border controls with Afghanistan in order to crack down on smuggling, which drove up Afghan wheat prices and caused the Afghan currency (the afghani) to fall sharply. In response, relations between the Taliban and Iran thawed quickly, and in late November 1999 the Afghan-Iranian border was reopened for trade at Islam Qala, west of Herat. A flurry of diplomatic activity ended 1999 and began 2000, led by Musharraf's visit to Iran in December, where he attempted to coordinate Pakistani-Iranian policy on Afghanistan. The Taliban leadership sought to normalize relations with Iran while developing good ties with the new Pakistani regime, and Taliban president Mullah Mohammad Rabbani headed high-level visits to Pakistan in January and February 2000 to promote this effort. Northern Alliance president Burhanuddin Rabbani rushed to Iran in December 1999 to shore up that critical relationship.

In addition, Islamist opponents of the Uzbekistan and Kyrgyzstan governments were given refuge in Taliban-held northern Afghanistan during the fall of 1999, heightening Central Asian concerns about Taliban support for extremism. In December, Uzbekistan claimed the Taliban were training the Uzbek Islamist rebels, while Russia made similar allegations about Taliban support for Chechnya. In January 2000, the Taliban recognized Chechnya, which promptly established an embassy in Kabul.

The year 2000 began in Afghanistan with two airplane hijackings, one from India to Kandahar and one from Kabul to London. But more important developments occurred during the year that were characteristic of the general trends of stage eight. First, legendary Herati commander Ismail Khan escaped in February from Kandahar, where the Taliban had held him captive since 1997. His escape sparked an Iranian-backed effort during the spring to construct a more formidable northern alliance, including other marginalized and exiled former leaders such as Abdul Rashid Dostam and Abdul Malik. Despite the return to northern Afghanistan of both Dostam and Malik in December 1999, they could not regain their previous leadership positions, and the defense of the northern stronghold fell primarily on Massoud once again. Second, a terrible drought hit throughout sourthern and central Asia, but its effects were especially punishing on the already marginal Afghan population, driving up food prices and sparking yet another refugee crisis. This time, though, Pakistan closed its border to Afghan refugees (in November 2000) and the "donor fatigue" of the international community produced no major humanitarian effort to respond to the crisis. More than one million Afghans were at grave risk of starvation by the end of 2000. Third, the Musharraf government in Pakistan openly announced its military support for the Taliban and assisted them in their July–September campaign into the northeast, which led to the fall of Taloqan and the cutting off of Massoud's supply lines with Tajikistan by the end of the year. Fourth, the Taliban took several steps during the year to improve their international image, including announcing a ban on opium poppy farming in July and relaxing their ban on girls' schooling, in an unsuccessful attempt to gain Afghanistan's seat at the United Nations and, more generally, international recognition. Instead, the UN Security Council slapped on new sanctions in December 2000, led by the United States, which wanted the Taliban to give up Osama bin Laden, following his suspected complicity in the terror bombing of the USS *Cole* in Aden, Yemen, in October 2000; and Russia, which was increasingly concerned about Taliban exporting of Islamic extremism, especially in Chechnya and Central Asia. However, the Taliban successes on the battlefield during the summer–autumn fighting season forced its neighbors like Uzbekistan and Kazakhstan to reconsider their chilly relations. Indeed, despite the official isolation imposed by the United States and Russia, by early 2001 it was increasingly clear that the Taliban controlled almost all of Afghanistan, with Massoud bottled up in the Panjshir Valley and remote northeastern Badakhshan and his Hazara allies isolated in the central highlands.

Thus, the fighting of stage eight seemed to represent the endgame to Afghanistan's long war, although Massoud's forces hung on grimly during the 2000–2001 winter and the leaders of the international community continued to isolate the Taliban regime. The gradual gains made by the Taliban during the fighting of 1999–2000 saw them finally take control of most of the country. By early 2001 the Taliban controlled 90 to 97 percent "of national territory, although in many areas this control amounts to little more than a small armed presence in the major towns."[85] As of early 2001, the opposing forces in Afghanistan were arrayed as follows. The Taliban controlled most of twenty-nine or thirty of the thirty-one provinces and could call upon perhaps forty-five thousand fighters.[86] For most of their time in power the Taliban had controlled areas populated predominantly by Pushtuns, along with some areas of mixed populations (such as Kabul and the northwest region centered on Herat). They now have added outright control of virtually all of the Hazarajat and the Turkestan plains, areas inhabited almost entirely by the ethnic minorities (Hazara, Uzbek, Turkmen) who have resisted their ascendance. In the fall of 2000 they pushed firmly into the Tajik northeast.

Prior to the summer 1998 offensive, three major groups opposed the Taliban in the loose Northern Alliance. It is now unclear to what extent these forces are still militarily and politically viable. One of the three, the Tajiks of Shura-i-Nazar, led by Massoud, are down to fifteen thousand fighters but still are hanging on in Badakhshan and the strategic Panjshir Valley, key to the Salang Tunnel, which provides Kabul and southern Afghanistan access to northern Afghanistan during the long winter months. Dostam and Malik headed the Uzbek militia Jumbush-i-Milli and some affiliated Turkmen forces—the second major group—prior to mid-1998; they were reported to have had at their height sixty-five thousand trained troops in the five north-central provinces. Little of that organization survived the fall of those provinces to the Taliban, and despite small-scale guerrilla activities there during late 1998, 1999, and early 2000, as well as simmering resentment against Taliban occupation in Mazar-i-Sharif, little organized opposition has emerged. Both Dostam and Malik returned to northern Afghanistan in late December 1999 and began reorganizing their former troops, several thousand of whom had rallied to their respective banners by early 2000, but efforts to reintegrate them into the Northern Alliance failed by the summer of 2000.

The third group, the Hazara Shia Hezb-i-Wahdat, was split and possibly shattered by the fall of its base in Bamiyan. One faction, led by Ustad Akbari, defected to the Taliban in November 1998. Another, larger faction, led by Abdul Karim Khalili, previously had nearly fifty thousand fighters, but they were scattered by their defeat and have yet to regain the capacity for conventional combat operations. A third, smaller Shia faction is the Harakat-i-Islami (Islamic Movement), which under the leadership of Sayed Hossein Anwari has conducted active military operations during 1999 and 2000, especially in Balkh and Samangan provinces. Collectively, the Shia forces were estimated to number no more than five thousand during the year 2000.

April 2000 marked the end of twenty-two years of continuous war in Afghanistan. As the year 2000 ended, the country was more unified than it had been at any point in the preceding two decades, but for all that, it was still deeply divided. The ascendance of the Taliban had left them in control of 90 to 97 percent of Afghan territory, but the remaining area was held fiercely by Massoud's Tajik army, and the other ethnic minority areas are still being contested despite current Taliban preeminence there.

Ethnic and sectarian differences have been deepened by the Taliban's successes and the atrocities that have occurred, especially the massacres in Mazar-i-Sharif in 1997 and 1998, the massacres in Bamiyan in 1998, the forced expulsions and wanton destruction north of Kabul in 1999, and the flight of over 150,000 refugees in the face of the Taliban advance into Takhar province in 2000. Whatever mandate the Taliban enjoyed in their early days is now gone, in a conflict that is increasingly drawn along ethnic and religious lines. The ethnic minorities of the center and north of Afghanistan continue to reject Taliban control over their areas, and it can be expected that violent resistance to Taliban hegemony will continue in these regions during the new century. Largely because outside powers continue to supply all the warring parties, both the Taliban and their opponents continue to seek a military solution to the questions of who should control Afghanistan and what manner of government the country should have.[87] Thus, the foundation for continued conflict is in place. Despite the recent downward spiral in combat intensity in Afghanistan, the ethnic foundations for continuing violence there make it difficult to feel certain that stage eight will be the last stage of the Afghan War. Tragically, this war continues grimly on, now in its third decade.

Still, for all the mind-numbing sameness that this protracted war often seems to have had, I believe that in fact it has progressed through seven relatively distinct and identifiable stages. They reveal a pattern of first increasing and then decreasing intensity and, at the war's height, a propensity to widen into neighboring countries. Now the war has entered an eighth and, it is to be hoped, final stage. This most recent stage is troubling, however, because despite its inauguration by the apparent military conquest of virtually the entire country by the neofundamentalist Taliban movement, it has also been marked by the first increase in the conflict's intensity and propensity for spillover in several years.

A summary of the conflict's stages is set out in table 3.1. The seven

TABLE 3.1. Stages of the Afghan War

Stage	Dates	Duration in Months
1	4/78–12/79	21
2	1/80–3/83	39
3	4/83–5/86	36
4	5/86–2/89	34
5	2/89–4/92	38
6	5/92–10/94	30
7	11/94–9/98	47
8	10/98–present (1/01)	28–

Range = 21–47 months per stage; mean = 35.0 months;
standard deviation = 7.5 months.
Note: See also Table 2.1 (p. 46) to compare Afghan periods and rulers.

completed stages of the war averaged 35.0 months in length, or almost three years each. Events of signal importance that constituted a major change in the strategy and/or tactics of one or more key actors in the conflict demarcated each stage from its predecessor and successor. Thus, stages were characterized by significant differences in military or political activities. Whereas stages two through six were closely clustered around the mean (30–39 months), the brief first stage (21 months, or less than two years) and the long seventh stage (47 months, or almost four years) limit our ability to use them for predictive purposes.[88] Moreover, the complexity of events bearing on the long Afghan conflict, especially in the post–Cold War era, makes it difficult to predict with any confidence what will happen next, much less when. Until recently, however, there was a clear pattern of intensity in the stages of the war (table 3.2).

Intensity can be assessed in several ways, including number of casualties, frequency of combat, and territorial coverage of combat. Considering such determinants as these, the analysis of the war over the previous stages reveals the following pattern of intensity.

From its localized beginnings in Kabul, the war grew in intensity throughout the 1980s. Combat operations and deaths mounted, and the war was transformed from a local uprising into a regional rebellion, then into a national civil war, and finally into a major international conflict that spilled over into neighboring countries and had far-reaching implications. After the Soviet withdrawal in 1989, the conflict began to decline in intensity, and much of the country began to have periods of peace. The previously unassailable Kabul now became the center of continued, high-intensity combat. The pattern of intensity over the

TABLE 3.2. Intensity of the Afghan War

Stage	Intensity	Increasing/Decreasing
1	Low	Increasing
2	Medium	Increasing
3	High	Increasing
4	High	Stable
5	High/medium	Decreasing
6	Medium	Decreasing
7	Medium	Decreasing
8	Low	Increasing

seven identified stages suggests that stage eight could be the last stage of this long and deadly conflict, but the deepening ethnolinguistic-religious divisions among the current Afghan combatants (manifested most clearly in the genocidal behavior of both the Taliban and their opponents in 1997–2000) might provide the foundation for a new spiral of conflict in Afghanistan and the surrounding region. This possibility is made more likely by the continued involvement of various outside actors in the war in Afghanistan, either because of their ethnolinguistic and/or religious ties to certain groups there (this applies to all of Afghanistan's immediate neighbors except China) or because of their geopolitical and geoeconomic goals (Russia, India, Saudi Arabia, China, and the Ukraine can then be added to the mix). Iran's saber-rattling in the autumn of 1998 and Pakistan's blatant involvement in Afghan combat in the summer and early fall of 1998, 1999, and 2000 (as well as earlier) are warning signals of a widening and deepening of the Afghan War should UN or other efforts at negotiation not be taken seriously by all parties to the conflict.

Transition from the current conflict to peace can occur only if the United States and interested regional powers exercise sufficient leverage on their Afghan clients to put in place and maintain a broad-based government. For this to happen, the outside actors would have to agree to curtail support for their Afghan proxy forces, and a mechanism for power sharing between intransigent groups would have to be devised —both daunting prospects. If the Taliban are willing to control the Pushtun-dominated territory and the national government while allowing the minorities some local autonomy, this could occur. However, they would have to revise some of their earlier ideological positions, which they have so far exhibited great reluctance to do.

The alternative is continued war in Afghanistan, probably increasingly along ethnic and sectarian lines, possibly producing national fragmentation or disintegration.[89] In this scenario, outside powers will remain involved, and the war will probably continue at a relatively low level of intensity, with occasional flare-ups. Continued war of any sort, however, means continued delay in the reconstruction of a ravaged country.

Indeed, how can Afghanistan stand any more war? Today the situation there is terrible, and prospects for the future are dismal. The country has been ravaged by a war as destructive as any in its history, including those of Genghis Khan and Tamerlane. Standards of living have dropped precipitously. Average life expectancy has fallen to forty-seven years, and infant mortality is now over 144 per 1,000 life births.[90] Per capita income has declined to essentially nothing for many families, who lost homes, land, animals, and jobs in the war. Disruption of limited social welfare, education, transportation, and communication systems further deepened the existing social problems. Destruction of the traditional agricultural economy opened the door to the growth of a narcotics subsector that has become increasingly important.

Furthermore, sociocultural traditions in Afghanistan atrophied during the war years as children grew up in refugee camps and mine fields rather than in villages and wheat fields. A surge of Islamic fervor, an important unifying force for the otherwise fractious mujahideen, also bore a stiff price. Women were forced to retreat behind the veil, and earlier progress toward development was held hostage to the conceptions of morality and propriety of petty mullahs. Traditional channels and mechanisms of authority were disrupted or destroyed. These forces combined to produce new elites with limited governing capabilities whose qualifications often derived from their gun barrels and misunderstanding and misapplication of Islamic law. The rise of the Taliban provides a perfect example of what two decades of high-intensity war can do to pervert and distort a society. Moreover, ethnic and tribal differences were magnified, and a local arms race of epic proportions introduced the equipment necessary to take these disputes to unimaginable heights of violence. In short, the Afghan population, political and economic systems, society and culture—even the ancient land of Afghanistan—have all been indelibly scarred by this long war.

4/Impact of the War on Afghan State and Society

The destructiveness of modern war is widely understood, but the war in Afghanistan has been uniquely and comprehensively destructive. Its impact on Afghanistan's population has been, if not unprecedented in a century of extraordinarily destructive conflicts, then certainly as enormous as that of any other conflict in the modern era. First, the war has remained at relatively high intensity for twenty-two years. Second, for nearly a decade the war pitted an impoverished developing country against a military superpower. Like the United States in Vietnam in the 1960s, the Soviet Union in Afghanistan in the 1980s attempted to use its superior firepower and command of technology to overcome the sheer determination of the Afghan rebels. As in Vietnam, the outcome was widespread and conscious destruction of the countryside. Third, at different points during the war, various participants engaged in murderous tactics against their opponents. The aim of the war became not merely the defeat of opponents but their comprehensive destruction, even extermination. Again, the Vietnam War provides a parallel, at least in terms of the massive destruction a superpower can wreak on a developing country (although the Vietnam War spilled over into its surrounding region in a way that the Afghan War did not—or has not so far). Fourth, since the end of the 1980s a civil war between rival factions supported by outside powers has shattered areas (especially Kabul) that had previously escaped destruction.

Last, throughout the years of war, the geographic and demographic factors discussed in chapter 1 helped isolate Afghanistan from the influence of the rest of the world and make resolution of its conflict a difficult matter. The plight of Afghanistan never stirred Western public opinion because the war itself seemed to fall outside of Western interests, and the Western media found it difficult to cover and explain. Afghanistan is simply too remote and alien for many people in the West to care about it, and covering a war there has proved too arduous for most journalists.[1]

For this combination of reasons, the war in Afghanistan has been especially destructive of an entire nation and perhaps also of a regional and even worldwide political order and ideology. To understand the future of Afghanistan and the region, we must first understand how the Afghan War has affected the country. This chapter analyzes the war in terms of four major areas of impact on Afghanistan: physical destruction, economic and political disarray, the rise of the Taliban (especially as it has affected Afghanistan's ethnic and religious balance), and sociocultural change.

PHYSICAL DESTRUCTION

The Afghan War totally destroyed the progress toward nation building of more than two centuries. It also destroyed much of the country. Nearly two million Afghans were killed, perhaps as many as two million more were injured, more than six million were driven out of the country as refugees, and an additional two million became internally displaced. Massive destruction was wrought on the nation's infrastructure, with more than half of Afghanistan's twenty-four thousand villages destroyed, large sections of the major cities reduced to rubble, roads turned into dirt tracks, and farms made unsafe after being sown with mines instead of seed.[2] Social and political institutions were destroyed or irrevocably altered, especially governmental institutions, the armed forces, political organizations, universities, the religious hierarchy, and the media. Similarly, power groups including the khans, urban capitalists, military officers, the intelligentsia, the 'ulama, and tribal leaders could not survive the war unaffected. The entire framework of Afghan society was altered.

The physical destruction of Afghanistan is the most obvious way in which the long war there has affected the country. Furthermore, it is this physical destruction that underlies the rest of the changes wrought by the war. Physical destruction takes two major forms: destruction of population, measured in numbers or percentages of people killed, wounded, and displaced by the war; and destruction of property, measured in damage to infrastructure such as houses, other buildings, roads, bridges, orchards, and fields. The heavy use of mines throughout Afghanistan must also be taken into account, for they not only continue to cause death and injury but also make fields unusable.

Although quantitative measures are always suspect in Afghanistan (I know from experience there that numbers are always exaggerated), estimates of the physical damage do exist and are valid enough to give a sense of the comprehensiveness of the destruction. Population destruction is most obviously understood in terms of the numbers of people killed in the war, but it is also useful to consider those wounded and/or displaced. As the publication *Refugees* put it: "In Afghanistan virtually everyone is a victim."[3]

Afghanistan's 1979 census suggests a prewar population of 13.05 million, but various authors have argued that slightly higher figures (15–17 million) might better approximate the true population size when the nomadic population is taken into account. Noor Ahmed Khalidi calculated that 876,825 Afghans, constituting some 7 percent of the total population, were killed by the war in its first decade (1978–1987).[4] Marek Sliwinski presented a higher figure for this time period: approximately 1.25 million war deaths, or 9 percent of the prewar population.[5] Siddieq Noorzoy suggested an even higher figure of 1.71 million war deaths for the same decade.[6] The year of greatest intensity during this period, in terms of war deaths, was 1984.[7]

Intensity declined during the second half of the war (following the Soviet withdrawal in 1989), but people continued to die (and still do today). Recent reports suggest that from 1.5 million to more than 2 million war deaths have occurred in Afghanistan since 1978,[8] with an average of 350 combat deaths per month in 1997.[9] Higher intensity resulted in 1998 because of the massacres carried out against ethnic minorities following the fall of Mazar-i-Sharif to the Taliban in September 1998 and the fall of Bamiyan in October 1998.[10] Likewise, in 1999 the late summer offensive by the Taliban and counteroffensive by the Northern Alliance produced high casualty figures, as did the late summer campaign by the Taliban in 2000.

Numbers of wounded and injured Afghans have also been high. Rasul Baksh Rais noted in 1994 that "the proportion of those incapacitated by the war is 31 per thousands of the entire population of the country."[11] Current population estimates vary widely (17–23 million persons), but at 22 million that would mean 682,000 persons wounded in the war. This estimate seems low, and substantially higher estimates are also available.[12]

Afghanistan's displaced population has been the highest in the world since 1981, peaking at 6.2 million refugees in countries of first asylum in 1990, with more than 2 million internally displaced persons (IDPs) during this time as well. Substantial repatriation has occurred since the fall of the communist government in 1992, but a stable population of 2.7 million refugees remained, primarily in Pakistan and Iran, in 1996 and 1997. As fighting over Kabul raged in 1994, Pakistan closed its border to prevent another massive refugee flow, which led to a dramatic swelling of the IDP population in Afghanistan. More than 1.5 million IDPs were created in Afghanistan between 1992 and 1997 alone. The 1997–2000 Taliban push into northern Afghanistan, along with the drought of 2000, prompted several hundred thousand more Afghans to flee their homes.[13]

In short, the direct effect of the Afghan War on the Afghan population has been stunning. Although all figures are estimates, some rougher than others, it is clear that more than 50 percent of Afghanistan's population has been directly harmed by the war through death, injury, or displacement. If we include the loss of family members in this category, it is unlikely that any Afghan has not been affected directly and tragically by the war. The level of destruction is even worse when we consider the widespread damage to Afghanistan's infrastructure as well.

The damage to Afghanistan's physical infrastructure has been all the more dramatic for being so multifaceted. At one point or another since 1978, virtually everything in Afghanistan has been a target. Cities, towns, villages, houses, mosques and minarets, schools, hospitals, industrial structures, other buildings, roads, bridges, orchards, and fields have all been damaged or destroyed during combat. The heavy use of mines throughout Afghanistan is another manifestation of property destruction there, because they make fields unusable (and continue to cause death and injury).

That such widespread destruction should occur in such a remote, rugged, and underdeveloped country is due to at least four factors. First, Soviet tactics designed to destroy the base of popular support for the mujahideen, especially in stages two and three of the war (1980–1986), directly targeted villages and rural areas. This "rubbleization" strategy was supposed to drive people out of the rural areas that the Soviets and their regime in Kabul were unable to control. At least half of Afghanistan's twenty-four thousand prewar villages were destroyed and turned into ghost towns, and millions of antipersonnel mines (especially the little "butterfly" mines, designed to maim) were scattered throughout the countryside.[14] The effort to drive people out of the countryside, especially along the Pakistani border, was intense and also included destruction of orchards, irrigation systems (such as the centuries-old underground *qarez*), and fields, often when they were ready for harvesting.[15]

Mujahideen attacks on Soviet-DRA-held cities and bases were rare and, when they did occur, generally ineffective during this part of the war. The very length of the war, however, is the second reason for the comprehensiveness of the property destruction, because when the mujahideen finally took over the government in 1992 and then embarked on their civil war, Afghanistan's cities, which had been spared much of the earlier destruction, became targets as well. As of early 2001, many buildings in Kabul had been reduced to rubble, including Darulaman Palace, the Ministry of Defense, and entire residential quarters. Large sections of Kandahar were in ruins, and for much of the late 1990s Herat suffered from a lack of electricity (except through the use of private generators). Smaller cities and towns faced similar problems.

Third, Afghanistan's underdevelopment and isolating geographic characteristics also contributed to the depth of the property destruction. By comparison with many other countries, there was little to destroy in Afghanistan to begin with, and a war lasting for twenty years has provided ample opportunity for the various combatants to hit most of the worthwhile targets. For example, Afghanistan's limited major road network (basically the Ring Road) is now little better than a jeep track, degraded and destroyed by misuse, combat, and lack of maintenance. Part of the Salang Tunnel was dynamited in May 1997, as was the entrance to the Panjshir Valley in October 1996 (and since).

Finally, Afghanistan has attracted significant attention from outside actors during its more than two decades of war, but most of that attention has come in the form of military aid, consumption-oriented economic aid, and refugee relief. Even in 1999 and 2000 most of the international assistance effort in Afghanistan was aimed at relief and short-term assistance, with little aimed at reconstruction. Furthermore, "donor fatigue" is a significant problem in Afghanistan, and the UN has been unable even to meet its relief targets (for example, the 1999 UN appeal for $112 million in high-priority funding had garnered only $29 million by late June 1999, with a further $12 million pledged for relief efforts outside the appeal; previous appeals never reached 75 percent of their targets).[16]

The combination of the four factors just described has produced widespread, comprehensive property destruction. As of early 2001, Afghanistan was a country reduced by the technology of modern war to a premodern level of existence. Its formal economy had essentially collapsed. Virtually no industry functioned, and the most vibrant economic activities were transit trade, opium growing, heroin manufacturing and smuggling, and other small-scale agriculture. Gross domestic product (GDP) in 1997 was approximately $5 billion, half of which was from the transit trade, primarily the smuggling of duty-free goods into Pakistan.[17] Reportedly, the Taliban government in Herat made $30,000 per day in customs duties on transit trade there, prior to closing the border with Iran in early 1997.[18] The overall annual value of Afghanistan's legal exports declined steadily during the 1990s to a value of well under $100 million, whereas the illegal narcotics industry grew to the point that Afghanistan in 1999 produced 4,800 tons of opium, 75 percent of the world's total of 6,000 tons. Now the only significant domestically produced exports are narcotics and some timber and gemstones.[19] The only significant economic activities in Afghanistan today, other than subsistence agriculture, are illegal or quasi-legal, at least outside of Afghanistan—narcotics manufacturing and export, arms trafficking, and smuggling of duty-free goods. Economic reconstruction has also been constrained by the continued threat posed by mines and other unexploded ordnance throughout the country. Although mine clearing has been under way for over a decade, there are still an estimated ten million mines throughout Afghanistan, making resettlement of some areas and resumption of traditional economic activities there still dangerous.[20]

The physical destruction of Afghanistan can be characterized as nothing less than the destruction of a country. It stems from a conscious effort on the part of various combatants, especially the Soviet-DRA forces, to depopulate the country by making it uninhabitable. It rivals the level of destruction recorded in other major wars of the twentieth century but was inflicted on a small, underdeveloped country that, in the post–Cold War world, other countries have found easy to ignore. Thus, there has been no Marshall Plan to rebuild Afghanistan, nor will there be. This comprehensive destruction has had profound effects on Afghanistan, altering every important institution in that society. The rest of this chapter traces the path of these alterations in three broad categories: first, the impact of the war on Afghanistan's political and socioeconomic institutions; second, the socioethnic and religious transformations produced by the war, especially the causes and effects of the rise of the Taliban; and third, the damage done to Afghanistan's underlying sociocultural framework.

ECONOMIC AND POLITICAL DISARRAY

The long Afghan War profoundly altered and in some cases even obliterated important components of Afghanistan's economic and political framework. For example, much of the economic infrastructure has been destroyed by war, including urban factories, power supply and transportation links, and important agricultural areas. Political institutions were affected less by the physical destruction of buildings but more by the targeting of individuals. The communist regime in Afghanistan eliminated the existing political elite in order to construct a new political system in its place. It introduced a new form of government built around a political party and an ideological system alien to Afghanistan, which now in turn have become obsolete. These changes have had sweeping and dramatic transformative effects on Afghanistan and merit careful examination.

Three major changes can be noted. First, the war has destroyed the prewar elites and the social system that supported them, leading to the development of new political elites (mujahideen and Taliban) that are founded on a newly prominent role for youths and Islamist ideologues. Second, the war transformed the role of violence in society, even in non-combat situations. Not only did Afghan citizens become more inured to everyday violence, but also the collapse of functioning government and social institutions made violence a more common means of settling disputes. The near anarchy that resulted was made possible by the proliferation of high-technology weapons in the country; accordingly, it was dubbed "Kalashnikovization." The continuation of the Afghan conflict long after the Soviet withdrawal has delayed the rebuilding of state institutions and maintained new elites in power, leaving Afghan society today with a rudimentary political system that barely functions. Third, the war so shattered the traditional Afghan economy that an opium-heroin economic sector based on drug trafficking emerged to replace it.[21]

Looking more closely at the first change, it is no exaggeration to say that the war has destroyed the social and political order in the countryside. Early in the conflict, most of the khans were co-opted or executed by the government, or they fled abroad. Land reform and the air war policy of "rubbleization" eliminated the traditional source of the khans' power, and their failure to protect their supporters from the government eroded their authority.[22] Though the assembly of elders, or jirga, was retained as a symbolic mechanism of national decision making, in reality during the war policy radiated outward and downward in those areas under Kabul's control. The attack on the communal qawm groups was not unrelenting, however, especially in the Najibullah period (1986–1992), as various tribal groups (and their militias) were induced to join the government in temporary alliance. Nonetheless, the traditional socioeconomic system of rural Afghanistan, based on wealth derived from land and agriculture and on jirga governance of social and political affairs in the qawm, has been altered, perhaps permanently.[23]

Also, the failure of the Durrani tribe to assert its traditional dominance during the military struggle against the Soviet-supported Kabul government has raised questions about its role in the future political order. Many leading Durrani tribesmen were relatively uninvolved in the war because of the absence of Durrani khans in opposition to Kabul. Even former king Zahir Shah kept a low profile throughout the war. Interestingly, as Shah M. Tarzi noted, "immediately after the Soviets withdrew and the external threat dissipated, prominent figures of the Sadowzais, Popalzais, Achekzais, and Barakzais, the four major Durrani sub tribes, openly protested against, and have questioned the legitimacy of Hekmatyar, Rabbani, and Khalis."[24]

In the absence of the Durranis and khans, new groups entered the picture, such as the non-Durrani resistance leaders mentioned by Tarzi. Some of these party leaders enjoyed traditional networks of support, but the most important ones (ousted president Burhanuddin Rabbani, former prime minister Gulbuddin Hekmatyar, Maulavi Yunus Khalis, Rasoul Abdur Sayyaf) represented the Islamist movement that injected fundamentalism into Afghan society.[25] In addition to the party leaders, important new actors included the commanders inside Afghanistan (such as Ahmed Shah Massoud and Ismail Khan of the mujahideen, and Abdul Rashid Dostam of the Jowzjani Uzbek militia) and the refugee populations in Pakistan and Iran.[26] The cynical and continuous struggle for power among these actors led ultimately to the appearance in October 1994 of the Taliban, Afghanistan's newest elite. Wresting the Islamist position away from Rabbani, Hekmatyar, and others, and arising out of the marginalized Kandahari Pushtuns, the Taliban have come the closest yet to taking over the whole country, with profound implications for Afghan culture and society.

The Taliban have simultaneously allowed the Durrani Pushtuns (as well as non-Durrani Pushtuns from the Kandahar area) to reassert their traditional claim to power while opening the door to a much younger base of leadership than is customary in Afghanistan. The Taliban leadership is composed almost exclusively of young men (mid- to late thirties in age) whose experiences in the early days of the war were as rank-and-file mujahideen or small-unit commanders. Before being welded into the Pakistani-supported religious militia of today, most of the Taliban leaders also spent several years as virtual mendicants in Pakistani madrasahs affiliated with the conservative Deobandi Islamist movement. Although the Taliban leaders all claim religious titles such as *maulavi* (teacher) or *mullah* (preacher/priest), only a few of them have much serious formal education or administrative experience. Older Pushtun leaders have been kept at arm's length and are angry about their inability to exert more influence over the Taliban movement. The emphasis on youth is even more telling among rank-and-file Taliban soldiers, who are generally in their middle to late teens. The average Taliban teenager is illiterate, often orphaned or from a family fragmented by the war, and deeply ignorant of the wider world. His only knowledge comes from within a very conservative Islamist framework.[27]

The horrific and widespread destruction wrought by twentieth-century weaponry transformed the Afghan battlefield forever—the second major change in the country's political and socioeconomic institutions. Prior to the Afghan War, most rural Afghan men possessed weapons, but generally the most advanced were Lee Enfield .303 rifles. Those days are gone forever. The Soviet Union supplied $36 billion to $48 billion worth of military equipment to the communist regime in Kabul from 1978 to the early 1990s.[28] Over the course of the Soviet phase of the war, the United States, Saudi Arabia, and China supplied $6 billion to $12 billion worth of weapons and military supplies to the mujahideen. The end result of all this has been not only the destruction of the Afghan physical infrastructure (for example, more than fifteen hundred SCUD missiles were used in Afghanistan as compared with fewer than one hundred in the Gulf War) but also the dissemination of modern weapons to people living in a segmentary social system with a cultural tradition of violence.[29]

The term "Kalashnikovization" first appeared in Pakistani newspapers in the mid-1980s to describe the deterioration of law and order brought about by the dissemination of AK-47 rifles (Kalashnikovs) that spilled out of the covert CIA arms pipeline to the mujahideen.

Kalashnikovization has been even worse in Afghanistan, where it has come to stand for war fought at a level of technology inconsistent with national development. Moreover, increased banditry and lawlessness resulted from it, reducing parts of Afghanistan during 1992–1994 to anarchy.[30] Local groups of erstwhile mujahideen controlled small areas in the name of a mujahideen party with which they had at least a nominal affiliation. They extracted resources from the citizens in their areas of control, often by quasi-legal methods at best, and extortion, robbery, rape, and murder became common. I well remember riding a bus from Kabul to the Khyber Pass in August 1992 and passing through nineteen different checkpoints representing a hodgepodge of groups en route. The Taliban leaders claim they began their campaign in order to end this state of anarchy and the un-Islamic practices it fostered, and their insistence on confiscating weapons in areas they control has helped to reduce the level of violence in Afghanistan somewhat. Indeed, that same bus ride in July 1997 went through territory controlled entirely by the Taliban and was held up only by two flat tires. There were, however, reports in 1999 and 2000 of increased lawlessness and banditry along the roads in Taliban-held Afghanistan.[31]

The widespread dissemination of weapons also helped destroy the Afghan military, which essentially ceased to exist in all but name. The Afghan Army had been a key institution in Afghanistan's state-building process since the late nineteenth century, but the Soviet phase of the war saw it shrink in size and effectiveness until, by the early 1990s, it had been transformed into a number of ethnic-based militias. Today the largely Pushtun Taliban militia (augmented by thousands of Pakistani "volunteers") faces off against the ethnic minority militias of Afghanistan's north, demonstrating that a revival of the national army as a twenty-first-century state-rebuilding institution is still a long way off.[32]

After long years of war, killing has become a way of life in Afghanistan, as is suggested by the massacre of captured Taliban soldiers in northern Afghanistan in the fall of 1997, the retaliatory massacre of eight thousand or more ethnic minorities (especially Hazara) by the Taliban upon their military successes in north and central Afghanistan in August–November 1998, and the ethnic cleansing by Taliban forces north of Kabul during their July–September 1999 offensives. Conflict in Afghanistan seems to have become increasingly defined in ethnic terms, which suggests that Kalashnikovization has contributed to ethnic cleansing and even genocide there.

A third important change that the war has produced in Afghanistan has been to its economy. Long accustomed to a rentier economy, Afghanistan had always relied heavily on outside sources of income, but during the war this reliance increased dramatically. Barnett Rubin detailed how the Kabul government during the 1980s and 1990s derived virtually all of its revenue from Soviet aid, sales of natural gas to the USSR, and borrowing from the Central Bank (producing high inflation).[33] Since the fall of the Najibullah government in 1992, virtually all of Afghanistan's relief and reconstruction effort has been undertaken by the UN and nongovernmental organizations (NGOs), not by the mujahideen or subsequent Taliban government, both of which have spent most of their resources on continued military struggle. Virtually all of the Taliban government's $10 million annual budget is provided by grants from Pakistan.[34] Much of Afghanistan's domestic economic production was centered on subsistence agriculture, which was severely disrupted by the war. Thus, in the 1980s and 1990s Afghanistan's cash-strapped farmers turned to growing opium, a much more lucrative crop than wheat.

Afghanistan, like most of South Asia, has a long history of opium production, but the cultivation of opium poppies has increased tremendously since the beginning of the Afghan War, and local processing of heroin is entirely a post-1980 phenomenon. Today, Afghanistan is the world's largest opium producer, with the unprecedented record of an estimated 4,600 metric tons produced in 1999 on 91,000 hectares of land.[35] This makes Afghanistan the biggest producer of illicit opium by far, with more than 75 percent of the estimated 1999 global output of 6,000 metric tons. Moreover, while other countries were bringing their opium-heroin production under control, Afghanistan's narcotics industry grew steadily. Bad weather limited the 1998 crop to 2,100 tons from 64,000 hectares, as compared with 3,100 tons of raw opium in 1997[36] and 1,230 metric tons produced in 1996 on 37,950 hectares of land.[37]

As the key producer of opium in the Golden Crescent, which also includes Iran and Pakistan, Afghanistan sits at the epicenter of a burgeoning regional drug economy and culture that also includes hashish. In particular, Pakistan has now developed one of the world's most significant domestic drug problems, even as pressure from the Pakistani government on narcotics manufacturers caused them to move most of the poppy fields and heroin labs into Afghanistan in the early 1990s, out of the reach of organizations like the US Drug Enforcement Agency (DEA) and the UN Drug Control Program (UNDCP). Although the

Golden Crescent heroin was initially manufactured primarily for sale in the West, enough spilled over into the local market for Pakistan's indigenous addict population to explode from fewer than 10,000–12,000 persons in 1979 to more than 500,000 in the mid-1980s and as many as 3–4 million in 1999. Throughout the 1990s Pakistan's addict population grew while its opium-heroin production declined, but record production in Afghanistan more than filled the demand. For example, in 1992 Pakistan's 1.1 million to 1.2 million addicts consumed some 55 tons of heroin, only 18 tons of which were produced domestically. The rest came from Afghanistan's poppy fields.[38] Today, Pakistan's addicts require three to four times as much heroin, almost all of which comes from Afghanistan. Approximately 97 percent of the poppy-growing land of Afghanistan is under Taliban control, and the Taliban levy a tax on opium, so it is Pakistan's proxy army in Afghanistan that is growing the opium used to feed the demands of Pakistan's heroin addicts.[39]

Much of the poppy growing in Afghanistan takes place in the southwest (especially in Helmand and Kandahar provinces), the east (Nangarhar), and the northeast (Badakhshan). These are the major growing regions, but poppy cultivation has spread dramatically over the last twenty years and in 1999 was found in 104 districts in 18 of the 31 provinces (although some areas, such as Kunar province under Jamilur Rahman in the early 1990s, saw a decline in opium production).[40] This is because the agricultural infrastructure of Afghanistan has been ravaged by the war, with fields made unusable by mines, orchards cut down, irrigation systems destroyed, and roads and factories reduced to rubble. Opium has become the most lucrative cash crop available in the short term. Repatriating refugees are unable to grow enough food to meet their immediate needs, nor are they able to make money off high-return crops such as fruit for several years. Thus, they turn to growing poppies.[41]

There is also a clear linkage between opium-heroin production and weapons, which are used to protect the drugs and are bought with drug profits. It is less clear who fostered the growth of the opium sector during the Afghan War, but it became a source of income for both the mujahideen (and now the Taliban) and those farmers whose regular means of livelihood were disrupted by the war.[42] Despite early Taliban claims that they would eradicate opium-heroin production, since 1994 it has increased in the areas they control (which constitute virtually all of the opium-producing territory in Afghanistan).[43] Their half-hearted justifications for their continued tolerance of an obviously un-Islamic practice reflect the industry's strength and its influence in high government circles in both Afghanistan and Pakistan. The Taliban made no serious narcotics interdiction or poppy eradication efforts during 1998 or 1999, and they derive a significant portion of their revenue from an opium tax.[44] In July 2000 Taliban supreme leader Mullah Omar issued an edict outlawing opium growing, and some Taliban efforts to curtail its production followed. International narcotics officials were skeptical about the Taliban's commitment to ending the drug traffic, however, and although they expected the 2000 crop to be far less than the 1999 output, they attributed this to the drought, which provided less than ideal growing conditions.

As we have seen, the Afghan War has brought about at least three major changes in Afghanistan's socioeconomic and political institutions. First, it has created powerful new actors in Afghanistan, many of whom represent a new generation and derive their claims to legitimacy from nontraditional sources. Their emergence and empowerment issued from the power vacuum resulting from the destruction of the prewar political system and the elimination of many prewar elites, as well as from the destruction of the communist political system and elimination of those elites. In the absence of traditional sources of legitimacy, the new elites have relied on the remaining two changes to bolster their claims to leadership.[45] The proliferation of high-technology weapons has provided them with the ability to use force, while the rapid growth of the narcotics industry in the region has given them a source of funding. Similarly, the use of an Islamist lexicon and symbols, a subject considered in the next section, has provided the new elites with an ideology.

The spillover of arms from the Soviet and American pipelines and the profitability of the opium-heroin industry have promoted the Kalashnikovization of society in Afghanistan.[46] This cult of violence produced by the local and regional proliferation of arms has deepened and exacerbated existing ethnic, linguistic, and religious cleavages. The rapidly developing narcotics industry, combined with traditional Pushtun political culture, encouraged resistance to disarmament during the tumultuous early 1990s. The result has been greater militarization and internal instability. The implication for the future is that Afghanistan will be resistant to nation building and will be characterized by continued fragmentation and internal instability.

Afghanistan today has become a violent society, bereft of political institutions that function correctly and an economy that functions at all.

When this is coupled with the destruction of population and the physical infrastructure described in the preceding section, it becomes clear that Afghanistan is a country on the edge of collapse, or at least profound transformation. Perhaps the most significant alterations to Afghanistan wrought by its long war, however, have been to its fragile ethnolinguistic-religious balance and its underlying sociocultural framework.

THE RISE OF THE TALIBAN

The Afghan War's comprehensive impact on Afghan society has put special pressure on the fragile ethnic and religious balance there. Afghanistan's new elites cannot, for the most part, ground their claims to leadership in traditional bases, because Afghanistan's traditional leaders either fled or were destroyed, co-opted, or discredited by the war. The new and younger elites who have emerged must legitimate their claims to leadership in some other way. Almost all have done so through references to Islam,[47] a trend that has been most dramatic in the case of the Taliban. Afghanistan's increasing Islamization consti-tutes a major change for Afghan society and for neighboring countries. The Taliban represent the latest, most successful, and most vehement of these new Islamist elites, and many of their policies have had profound effects on Afghanistan's ethnic and religious balance.[48]

Since the emergence of the Taliban movement in the autumn of 1994, nowhere in the Islamic world have religion and politics intersected in such dramatic fashion as in Afghanistan. With their white banner fly-ing and Korans held high, the Taliban have swept across Afghanistan to now control more than 90 percent of the country and its five largest cities (Kabul, Kandahar, Herat, Jalalabad, Mazar-i-Sharif). In the process, they have inflamed deep ethnic and religious divisions in Afghanistan and further contributed to the fragmentation of that war-torn country. Their essential monoethnicity and close relationship with Pakistan have disrupted the tenuous post–Cold War regional stability, raising tensions with various of Afghanistan's neighbors, including Iran, Uzbekistan, and Tajikistan (as well as states a little farther removed, such as Russia and India). Their secretive leadership and the obvious puritanical zeal of their followers, combined with their stunning successes in taking and keeping control of large areas of Afghanistan, mark the Taliban as the Islamic movement of the 1990s.

But numerous questions about the Taliban remain. Are they truly an indigenous religious movement with limited political goals, or are they being using as a proxy for Pakistan, a country with a clear geopolitical agenda for Central Asia? Do the Taliban represent a new form of political Islam, and if so, will this be exported into Central Asia? Are the Taliban the future of Afghanistan, a unifying force devoted to purifying the country of the detritus of its experiment with secularization, or will they be the catalyst for the final shattering of Afghanistan?

Olivier Roy suggested three possible meanings for Islamization in Afghanistan: the implementation of sharia (Islamic law), the purifying of society through preaching and a return to fundamental religious practices, and the establishment of an Islamic state through violence if necessary.[49] All of these meanings have been at play among groups wishing to Islamize Afghanistan, a society that has such a strong traditional adherence to Islam that any claimant to political power has had to use it as a legitimating factor.[50] The present trend toward Islamization in Afghanistan has its roots in the struggle between communists and Islamists within Kabul intellectual circles dating back to the mid-1960s,[51] and more generally in the century-long struggle between modernizers and traditionalists.[52] The successful communist coup that sparked the war in 1978 helped mobilize an increasingly militant Islamist resistance movement. The structure and bases of support for that movement empowered the Islamist factions among the Afghan resistance such that throughout the war the more "fundamentalist" groups and leaders (such as Gulbuddin Hekmatyar and his Hezb-i-Islami faction) received the most support, especially as Pakistan under Zia ul-Haq in the 1980s was undergoing its own Islamization. Modernization became affiliated with the "evil" communist government, while the "noble" mujahideen fought a jihad for the redemption of the nation. There was little room for a secular or moderate alternative among the resistance, and even the "moderate" mujahideen parties were headed by traditional leaders whose legitimacy rested on their Islamic credentials and who were not opposed to Islamic government in Afghanistan.

The power struggle that erupted among mujahideen leaders and some former supporters of the communist government (such as the Uzbek warlord Abdul Rashid Dostam) after the fall of the communist regime in 1992, which then continued through 1993 and 1994, undermined whatever legitimacy these leaders had outside of their own local or regional bases of support and paved the way for the emergence of the Taliban. By the fall of 1994, Afghanistan had been free of communist rule for more than two years, but from almost the beginning of the post-Najibullah era, squabbling among contenders had degenerated into violence. Kabul lay in ruins, destroyed by the battle for its control between various forces, most prominently those of President Burhanuddin Rabbani and his military chief Ahmed Shah Massoud against troops loyal to Prime Minister Gulbuddin Hekmatyar. The capital was also partitioned, with different sectors controlled by different factions, symbolic of the fragmentation of the country. The quality of government in different regions and cities varied widely, depending on the personal idiosyncrasies of local warlords and commanders.

The Pakistani government grew increasingly frustrated with the lawlessness and political instability of Afghanistan, which showed itself in the increased impact on Pakistan of both the narcotics traffic and Kalashnikovization, in the slow and incomplete repatriation of Afghan refugees from Pakistan, and in Afghanistan's inability to develop trade routes to the emerging markets and primary resources of Central Asia. Given the resurgent regional aspirations of Iran and even Turkey in the post-USSR political environment that Afghanistan had helped to usher in, Pakistan felt compelled to attempt to stabilize the Afghan situation once and for all. This goal certainly fit with its previous support for mujahideen parties operating from bases in Pakistani territory, but supporting the Taliban constituted a major change in Pakistan's patron-client Afghanistan policy—away from its traditional client (Hekmatyar) and toward a new one (the Taliban) that shared the same Islamist ideology but came from a more acceptable tribal background (more Durrani rather than solely Ghilzai Pushtun) and was encumbered with less political baggage than Hekmatyar. Thus, the Taliban were born.

Much about the Taliban remains shrouded in mystery, and Western scholarship on the movement is just beginning to appear.[53] Thus, before considering the reasons for the success of the Taliban and the prospects for their future, we need a basic description of the movement. Who are the Taliban, where did they come from and when, and what are their goals? Answers to these questions will allow us to explore their success so far and examine their role in Afghanistan's future. These questions provide a framework not only for understanding the Taliban movement but also for assessing its impact on Afghanistan's ethnic and religious stability.

Who Are the Taliban?

Although *taliban* means religious students, this movement has grown beyond its original roots in the madrasahs of Pakistan's tribal belt and can no longer be seen in monolithic terms. Its key leaders are young veterans of the Afghan-Soviet War (in their mid-thirties to early forties), many of them physically scarred from that conflict. As the Taliban spread their control over larger sections of Afghan Pushtun territory, the movement expanded to include elements that did not originate in the Pakistani madrasahs. Still, even now the Taliban rely on those madrasahs to supply rank-and-file soldiers, many of whom are poorly educated, impoverished teenagers. For example, during the Taliban's successful 1998 campaign to capture most of northern and central Afghanistan, thousands of Pakistani madrasah students were given extended holidays in order to participate. Likewise, in August 1999 Taliban leaders asked for and received thousands of additional Pakistani religious students following heavy losses in their attack on northeastern Afghanistan. Ahmed Rashid estimated that eighty thousand to one hundred thousand Pakistanis fought or trained in Afghanistan during the 1990s.[54]

If the relative youth of the Taliban leadership represents an important generational change in Afghan affairs, their origins also represent a change, but of a different sort. The key leaders of the Taliban (all of the Inner Shura and most of the Supreme Shura) are Kandahari Pushtuns, and many are Durranis, the tribal group of Afghanistan's royal family and national leadership.[55] The Durrani Pushtuns were underrepresented in Afghan politics after 1978, at least relative to their traditional role of national leadership. Much of the communist government leadership and most of the leading mujahideen figures were from other Pushtun tribes (especially the Ghilzai) or other ethnic groups, and the period of Durrani dominance appeared to have ended.[56] The rise of the Taliban appeared to mean the ascendance of the Durranis once again. As the Taliban gained territory, however, they had to expand their ranks to include others, especially eastern Ghilzai Pushtuns and local commanders willing to switch sides, as well as ex-Khalqi communists with more advanced combat skills and training. This led to increasing friction within their ranks, centered on differences in ideology, tactics, and background.[57] The friction ignited a purge in the late autumn of 1998, especially of former Khalqis in the Taliban ranks. On several occasions the Taliban have also removed civil servants from their positions if their piety was deemed inadequate.

The original core Taliban received religious instruction in rural madrasahs located in the North-West Frontier Province (NWFP), Baluchistan Province, and the Federally Administered Tribal Areas

(FATA) of Pakistan. Most of these madrasahs are affiliated with or run by the conservative Islamist Pakistani political movement, the Jamiat-ul-Ulema-i-Islami (JUI) party, and have their intellectual roots in the Deobandi tradition.[58] Thus, the Taliban represent the resurgence of the rural mullah, come to cleanse the country of the impurities produced by its flirtation with modernization, a recurrent theme in Afghanistan's twentieth-century development.[59] Recently, William Maley has argued that the Taliban exhibit elements not only of traditionalism resurgent but of fundamentalism and totalitarianism as well.[60]

The Taliban first appeared on the scene in the late summer of 1994, and various theories have been advanced about the precise nature of their origins, including the degree to which they represent the geopolitical aspirations of Pakistan's governing elite. The supreme leader of the Taliban, Mullah Mohammad Omar Akhund, gathered together a small group of Kandahari Pushtun war veterans, many of whom had seen combat with Nabi Mohammadi's Harakat-i Inqilab-i Islami. From this early group of fewer than fifty men would come most of the Taliban's present leaders. The Taliban first conducted an operation in Afghanistan in October 1994, when they captured the southern border town of Spin Buldak and then "rescued" a Pakistani trade convoy near Kandahar. The expansion of their territorial control since then has been steady, despite some spectacular defeats, most notably the Mazar-i-Sharif debacle in May 1997 and Massoud's counterattack in August 1999. Key dates include their capture of Kandahar in November 1994, of Herat in September 1995, and of Kabul in September 1996, their capture and subsequent loss of Mazar-i-Sharif in May 1997,[61] their recapture of Mazar-i-Sharif in August 1998, and their capture of Bamiyan in September 1998.

What are the goals of the Taliban? These were not initially and are not even now entirely clear. The Taliban present themselves as a movement motivated by Islam, desiring to unify and purify Afghanistan. Many noncombatant Afghans initially perceived them as a front for the former king, himself a Durrani Pushtun, or for the Americans, eager to curtail Iranian influence in Central Asia and support the US-led natural gas consortium in Turkmenistan.[62] Their Afghan opponents perceive them as the tool of Pakistan and/or a Pushtun nationalist element.[63] The Russians and Central Asians fear the possibility that their brand of Islam might spill over north of the Amu Darya River. Even the Taliban do not speak with one voice about the goals of their movement, probably because the movement has grown far beyond anyone's expectations of its success. For example, Mullah Bismullah, a member of the Supreme Shura, said during an interview in Herat, "We [the Taliban] will establish a moderate Islamic system in Afghanistan that others will learn from. Neighboring countries that fear the Taliban—they are like a sick person. The first taste of medicine is bad, but it tastes better with time. They will ask for more. Islam—they have forgotten the taste of Islam."[64] Several days later, Mullah Omar's spokesman, Maulavi Wakil Ahmed (now the Taliban foreign minister), presented a different point of view, saying, "We never want to interfere in any neighboring country. We want good relations with all our neighbors. We wish to understand them and they us."[65]

How can the success of the Taliban be explained? Five factors have been most important. First and most telling has been the shared Pushtun ethnicity of the Taliban and the majority of the noncombatant population in most of the area they have come to control. Until their military successes in northern and central Afghanistan in 1998, the area the Taliban controlled was overwhelmingly Pushtun, and the area they were unable to take over was populated primarily by ethnic minorities (with the major exceptions of Herat and some sectors of Kabul). Thus, although the Taliban's appeal has not been consciously ethnic (indeed, the ethnic dimension has been downplayed), they nonetheless have been perceived and responded to as a Pushtun movement. This factor has partially changed now that the Taliban control large areas of Hazara (Imami Shia), Ismaili Shia, Uzbek, and Tajik territory, and also now that the Hazara Hezb-i Wahdat faction leader Ustad Akbari has defected to the Taliban. Nonetheless, in August 2000 Pakistani leader Gen. Pervaiz Musharraf announced that Pakistan supports the Taliban in part due to the movement's dominant Pushtun ethnicity, which is shared with the Pushtuns of Pakistan's NWFP, FATA, and Baluchistan.

The next two factors in explaining the rise of the Taliban are interrelated. These are their emphasis on religious piety and the war-weariness of the Afghan civilian population. From the beginning of the Taliban's existence, and continuing even today, they have presented their movement in fundamentalist religious terms that are very appealing to many Afghans (especially conservative rural Pushtuns). Early on, they often avoided combat by carrying the Koran in front of their advancing troops, and their first actions upon taking control of new territory have always included religious activities such as compelling men to attend prayers in mosques, forcing women to veil themselves, and banning practices deemed un-Islamic, such as listening to popular music. Perhaps equally important, since all of the mujahideen groups have also presented themselves as Islamist, has been the Taliban's relative lack of corruption, although reports of growing lawlessness in Taliban territory during 1999 suggest that this positive feature of their movement may be under pressure. Part of the Taliban's appeal has been based on the perception by the Afghan public that the movement's leaders are extremely pious and devoted to creating an Islamic society and state. In addition, many people were exhausted by the long war, disgusted by the infighting among mujahideen groups for personal gain, and ripe for the emergence of a new and purer movement. So war-weariness was also a factor—not just exhaustion from the years of fighting but also specifically exhaustion from the civil war between mujahideen groups. This factor was most prominent in Kandahar and Kabul.

A fourth factor that explains the rise of the Taliban is money. Numerous knowledgeable observers of modern Afghanistan report that the Taliban used money to induce opposing commanders to switch sides or surrender. Bribing or buying the loyalty of opposing commanders has been especially important to the Taliban's success; so far every significant Taliban advance has been preceded by the liberal disbursement of Taliban funds to opposition commanders whose loyalty could be purchased.[66] Reportedly the money for this purpose came from Saudi Arabia and other Persian Gulf countries, the "truck transport smuggling mafia based in Quetta and Chaman in Balochistan,"[67] heroin smugglers,[68] Osama bin Laden, and the Pakistani government. Customs duties, including a heroin tax, are now the major legitimate source of revenue for the Taliban government.[69] Taliban religious piety and the judicious use of financial incentives to opposing commanders proved to be a potent combination in the early days of the Taliban movement (1994–1995). Indeed, the Taliban fought few real battles until their defeat outside Kabul in April 1995.

Finally, the fifth factor that explains the success of the Taliban is Pakistani support. Support for the Taliban within Pakistan's government, army, and society is deep and multifaceted. Indeed, it is not incorrect to say that the Taliban are Pakistan's proxy army in Afghanistan, even though the Taliban leadership has not always followed Pakistan's preferences. And yet the Pakistani government has consistently denied supporting the Taliban, or at most has admitted to giving them minimal logistical support, even though the evidence overwhelmingly indicates the contrary.[70] Even in the middle of the July–August 1999 offensive into northeastern Afghanistan, in which thousands of Pakistani "volunteers" took part, the Pakistani government firmly maintained that it played no role in Afghanistan.

In fact the Taliban were helped from the very beginning by Pakistan's interior ministry, headed by Naserullah Babar under the Benazir Bhutto government of 1994, and various Pakistani actors have continued to provide support for the Taliban ever since. Whether they were intended from the outset to be Pakistan's militia in the ongoing Afghan civil war or were merely another recipient of Inter-Services Intelligence Directorate (ISI) largesse is not yet entirely clear. But their spectacular rise quickly eliminated other possible clients for Pakistan, so that today they represent Pakistan's only real client of significance in Afghanistan. Of course, Afghan history is replete with examples of politically defunct leaders being resurrected to play new roles in national politics, often being restored to the throne by the very power that brought them down earlier. Perhaps such a fate yet awaits Gulbuddin Hekmatyar, Sibghatullah Mojaddidi, or some other formerly significant actor now relegated to the sidelines by Pakistan's commitment to the Taliban—though it is hard to conceive of a scenario in which that will occur in the foreseeable future. So long as the Taliban enjoy Pakistani support they can control at least the Pushtun areas of Afghanistan. By the same token, the northern and central areas inhabited by non-Pushtuns will under those circumstances never view them as anything other than foreign pawns.

The details of Pakistan's support were initially unclear, because the Taliban could not be revealed to be a Pakistani government client until Hekmatyar, at least, was driven from the stage. That the Taliban were Pakistan's military client from the start, however, was quickly apparent in the nature of their earliest military operations in Afghanistan, their anti-Iranian posture, and their replacement of Gulbuddin Hekmatyar's forces on the southern edge of Kabul in early 1995.[71] It is now known that the Taliban received significant Pakistani assistance from the very beginning, including help in recruitment and training, weapons and ammunition, logistical support, financial assistance, and even the direct involvement of Pakistani military intelligence officers and regular forces (firing across the border in support of the Taliban's attack on Spin Buldak in October 1994).[72] As time passed, Pakistan's involvement with the Taliban, which came from various sectors of the Pakistani government and society, became so comprehensive that it began to drive Pakistan's policy toward Afghanistan. Pakistani support for the Taliban included direct and indirect military involvement, logistical support, recruitment, financial aid, and diplomatic recognition.

The Taliban are, at heart, a movement devoted to military activity. Thus, most of their foreign support is related in one way or another to that aspect of their program. Pakistan's military assistance to the Taliban has run the gamut, from direct involvement of their own forces in Afghanistan to the training of Taliban soldiers in Pakistan. Reportedly, Pakistani military personnel have maintained and operated Taliban aircraft and tanks, and Pakistani officers have played combat advisory roles for the Taliban.[73] Several hundred "Pakistani Taliban" have been captured and an indeterminate number killed in fighting against the northern Afghan groups. Iran, Russia, Tajikistan, and Uzbekistan, along with the Afghan opposition government, all have alleged that the Taliban victories in northern Afghanistan in 1998 were due in part to direct Pakistani military involvement, including more than fifteen hundred troops and numerous combat sorties by the Pakistan Air Force.[74] Similar allegations were made during the summer offensives of 1999 and 2000.[75]

Taliban combat operations have revealed a tactical sophistication generally lacking among the mujahideen forces. The Taliban have combined careful planning and political groundwork with such tactical innovations as night attacks and high mobility. Their command-and-control network has been highly efficient. All of this is at odds with the picture they presented to the outside world of their being simple religious students, and even with the more accurate picture of their being former mujahideen. The reality is that not only have the Taliban been strengthened by the assistance of Pakistani forces, but their personnel have also been trained by Pakistani military instructors to fight a different kind of war from the one they had fought during the jihad days of the 1980s.[76]

Pakistan has also provided critical logistical support, without which Taliban military operations would not have been so successful. This support has included weapons, ammunition, fuel, communication equipment, maintenance of armor and airplanes, and transport for men and materiel. Perhaps of even greater significance, Pakistan has been the primary recruiter for the Taliban, to the point that today the movement's rank-and-file soldiers include more than ten thousand Pakistanis.[77] The ISI has recruited thousands of Pakistani youths since 1994, primarily from madrasahs, to fill Taliban ranks. It also provided the Taliban with many former Khalqi army officers who were part of the failed Shanawaz Tanai coup against the Parchami-led Najibullah government in 1990.[78] Rashid reports that "by the time the Taliban captured

Kabul, their entire air force and a large section of their armour and heavy artillery were being manned by former Khalqis."[79]

Various elements of the Pakistani government have been involved in supporting and assisting the Taliban, notably the Frontier Constabulary (training and field communications) and the National Logistics Cell (logistical support, basically transport). Former interior minister Babar was the architect of the Taliban support structure. He allegedly set up "an Afghan Trade Development Cell in the Interior Ministry" that coordinated the support activities of numerous other Pakistani ministries and offices, including Pakistan International Airlines, Pakistan Railways, Pakistan Telecom, the National Bank of Pakistan, Radio Pakistan, the Water and Power Development Authority, and the Public Works Department.[80] The provincial governments of the NWFP and Baluchistan gave the Taliban significant support as well, often for local political reasons that had little to do with Pakistan's foreign policy.[81]

Various private Pakistani actors have provided support to the Taliban, notably in recruitment and financial aid. The JUI and even more radical Islamist organizations (such as the Lashkar-e-Toiba, Hizbul Mujahideen, Harkatul Mujahideen, and Tehrik-e-Jehad) provide recruits for the Taliban in Afghanistan. The JUI has encouraged students in its madrasahs to join the Taliban by declaring the Afghan struggle a jihad, giving students vacations so they can join the fighting, and even closing their schools altogether. In 1997, 1998, and 1999 the Taliban faced at least one major defeat or military crisis per year, and each time, Taliban supreme leader Mullah Umar issued special appeals to the JUI seminaries for more recruits, producing thousands of volunteers in short order.

Many of the organizations just mentioned have contributed monetary aid to the Taliban in addition to whatever other support they provided, but there are also private individuals and nongovernmental actors who have contributed only money to the Taliban cause. A notable Pakistani example of such an actor is the transport "mafia" centered in Quetta, which provided financial support (through both customs duties and special collections prior to major offensives) and much of the initial impetus for the rise of the Taliban.[82] Arab terrorist financier Osama bin Laden, US oil company Union Oil Company of California (Unocal),[83] and Pakistani and Afghan drug barons are or have been other important private actors in Afghanistan. The collapse of Afghanistan's formal economy has empowered many of these private actors, especially the drug barons and smugglers with Pakistani connections, because they provide most of Afghanistan's tiny annual GDP, and much of their goods go to or through Pakistan. Pakistan also provided most of the official government budget of $10 million in 1998.[84]

Finally, Pakistan accorded the Taliban diplomatic recognition in 1997, in that brief moment when Mazar-i-Sharif had fallen to the Taliban for the first time and the movement appeared on the verge of conquering northern Afghanistan. Since then, only Saudi Arabia and the United Arab Emirates have joined Pakistan in recognizing the Taliban as the official government of Afghanistan. All three countries have since faced substantial pressure from the West to revoke or downgrade their recognition, and both Pakistan and Saudi Arabia did downgrade relations under intense US pressure in 1998. Pakistan, however, remains the Taliban's unofficial spokesman in the international arena.

Since 1994, Pakistan has, in numerous ways and through numerous actors, fostered the rise of the Taliban militia to power in Afghanistan. Today the Taliban are Pakistan's proxy in Afghanistan, the latest indigenous group to be manipulated by the Pakistani government in order to advance Pakistan's foreign policy aims there. But they are not a movement that Pakistan has been able to control with ease, and their existence and success pose serious implications for Pakistan. As Rashid commented: "The Taliban's close links with Pakistani society, their uncompromising stance on their version of Islamic values and the fact that they represent a new form of Islamic radicalism which is admired by a younger generation of Pakistani madrasasa students, give them far more clout inside Pakistan than other Afghan Mujahideen groups. For many Pakistanis, the Taliban are an inspiration."[85]

The rise of the Taliban to power may be somewhat artificial, and thus their appearance on the Afghan stage may be transitory, precisely because key elements are missing that could make their role more natural and permanent. Specifically, the Taliban lack talented political leadership, competent military performance, and ideological creativity. Their leader, Mullah Mohammad Omar, is by all accounts a simple man who seldom meets with outsiders, and few of the other Taliban leaders have any political background at all. They are a mixture of former small-unit military commanders and madrasah teachers. Despite their wealth of first-hand military experience, their performance in their few actual battles has been mixed at best. Even Anthony Davis, who is impressed by their "planning; impressive command-and-control and intelligence in a fluid tactical situation; unfailing logistics support; and unrelenting, overwhelming speed," attributes the Taliban's martial capability to Pakistan.[86] Most of their success has been due to avoiding battles rather than winning them. Indeed, despite the aura of invincibility enjoyed by the Taliban, they have suffered at least three significant defeats so far (Kabul in March 1995, Herat in April 1995, and Mazar-i-Sharif in May–June 1997). Their best Afghan infantry now appear to be battle-hardened eastern Pushtun tribesmen, many from Ghilzai or other non-Durrani clans, under the command of Maulavi Jalaluddin Haqani. Meanwhile, they rely increasingly on Pakistani recruits, fighting in their own units and led by Pakistani noncommissioned and commissioned officers. The Taliban air force, armored units, and artillery are reportedly staffed by ex-Khalqis and maintained by Pakistani military personnel.[87] Few Taliban leaders have command experience in large-scale military operations. Finally, the Taliban appear to be devoid of ideas about how to confront Afghanistan's myriad development problems. As I will explain later, some Taliban policies have proved unpopular, but more importantly, there is little sense that policies are based on an overall plan.

It is clear that the Taliban are the most important force in Afghanistan today, and almost certainly they will continue to be a major player in Afghanistan's future in the short term (one to two years) and medium term (three to five years). Why the Taliban will be a critical factor in Afghanistan's future requires deeper analysis, but one key reason is that they represent the first significant Pushtun-led government in Kabul since the fall of the communist regime in 1992 (not counting Sibghatullah Mojaddidi's brief rule in 1992). Whether they can be a critical force in the future of Afghanistan and the region will depend heavily on whether they can govern the country and on what policies their government undertakes, areas in which the Taliban have so far been significantly weak.

The Taliban are a social movement and tribal militia running a country.[88] Perhaps at no time since the Wahhabi movement in Saudi Arabia in the 1920s has a similar situation existed in the Islamic world. Such a situation does not readily lend itself to the kind of structural-functional or institutional analysis of governance that has become standard in political science since the 1960s. With the Taliban, there are few meaningful governmental structures and little that actually functions. Nonetheless, in an effort to understand how the Taliban actually govern, I turn to a consideration of how the Taliban government is structured and then consider broad areas of Taliban policy.

The Taliban as a Governing Body

The Taliban government is headed by a Supreme Shura of thirty to forty members,[89] which is itself headed by Mullah Mohammad Omar Akhund, Amir ul-Moemineen (Commander of the Faithful), a title considered by his followers to extend to all Muslims worldwide. Indeed, in October 1997 the Taliban renamed the Islamic Republic of Afghanistan the Islamic Emirate of Afghanistan. Mohammad Omar himself was virtually unknown prior to his emergence in the summer of 1994, and his unwillingness to meet with anyone outside of his inner circle makes him still a mystery to the world today. A mid-level commander in Nabi Mohammadi's party (Harakat-i Inqilab-i-Islami) during the 1980s,[90] Omar was wounded fighting against the Soviets and now has full use of only one eye. Reportedly, his disgust with the anarchy and un-Islamic practices following the fall of the communist government in Kabul in 1992 led to his call to arms; other stories attribute his inspiration to visions from Allah.[91] He does not meet foreigners, does not leave Kandahar, and thus has little direct influence on the day-to-day operations of the Taliban. Still, key Taliban leaders all claim that he makes the final decisions for the Taliban government, upon the advice of the Supreme Shura.[92]

The Supreme Shura has seen its membership (which is not known precisely) change numerous times as the Taliban movement has grown. Originally numbering no more than fifteen, all Pushtuns from the Kandahar area, today the Supreme Shura has grown to more than twice that size and includes Ghilzai and other eastern Pushtuns. The inner core of the Supreme Shura (the Inner Shura), however, has perhaps six to eight members and includes Premier Maulavi Mohammad Rabbani, Deputy Premier Maulavi Mohammad Hassan, and Foreign Minister Maulavi Wakil Ahmed. The full membership of this inner council is not known and probably is not fixed, but some Taliban leaders who have been thought to be members include Defense Minister Mullah Ubaidullah, Deputy Defense Minister Biradar, Interior Minister Abdul Razzaq, and Mullahs Ehsanullah, Abbas, Mohammed, and Pasani.[93] Maulavi Ahmed describes the Taliban system as follows: "We have an emirate system, which means government power is based on a shura, which selects the amir. Then the government [i.e., its executive and administrative functions] is [the] second rank. Shura members are spread around in different provinces. The majority are in Kabul but meet here [Kandahar] and advise Mullah Omar, and then decrees are issued."[94]

Ministries and provincial and city governments remain essentially unchanged, often staffed at lower levels by pre-Taliban personnel. There are twenty-seven ministries, based primarily in Kabul, but they are characterized by little activity. In November 1997 the Taliban purged all ministries of forty to fifty workers each, firing those whose records included letters of commendation from previous governments.[95] Ministry employees in Kabul were not paid for more than eight months in 1997,[96] and since then pay has continued to be irregular and morale low among civil servants.

All ministries were headed by acting ministers from September 1996, when the Taliban captured Kabul and formed their government, until October 1999, when Mullah Omar announced a reorganization of the government and dropped the pretense that the Taliban were a temporary phenomenon. Prior to that decree, the Taliban maintained that they were merely an interim government, holding power only until the Afghan people could have the opportunity to select a permanent government. Kabul itself is headed by a six-man supervisory council that includes key Taliban leaders such as Mohammad Rabbani and Mohammad Hassan.

A significant new addition to the government is the religious (or morality) police, known as the Ministry for the Promotion of Virtue and Prevention of Vice (Amr bil-Maroof wa Nahi An il-Munkir). It patrols the streets enforcing social policies concerning attire, beards, games, entertainment, interaction with foreigners, and, especially, the appearance and role of women in society. There appears to be substantial latitude on the part of local Taliban commanders in the application of such policies, and numerous human rights abuses have resulted.[97] This ministry began as a semi-independent department of the Ministry of the Interior, and through 1998 it was supposed to take cases of violations of public morality to that ministry, which in turn would present them to the Ministry of Justice. The religious police clearly are modeled on the similar institution in Saudi Arabia and reflect the Saudi influence among the Taliban leadership. This organization has separate access to Gulf funds, which helped it achieve ministerial status in 1999 and become the most active and significant of the Taliban ministries. All of the judges in the three-tiered Taliban court system are 'ulama.[98]

As essentially a tribal militia engaged in a military struggle that now finds itself at the helm of a government, the Taliban devote most of their attention to waging the war. Their formal military structure was somewhat loose at first,[99] and as late as 1997 Taliban leaders seemed to divide their time between a nominal ministerial and/or shura role and a more serious combat duty. At least three key Taliban leaders were killed in combat (Mullah Masher south of Kabul in 1995, Mullah Borjan at Sarobi in 1996, and Mullah Ehsanullah in 1998 after the capture of Mazar-i-Sharif), and many of the other leaders are obviously much more comfortable with military action than civil governance. A more formalized military structure was in place by 1999, with military corps based in each major Taliban city, but 25 percent or more of the Taliban forces were Pakistani.[100]

Taliban policy-making has been piecemeal and somewhat reactionary. Certainly no clear policy framework has been elucidated. Nonetheless, it is possible to examine the thrust of policies undertaken in three general areas: social life, economics, and criminal justice.

The most controversial and perhaps only well-developed part of the Taliban program has been in the area of social policy. It is there that the Islamization ideology has been most evident, especially with regard to Taliban policy toward women and girls, but also with regard to a range of other policies, such as those concerning religious practices, minority rights, and entertainment.

No other governance issue has attracted such negative attention to the Taliban as their policy toward women. From the beginning of their rule, the Taliban have turned the clock back on women's rights in Afghanistan by instituting a policy based on a mixture of conservative Deobandi teachings and traditional Pushtunwali conceptions of a woman's place and role in society. In traditional Pushtun areas, women have always led restricted lives, for their virtue is considered integral to family and clan honor. The tides of twentieth-century secularization and modernization in Afghanistan provided greater opportunities for women to participate in public life, especially in northern and urban areas. The recent ascendance of Islamists and the association of modernization with communism has undermined the status of women and introduced substantial restrictions on their lives once again. The Taliban, however, have made the issue of women's roles and status a cornerstone of their Islamization program. Indeed, policies toward women and girls, in conjunction with law and order policies, in many ways constitute the centerpiece of Taliban public policy.

Women have been virtually eliminated from public space by being forbidden to work outside of the home, forbidden to appear in public without being covered from head to toe (requiring adoption of the *burqa,* the head-to-toe form of the veil common among Pushtun women), and initially forbidden to appear in public at all. Girls have been forbidden to attend school, although the Taliban have claimed repeatedly that they only oppose coeducational facilities and that when Afghanistan returns to normalcy, girls' schools will be provided (education for girls is accepted under the major schools of doctrine of Islamic law). Although there have been some cases in which girls have continued to attend school, even in coeducational facilities,[101] the general trend has been to deny girls the opportunity to receive schooling, especially given that the Taliban have controlled certain areas of the country for more than six years now.[102] The banning of women from the workplace has had serious ramifications for many urban families headed by a war widow, and again, although there have been some exceptions, the general trend has been to prevent women from working. Many urban women have been driven to desperate begging and prostitution by the loss of their livelihoods (in 1997, forty thousand to fifty thousand widows existed in Kabul alone, many without a male relative to support them if they could not work). The beating of women for appearing in public without appropriate dress has occurred repeatedly.[103] The Taliban claim that these policies provide greater security for women, but although the widespread incidences of rape that occurred during stage six of the war have declined since the Taliban ascendance,[104] there continue to be cases in which women are molested.[105] Women have been denied political representation or civil rights to appeal their mistreatment.[106]

Under the Taliban women have also been denied access to adequate health care. Numerous Taliban edicts address this area of women's lives and collectively provide the greatest impact on their standard of living. These rules include the closure of public bathhouses and gender segregation in health care, including "a policy of segregating men and women into separate hospitals," which are usually lacking in even the most basic requirements for providing medical care.[107] Also contributing to the overall deterioration of health care services for females has been the prohibition on female employment, which has prevented thousands of female doctors, nurses, and pharmacists from providing health care even in segregated facilities. Physicians for Human Rights bluntly note that "Afghan women are thus caught in the paradoxical bind of being compelled to seek care only from female providers at the same time that governmental decrees ensure a dwindling supply of such providers."[108] The overall impact of Taliban policies on female health care has been to deny women (and many children, especially those from families headed by widows) health care. This has had clear negative effects on women's standard of living in Afghanistan. Life expectancy for women is only 43–44 years old, nearly twenty years less than the average for developing countries. It is so low because of maternal mortality rates (17 per 1000) and infant mortality rates (163 per 1000) that are the highest in the world, because less than 6 percent of births are attended by trained medical personnel, and because "only 29 percent of the population has access to health and 12 percent has access to safe water."[109] In a survey of 160 Afghan women (80 living in Kabul, 80 who had fled Kabul for Pakistan) conducted in 1998 by the Physicians for Human Rights, 97 percent of respondents met the clinical criteria for depression, 86 percent had significant symptoms of anxiety, and 42 percent suffered from post-traumatic stress disorder.[110] Thus, both the physical and mental health of Afghan women, already poor after years of warfare, have deteriorated sharply under Taliban rule.

The transformation of the position of women in Afghanistan over the last two decades of the twentieth century is an excellent illustration of the profound changes that have occurred in Afghan society during that period. Indeed, the ascendance of the Taliban represents the culmination of the Islamist trend in Afghanistan, but much of the groundwork for that trend was laid during the 1980s by the various mujahideen groups now held by the Taliban to be so un-Islamic.[111] Nonetheless, many Taliban policies based on their interpretation of sharia are unpopular outside of the rural Pushtun areas in which they have their roots.

Other notable social policies target urban men and also provide indicators of the Taliban's intent to Islamize Afghan society. These policies include forcing men into mosques to attend Friday prayers, requiring men to grow untrimmed beards as signs of piety, requiring men to trim and/or shave their heads and body hair, and otherwise insisting that men conform to the norms of southern, Kandahari Pushtun tribal society. Taliban policies on minority rights have been openly discriminatory, thus intensifying the ethnic divisions within Afghanistan. Not only did the Taliban kill Shia leader Ali Mazari in 1995, but on several occasions they have also been accused of rounding up minority residents of Kabul who subsequently disappeared. On at least one occasion, minority detainees were made to perform as human minesweepers on the battlegrounds north of Kabul.[112] More recently the Taliban degenerated into open ethnic cleansing during their successful northern offensive in August–September 1998. More than eight thousand minority residents were reportedly killed by the Taliban in and around Mazar-i-Sharif and Bamiyan, and there have been widespread fears among knowledgeable observers of Afghanistan that the Taliban may attempt the extermination of the Hazara Shia.[113] Likewise, the Taliban's scorched earth tactics north of Kabul during their July–September 1999 struggle with Massoud were clearly designed to force out the ethnic minority population living in this strategically significant area.

The Taliban have also banned or limited nearly all forms of secular entertainment (some of the limitations on popular culture were first initiated by Hekmatyar). Their policies in this area are discussed in further detail in the last section of this chapter.

The Taliban have virtually no program with regard to more traditional areas of social policy, such as public health, infrastructure reconstruction, and education. In these areas the Taliban rely almost completely on outside organizations for assistance, both in keeping with Afghanistan's traditional governmental preference for a rentier economy and the Taliban's focus on warfare to the exclusion of all else. Probably the most obvious area of policy failure in this regard has been inadequate infrastructure reconstruction. Herat and large areas of Kabul, for example, have had no regular supply of electricity for several years, and water throughout the entire country is unsafe to drink. There is no project in place to rebuild Afghanistan's degraded roads. Driving along, one periodically passes children, elderly men, and mine victims using crude shovels to scatter a bit of dirt into the larger holes. Their recompense is a few nearly worthless alghani notes tossed out of the windows of passing vehicles, and their activity is nothing more than creative begging. Taliban restrictions on women have had a very adverse effect on education, for boys as well as girls, because the majority of Afghanistan's teachers are women. Their inability to work has forced even boys' schools to close or operate with inadequate staffing.

Growing frustration with the Taliban restrictions, especially on women, has led many international relief and reconstruction organizations to close their Afghan operations or to consider doing so.[114] The disagreement between the Taliban and foreign aid organizations came to a head in July 1998, when the Taliban ordered all foreign NGOs in Kabul to close their operations and leave, nominally over their refusal to be relocated to a dilapidated dormitory in Kabul.[115] All foreign relief personnel, including those with UN agencies, were evacuated after American cruise missile strikes against Afghanistan on August 20, 1998, led to the killing of a UN military adviser in Kabul. UN and NGO humanitarian and development activities were resumed in Afghanistan in March 1999, after being interrupted for seven months, following "strong assurances" from the Taliban that the security of their personnel would be guaranteed. Foreign humanitarian operations in Afghanistan continued to decline in 1999, however, especially following an incident in June when Taliban soldiers beat and robbed Red Cross workers on the Bamiyan-Kabul road. The situation further worsened in 2000, with several incidents where aid workers were killed, expelled, or harassed. Prior to the UN Security Council sanctions of December 2000, all non-Afghan personnel working for the UN were temporarily withdrawn from the country.

The Taliban have complained that they can do little to rebuild Afghanistan so long as the fighting continues and outside powers fail to recognize their government. They do have revenue, but it appears to be spent primarily on the continuation of their military struggle. Their primary sources of revenue have been from outside actors such as Saudi Arabia and from customs duties imposed on the transit and smuggling trade, especially that of western and southwestern Afghanistan. Although they have attempted to close down the hashish traffic, heroin production has grown to the point that the "heroin tax" has become an important source of revenue. There is little evidence of any significant reestablishment of indigenous Afghan industry; virtually all factories are closed, and often they are only rubble.

Subsistence agriculture is the primary economic opportunity of most rural dwellers now, while the situation in urban areas differs from place to place. The security and stability that the Taliban brought to Kandahar in particular, as well as its key location as the terminus of the transit trade through southwestern Afghanistan, have made it possible for small businesses to thrive there. On the other hand, business has been moribund in Herat, especially from early 1997 to late 1999, when the border with Iran was partially or completely closed. In Kabul, many people are desperate, with unemployment running at more than 30 percent, most government employees going unpaid, high inflation, and shortages of vital goods. Until leaving the city in August 1998, the World Food Programme fed 25 percent of Kabul's population, and by December 1999 more than two-thirds of Kabul's population was relying on humanitarian assistance to survive.[116]

Both the Kabul government, under Rabbani as well as the Taliban, and Dostam's government in Mazar-i-Sharif printed Afghani currency, prompting the Taliban to make possession of the northern currency illegal. The new Pakistani military government tightened up on smuggling in October 1999, causing the price of wheat in Afghanistan to rise by more than 100 percent by the end of the year. That inflation, coupled with the continued influx of Northern Alliance–produced afghanis and a major currency heist in Kabul in January 2000, drove the value of the afghani down sharply.[117]

The Taliban hope to revive their moribund economy through traditional rentier means. Their hope is to acquire international recognition so that the Central Asia Gas Pipeline Ltd. (CENTGAS) consortium of oil and gas companies, led by Unocal,[118] can build a 1,500-kilometer (937-mile) gas pipeline from Turkmenistan through western Afghanistan to Pakistan. The Afghan leg of the pipeline will run 743 kilometers (458 miles), and the project is estimated to cost nearly $2 billion. If it is ever built, the pipeline will carry 20 billion cubic meters of gas per year and will produce billions of dollars in revenues for Afghanistan.[119] Likewise, the Taliban have recently explored or announced business deals with foreign companies interested in copper mines in Logar and the development of a cellular telephone system for Afghanistan. The imposition of economic sanctions on the Taliban by the US in July 1999 and the UN in November 1999 and December 2000 has undermined what little foreign investment the Taliban had been able to attract.

The last area of Taliban policy that I examine concerns criminal justice. Here again, the application of sharia, as modified by the customs of Pushtunwali, provides a clear illustration of the Taliban's intent to Islamize Afghan society. When taking over an area, the Taliban first establish law and order by confiscating weapons and imposing a curfew at night (still in place in all the cities they control). The Ministry for the Promotion of Virtue and the Prevention of Vice then begins to impose Taliban social policies on the population. Violators of certain laws have faced traditional *hudud* punishments (penalties prescribed in the Koran, such as amputations for robbery and stoning for adultery) as modified by Pushtun custom, including having the victim's family members execute murderers (by gun and knife), hanging rapists, amputating the hands (one hand and sometimes also one foot) of thieves, stoning adulterers, burying homosexuals alive, flogging fornicators, and publicly humiliating those convicted of lesser sentences.[120] Early pronouncements against the heroin traffic have been modified under economic and political pressure.

Other areas of Taliban policy include their domestic political policy toward rival groups, military policy, and foreign policy. Much of my examination of these topics comes in the final two chapters.

Popular opinion of the Taliban among Afghans today depends on whom you ask. Many people respect the Taliban for their piety and for bringing stability and security to areas they control, although some argue that they are not really pious and/or that the areas they now control were already stable before they took over.[121] Nonetheless, they are generally supported in Pushtun areas, especially in and around Kandahar. The Taliban are preferred in Kabul to the alternative of having Massoud back, at least among Pushtuns. On the other hand, the Taliban are viewed as an extremely unwelcome occupying force in Herat. The northern minority groups are also staunchly opposed to the Taliban, as are some moderate Pushtun leaders. Taking over the northern and central areas of the country during the summer and fall of 1998 and killing thousands of minority civilian residents of those areas cannot have endeared the Taliban to those local populations either.

Nonetheless, even those who respect them recognize that the Taliban are incapable of governing the country. The Taliban leaders are too inexperienced and uneducated in government and politics to rule effectively, and they may be too committed to their ideology to compromise. Also, as the Taliban have taken more territory, their movement has grown away from its core of Kandahari, Durrani Pushtuns to include Ghilzai Pushtuns, "reformed" Afghan communists from the Khalqi faction, ethnic minorities, and significant numbers of Pakistani youths. Numerous fissures have appeared within the movement, and not all who are now affiliated with the Taliban subscribe to their morality or social policy.[122] Thus, even if the Taliban do take all of Afghanistan, they will never govern it and will almost certainly fracture from within in trying to do so.

The Taliban's Transformation of Afghanistan

This analysis of the Taliban suggests at least three major implications for Afghanistan's ethnic, religious, and political divisions. First, the now-shattered Northern Alliance of ethnic minorities is deeply opposed to Taliban governance, thus exacerbating existing ethnic and religious divisions. The atrocities that occurred in the wake of the Taliban victories in Mazar-i-Sharif in August 1998 and Bamiyan in September 1998 show clearly the growing bitterness and depth of the ethnoreligious divide. The failure of UN-brokered negotiations between the Taliban and the Northern Alliance in Ashkhabad in March and Tashkent in July 1999 paved the way for Massoud's northern minority forces to dig in grimly for a fight to the finish. The fight came in July through September of

1999, and although they survived to endure another frigid winter in the high mountain valleys, the ethnic cleansing of the Shomali plains north of Kabul by Taliban forces only deepened the growing ethno-religious hatred. The late summer offensive of 2000 drove Massoud back even farther into the high northeastern mountains, where he faces the possibility of an attack on his Panjshir redoubt from northern Pakistan.

Second, the Taliban are internally divided between various Pushtun tribes and subtribes, ideological moderates and Islamist hard-liners, and native Afghans and Pakistani "volunteers." They cannot remain unified even if they achieve a military victory over their northern rivals. In the spring of 1998, Ahmed Rashid suggested that internal fissures within the Taliban were growing more serious and might lead to the movement's fracturing by the fall of 1998.[123] Rehmat Shah Afridi also argued that the Taliban would begin to split in 1998 as commanders from eastern provinces who joined for money became increasingly disillusioned and began to think of rejoining their old parties. According to Afridi: "The main contradiction is emerging between the Taliban groups controlling the lucrative border region with Pakistan where the transit trade flows, and the Taliban stationed deeper inside the central regions of the country where life means all work and no play."[124]

The arrest in September 1998 of former Khalqi communists within the Taliban ranks for plotting a coup seemed to suggest that this process of internal fragmentation had begun. That virtually all of those arrested also came from the eastern provinces of Kunar, Laghman, and Nangarhar further illustrates the internal division within Taliban ranks. Perhaps recent battlefield successes will help maintain Taliban solidarity a bit longer, but they may also lead to increased pressure from opposition forces to convince wavering Taliban commanders to switch back over, as was precisely the case in several northern provinces in late 1998 and 1999. Alternatively, a complete Taliban victory over the northern minorities would eliminate the primary factor unifying the Pushtun tribes. Furthermore, the widespread reports of substantial Pakistani military support for the Taliban in their 1998, 1999, and 2000 campaigns may mean that the Taliban no longer need their Khalqi soldiers. Taliban assertions that any excesses committed by their forces in the capture of northern areas in 1998, such as the killing of Iranian diplomats in Mazar-i-Sharif, were the actions of "rogue elements" within the movement may also reflect internal divisions within the movement.

Third, the Taliban have capped a thirty-year movement to Islamize

Afghan society and, in the process, introduced generational change into the country. The significance of this generational change must be emphasized. Afghanistan's prewar ethnic and sociopolitical framework is now dead, and even if the Taliban do represent the return of the tribes to prominence, as Olivier Roy has suggested,[125] their traditional jirga framework of governance has been clearly altered to make room for young men whose legitimacy grows out of the guns they control. Likewise, the Islamization of Afghanistan, although a recurrent theme in modern Afghan history,[126] occurs now in a changed national and regional environment that suggests it may well be deeper and longer lasting than in the past.

In addition, three facets of this regional-international environment may prove especially significant to the Taliban movement. First, the foundation of regional relations seems to be moving away from geopolitics and toward geoeconomics (despite the continuing India-Pakistan rivalry, intensified through nuclear tests on both sides in May–June 1998 and the Kargil Crisis in 1999), which may make the projected gas pipeline and transit trade from Central Asia through western Afghanistan key. Thus, it is vital to the success of their movement that the Taliban retain their hold on Herat, until recently their most fragile position. Second, the transforming face of Iran to the outside world may lead to a rapprochement with the United States, once again causing the superpower to abandon Pakistan. Thus, it is no surprise that Pakistan appeared to rethink its policy toward the Taliban and Afghanistan in 1998 and 1999.[127] Finally, increasing international pressure on the US to play a larger regional role is viewed as critical to achieving a settlement to the Afghan conflict. The US government was responding positively to that pressure by playing a more active role in Afghanistan in 1998, until the embassy bombings in Kenya and Tanzania prompted US retaliation against Osama bin Laden's bases inside Afghanistan. Since then, US policy toward the Taliban has been fixated on the capture of bin Laden, which on the one hand has led to greater US pressure on the Taliban, such as in the July 1999 US and November 1999 UN economic sanctions. On the other hand, the US government has been so focused on bin Laden that it may have lost its position as an honest outside broker. The change to a military government in Pakistan in October 1999 further strained the already-tenuous ties between the United States and the Taliban's biggest backer. In response to the subsequent iciness from Washington and its leadership of the international effort to isolate Pakistan (while the US simultaneously warmed up to

India), the Musharraf government openly embraced the Taliban in 2000, perhaps gambling that victory in Afghanistan would help bring about the moderation of the Taliban and change the international attitude toward both regimes.

SOCIOCULTURAL CHANGE

The last major way in which the war has changed Afghanistan has been the profound impact it has had on its culture. Afghanistan is peopled by many groups with differing cultural traits, including language, religious practices, physical appearance and attire, and customs. Intermarriage between ethnic or religious groups is relatively uncommon, and even the notion of being Afghan has always been weak; most individuals identify themselves in relation to their qawm.[128] Perhaps it is even inappropriate to refer to "Afghan culture," for Afghanistan is in many ways a society with differing ethnic cultures, both overlapping and clashing. Thus, Afghan conceptions of self and other are perpetually shifting, and rarely is "self" conceived broadly enough to incorporate members of other ethnic groups on the national level. Group identity usually extends no further than the qawm, which never extends beyond the tribal or ethnic group level and can be much narrower, depending on circumstances. Only outside threats such as the Soviet invasion in 1979 can produce a unifying response on the national level, and that is tenuous at best. The long war that resulted, however, has been so destructive to Afghanistan that it has produced dramatic and probably lasting cultural and social changes.

Much attention has been paid to the effects that Afghanistan's long conflict has had on the country's demographic profile, physical infrastructure, and political-economic development.[129] Popular culture, however, is often one of the first casualties of war as well, either sacrificed to the exigencies of war in the interest of life-and-death national struggle or transformed in various ways, often not benign, by the war itself. In Afghanistan the social framework and indigenous culture were direct targets of various combatants throughout the war, so it is no surprise that Afghan popular culture has been so damaged. Virtually every area of popular culture has been affected over the past two decades: the arts and music, architecture, customs, education, historical heritage, the intelligentsia, literature, publishing, and sports, to name a few. To write about Afghan popular culture now, with the decidedly anticulture Taliban apparently still ascendant, leads inexorably to negative conclusions about its future prospects. The Taliban are responsible, after all, for ruling virtually all secular forms of popular culture to be un-Islamic and thus forbidden. These include cinema, television, radio, music, and art. All photography has been banned, because it is considered un-Islamic to have depictions of human images. Televisions and videocassette recorders have been destroyed, as have films, videocassettes, and audiotapes. Because music is forbidden, vehicles are regularly stopped and searched for cassette tapes that, if found, are destroyed on the spot by teenage Taliban fighters who, if they were in any other country in the world, would be demanding to hear them louder![130] Leaving Kabul in July 1997, I sat in a long line of traffic formed so that each vehicle could undergo just such a search. My bus driver retained hidden cassettes of Pakistani pop music that he played throughout our journey, putting them away only at checkpoints and replacing them with a tape of Koranic recitation. Paradoxically, I also witnessed a traditional Afghan singer outside of Herat in July 1997 perform a cappella for a group of young Taliban; he sang songs of the Taliban movement and its heroes.

Similarly, the Taliban have curtailed or eliminated secular programming on radio and television and have continued the ban on cinema enacted by Gulbuddin Hekmatyar during his brief period as prime minister in the summer of 1996.[131] All photography and art involving human images has been forbidden. Popular sports such as football and activities such as kite flying and chess were banned by Taliban edicts in 1994, but the ban was later eased and sports and games are now played quite openly in all the Taliban-held areas. Appropriate attire (long pants and shirts with sleeves) must be worn, however, and games are interrupted at prayer times. Certain social policy edicts appear to have been relaxed over time, such as those dealing with sport, while others have been tightened, such as those dealing with photography and the human image. In July 1998, for example, the Taliban extended their restrictions to include the destruction of television sets and satellite dishes.

More ominously, Afghanistan's intellectual class and educational system suffered tremendously during the war. Intellectuals were targeted by the Soviets and Afghan communists in the early years of the war, and the subsequent destruction and dispersion of this tiny group dealt a blow to Afghanistan's educational system from which it has yet to recover.[132] Afghanistan now has the world's lowest recorded level of female literacy and is among the bottom five countries in total literacy.[133] With the Taliban's restrictions on girls' schooling and female employment, the majority of Afghan children are again going uneducated. For example, when I visited Kabul University in July 1997 it was devoid of females, who once constituted 60 percent of its students and teachers combined. With the passing of Afghanistan's intellectuals from the scene (some, like former Kabul University dean Sayed Bahouddin Majrooh, were assassinated; others, like renowned poet Khalilallah Khalili, are dead from old age; but the majority are now settled abroad, unlikely ever to return), there is no younger cohort of scholars, writers, and poets to take their place. Nor are there young engineers, physicians, and scientists to provide the technical and scientific leadership the ravaged country needs.

An important caveat must be introduced here. I have focused in this chapter on the changes produced in Afghanistan by its long war. Thus, I have largely ignored one of the most significant implications of the Afghan diaspora—that although most of the Afghan refugees languished in Pakistani camps or Iranian cities, the educated and skilled individuals migrated farther afield, usually to the West. The impact of this diaspora and its accompanying "brain drain" on Afghanistan have been profound. The absence of intellectuals helped make possible the Islamization of the vast majority of refugees in Pakistan and Iran, for the refugee camps provided a milieu in which Islamist education was emphasized, enabling a movement like the Taliban to germinate. It is primarily this latter group of Afghan exiles that has now returned to Afghanistan, whereas Afghans fortunate enough to have settled in the West have no intention of returning to their homeland. The dispersion of the intelligentsia has robbed Afghanistan of a voice for secular or at least moderate alternatives to Islamization and has also left Afghanistan bereft of much of its finest administrative and technical talent.

The attack on the Afghan educational system, first by the communists and later by the Islamists, has led to curriculum changes, school closings, a decline in teacher quality, and a host of other ills that have combined to lower literacy rates in Afghanistan, especially among females. Female literacy is now estimated to be only 3 to 4 percent.[134] With such low literacy it is perhaps unsurprising that there are few newspapers. Those that do exist tend to be affiliated with one or another political faction and are published sporadically. Kabul radio and television, the Voice of Shariat, produce mostly government pronouncements and religious programming.[135]

Likewise, Afghanistan's literature and publishing have declined during the war years, and only diaspora organizations such as the Writers Union of Free Afghanistan show any vitality. Indigenous publishing is virtually nonexistent today. One form of Afghan writing did blossom during the early days of the war, however—the *shabnamah* (night letters), which were antigovernment leaflets distributed clandestinely at night. These appeared in urban areas calling for uprising against the Afghan communists and their Soviet comrades and were instrumental in provoking, for example, the bloody February 1980 riots in Kabul.[136] Interestingly, shabnamahs have reappeared recently, at least in Herat, this time in opposition to the Taliban.[137]

Even Afghanistan's cultural heritage failed to survive the long war intact. In January 1993 the Kabul Museum was damaged in fighting, and over the next two years more than 90 percent of its priceless collection was looted by mujahideen from various factions and dispersed among illegal art and artifact buyers throughout the world. Ahmed Rashid noted that "archaeologists and historians say the losses from the museum amount to the destruction of a major part of Afghanistan's cultural heritage."[138] These losses included the Bagram collection, "one of the greatest archaeological finds of the 20th century."[139] Many of Afghanistan's important architectural sites, especially in and around Kabul, have been reduced to rubble in fighting, including the mausoleum of Nadir Shah, Babur's garden, Darulaman Palace, and the Victory Arch in Paghman.[140] Even sites not actively threatened by fighting, such as Herat's fifteenth-century Timurid minarets, totter and sway in the winds, with no funds available for restoration. The great cliff Buddhas of Bamiyan, relics from the pre-Islamic Gandharan era, were threatened in the summer of 1997 by advancing Taliban troops with plans to destroy them because they were not Islamic. A successful counteroffensive by opposition forces in the fall of 1997 drove the Taliban back and saved the Buddhas. Nevertheless, they suffered some damage due to nearby fighting and the use of the cliff cave complex by refugees, and when Bamiyan fell to the Taliban in September 1998 the smaller Buddha was partially damaged by errant gunfire. More recent reports maintain that both cliff Buddhas have had their heads blown off and that the carvings and murals at the site have been either destroyed, defaced, or removed.[141]

Even Afghanistan's crafts and traditions have begun to disappear. The blue glass makers of Herat are now down to one surviving elderly master craftsman.[142] Afghanistan's carpet weavers have modified traditional motifs to include war-related images such as the ubiquitous Kalashnikov rifle. The passing of the great polo ponies and master horsemen during two decades of war has reduced even Afghanistan's national sport of *buzkashi* (a game in which teams of horsemen struggle to convey the headless carcass of a calf to a predetermined spot on a large field) to a vestige of its vigorous past.[143]

Afghanistan is a country that has been severely damaged by its protracted war. That damage has been most apparent in its physical and property manifestations, but it extends into every corner of national life and has had a profound effect on Afghan society and culture. As described in this chapter, three major kinds of change have occurred to Afghanistan's political and economic institutions. First, the destruction of traditional society and its leaders enabled the emergence of young new elites, especially the mujahideen and Taliban, who have legitimated their leadership claims in terms of Islamic discourse and symbols and have brought about the Islamization of Afghan society. Second, these elites have grown powerful because of their access to and control of the massive amounts of high-technology weaponry provided to both sides of the conflict during the 1980s, which has led to a cult of violence known as the Kalashnikovization of society. Third, given the collapse of the traditional agricultural economy, the new elites have turned to narcotics production and trafficking for revenue, producing a drug culture that did not exist twenty years earlier and giving neighboring Pakistan at least four million heroin users. As these major social-cultural changes have taken place, various elements of popular culture have come under pressure as well. Music, television, and film are still banned in Taliban areas, as is photography, while sports are somewhat curtailed. Afghanistan's national treasures have been looted from the Kabul Museum and dispersed around the world, and the survival of its remaining architectural and artistic wonders is threatened by the continuing power struggle. Finally, the collapse of its educational system and the destruction of its intellectual class have left Afghanistan with an overwhelmingly illiterate population and few remaining masters. The transformation of Afghanistan after more than twenty years of modern war has left the country a cultural wasteland, and there is little expectation of the situation's improving soon. Discourse in Afghanistan today is extremely limited and actively curtailed, the legacy of warfare and decline. As Herat's great Timurid minarets crumble, so, too, does Afghanistan decay.

Yet there are some who do not see the destruction and decay as all bad. The Taliban recognize the need to rebuild much of Afghanistan's physical infrastructure, but they do not wish to follow a Western or secular model in doing so. Their Islamization of Afghanistan caps more than thirty years of movement in that direction by all the major players opposed to the communist government there. Afghanistan's deepening religiosity has at least two major ramifications, neither of which has played out fully yet.

First, the rise of the Taliban has sharpened ethnic, linguistic, religious, and qawm divisions in Afghanistan. Although those divisions were already apparent in stage six of the war as various mujahideen and militia factions battled for control of Kabul, the Taliban's manifestly Pushtun identity, ideological zeal, and ties to the Pakistani ISI and "religious right" have recast the fighting as a power struggle between ethnic and religious groups. The country may not yet be on the verge of ethnic disintegration, as Bernt Glatzer hopes, but "ethnic arguments are increasingly deployed in political agitation and there is a visible tendency toward ethnicisation of the conflict."[144] Indeed, recent events especially have moved Afghanistan to the edge of ethnic cleansing, beginning with the May 1997 massacre of Taliban forces in Mazar-i-Sharif, the atrocities committed by both sides during the fall 1997 campaign, the Taliban's blockade of food and relief supplies from the central Hazara region during the winter months of early 1998, their massacres of Hazara and Uzbek civilians in Mazar-i-Sharif in August 1998 and Bamiyan in September 1998, and their scorched earth tactics in the minority communities north of Kabul in July–September 1999. Where the intensification of Afghanistan's internal divisions might lead is considered in greater depth in chapter 6.

The other ramification of Afghanistan's Islamization is faced by its neighbors, all of which (except Iran) have secular governments but substantial populations of Muslims and important movements afoot to Islamize those countries as well. Not only is Afghanistan an important crossroads for regional trade, but its location also makes it a possible conduit of communication from the Taliban to groups with similar aspirations in neighboring countries. Thus, for a variety of reasons, including concerns about a regional Islamic revolution brought on by a snowball effect, shared cross-national ethnic identity, and geoeconomic and strategic maneuvering, Afghanistan's immediate neighbors and several other countries have all become actively involved in promoting their own interests in Afghanistan. Afghanistan's multifaceted role in regional affairs is the subject of the next chapter.

5 / Afghanistan and the Changing Regional Environment

Afghanistan on the eve of the twenty-first century has acquired a renewed importance on the regional and world stage. A linchpin country, it connects Central Asia with South and West Asia. In the new geopolitics of the 1990s, Afghanistan is once again the "crossroads of Asia." Despite its devastated infrastructure and economy and its limited natural resources (other than its opium crop, which it will be increasingly pressured to curtail), Afghanistan's geographical location and cross-border ethnic ties position it to play a critical role in trade between South Asia, Southwest Asia, and Central Asia. This is a novel situation for Afghanistan in the modern era, when it has more often served as a buffer state between empires or, as it has most recently, fought to avoid absorption into an encroaching superpower.

In this chapter I examine the regional environment in which Afghanistan now exists from three perspectives. First, I explore how the end of the Cold War, spurred to its conclusion at least in part by the debacle suffered by the Soviet military in Afghanistan in the 1980s, opened Central Asia to the outside world again and altered Afghanistan's geostrategic significance. Second, I consider how outside actors influenced Afghanistan during the war years of the 1980s and continued to do so during the 1990s. Finally, I examine Afghanistan's position in Asia in relation to its immediate and near neighbors of the twenty-first century.

The most significant post–Cold War change in Afghanistan's neighborhood has occurred in Central Asia. As the Soviet Union disintegrated as a political entity in 1991–1992, it was replaced at first by a loose confederation known as the Commonwealth of Independent States (CIS), which included eleven of the fifteen original Soviet republics (Estonia, Latvia, Lithuania, and Georgia did not join). The CIS never developed as a political entity, however, and almost as soon as it was formed its constituent republics began acting like independent countries. Three of the newly independent Central Asian republics—Tajikistan, Turkmenistan, and Uzbekistan—border Afghanistan directly (map 5.1). The very existence of the five new Central Asian states (Kazakhstan and

MAP 5.1 Central Asia in 1997. Source: ReliefWeb.

Kyrgyzstan are the other two) transformed the region in which Afghanistan exists.

The ways in which the Central Asian states have affected regional affairs have been multiple, but five deserve close attention. First, with the decline of communism in the former Soviet Union, previously forbidden religious practices are on the rise again, especially in Muslim Central Asia. The resurgence of Islam in the region threatens not only the internal stability of the new republics but also the stability of Russia. The former communist rulers of both the Central Asian states and Russia fear the consequences of the rapid spread of fundamentalist Islam in their countries and have taken a mixture of steps to prevent it, including the public and personal embrace of Islam by high-ranking leaders, rejection of a role for religiously based political parties, and outright repression. Despite these measures, Islam is growing more rapidly in the Central Asian republics than anywhere else in the world, and missionary activities there provide neighboring Islamic states (Iran and Afghanistan and, farther afield, Saudi Arabia, Pakistan, and Turkey) with ample opportunities for influence over Central Asian society.

There are other reasons for these countries to be interested in intercourse with the Central Asian states in the post-Soviet era, as will be detailed shortly, but the second major reason why these countries interact is that they share not only a common religious heritage but in many cases common ethnicity as well. Ethnic groups spill over political boundaries in Central Asia, despite the Soviet effort in the 1920s to create republics based on ethnicity. As of the 1989 Soviet census, for example, Uzbekistan's population included 71 percent Uzbeks, 4.7 percent Tajiks, and 4.0 percent Kazakhs; Turkmenistan was 72 percent Turkmen but also had 9 percent Kazakhs; and Tajikistan had 62.3 percent Tajiks but nearly 24 percent Uzbeks.[1] Indeed, Soviet decisions to internally colonize Central Asia and impose a cotton mono-agriculture in the region led to substantial Russian immigration there. According to the 1989 census, Russians made up 7.4 percent of Tajikistan's population, 9 percent of Turkmenistan's, and 8.3 percent of Uzbekistan's.[2] These Russian minorities are found especially in the capital cities of each republic. The 1989 census found Russians to compose 59.1 percent of the population of Alma-Ata (Kazakhstan's former capital) and 55.8 percent of Bishkek (Kyrgyzstan's capital), the highest proportions of any republic capitals outside of Moscow. Tashkent (the capital of Uzbekistan) had 34.0 percent Russians, Dushanbe (the capital of Tajikistan) had 32.8 percent, and Ashkhabad (the capital of Turkmenistan) had 32.4

percent, all substantially higher figures than the overall population of ethnic Russians in those republics.[3]

This last Soviet-era census came on the eve of dramatic demographic upheavals in the region, primarily the flight of large segments of the Russian populations of these countries following the collapse of the Soviet Union. Fears of ethnic conflict, especially in Tajikistan, have also sparked significant Russian emigration from the region since then. Thus, a decade later the ethnic distribution of these national populations has changed, as table 5.1 shows.[4]

In addition to ethnicity and religion, language and culture make it possible for other countries to have ties with the Central Asian region. Kyrgyz, Turkmen, and Uzbek are all Turkic languages, and all three countries have historical ties to Turkey (which that country is attempting to exploit once again). The Tajik language is a variation on Farsi, and Tajikistan has cultural ties to Iran. Kazakhstan is the least homogeneous of all the former Soviet republics and has cultural, historical, and linguistic ties with Turkey to the west, Mongolia to the east, and Russia to the north. Thus, the ending of more than seventy years of Soviet colonial hegemony in Central Asia opened the five new states there to a range of interactions with neighboring and nearby countries on the grounds of shared ethnicity, language, and religion.

TABLE 5.1. Ethnic Distribution of Population of Central Asian Republics

Country	Population (1998 estimate)	Major Ethnic Groups as Percentage of Population
Kazakhstan	16,846,808	Kazakh, 46%; Russian, 35%; German, 5%; Ukrainian, 5%; Uzbek, 2%; Tatar, 2%; other, 5%
Kyrgyzstan	4,522,281	Kyrgyz, 52%; Russian, 22%; Uzbek, 13%; other, 13%
Tajikistan	6,020,095	Tajik, 65%; Uzbek, 25%; Russian, 2%; other, 8%
Turkmenistan	4,297,629	Turkmen, 77%; Uzbek, 9%; Russian, 7%; other, 7%
Uzbekistan	23,784,321	Uzbek, 80%; Russian, 6%; Tajik, 5%; Kazakh, 3%; other, 6%

SOURCES: Mehrdad Haghayeghi, *Islam and Politics in Central Asia*, 1995; *World Almanac*, 1998, 1999.

The third and fourth means by which the opening of Central Asia has affected the region are both economic and are interrelated. They are the discovery of substantial reserves of oil and natural gas in the region, especially in Turkmenistan and Kazakhstan, and the trading opportunities that the expanding markets of these countries have brought to neighboring states. Kazakhstan, the richest and most developed of the former Soviet Central Asian republics, has a significant and diversified industrial base, produces more than 20 percent of the coal throughout the former USSR, and has one of the five largest oil fields in the world (Tengiz).[5] Uzbekistan is currently the leading cotton producer in the former Soviet Union, producing 1.45 million tons in 1992. Its levels of production were made possible only by significant over-irrigation that lowered the level of the Aral Sea to the point that widespread environmental damage has now occurred throughout the region.[6] Climate changes will have cut Uzbekistan's cotton production by more than 50 percent by the end of the year 2000, putting the foundation of its economic future in doubt.[7] Tajikistan and Kyrgyzstan are poorer, producing primarily agricultural goods and remaining economically tied to Russia. Kyrgystan, however, does have significant hydroelectric potential, while Tajikistan shares uranium deposits with Turkmenistan and Uzbekistan.[8]

Turkmenistan, which shares borders with Iran, Afghanistan, Kazakhstan, and Uzbekistan, perhaps best illustrates how economic forces are tying Central Asia to other regions. Although its economy under the USSR, like Uzbekistan's, was based heavily on cotton production, its future is defined more by its substantial oil and natural gas wealth and its position at the center of regional trading networks. As the CIS dawned on the world in 1992, Turkmenistan's economy had the highest reliance on trade of all the former Soviet republics, at more than 75 percent of its total economic output.[9] As its cotton production declines, Turkmenistan's development of its oil and natural gas reserves will become more important, as will its position as a convenient point of access to Kazakhstan's mineral wealth for countries outside the region.

It is in this context that tiny Turkmenistan (population 4 million) has already been so influential on regional geopolitics. With a "phenomenal 8.1 trillion cubic metres of natural gas reserves,"[10] Turkmenistan looks to a future linked to its ability to export that gas (and also its 700 million tons of proven oil reserves). Its existing pipelines run north into Russia and are maintained by Gazprom, the giant Russian gas company. At first Turkmenistan exported its gas at well below international market prices. By the end of 1992 it had raised its prices to international market levels, but resistance by other former Soviet republics to paying those prices resulted in the suspension of gas shipments for a period in the mid-1990s and the decline of gas production in Turkmenistan, which has thus looked to find other outlets for its gas. Various possibilities have been explored, including a project with Iran and Turkey to construct a pipeline to Western Europe that would cost $1.6 billion, run for 2,000 miles, and have an annual capacity of 30 billion cubic meters.[11]

Pakistan is also extremely interested in Turkmenistan's gas reserves, and this may well be a decisive factor in shaping Pakistan's policy toward Afghanistan. In October 1997, six major energy companies signed a deal in Ashkhabad to create CENTGAS, a consortium for the construction of a pipeline from Turkmenistan and across western Afghanistan to Pakistan. The American oil giant Union Oil of California (Unocal) led the consortium with 54.11 percent of the shares, followed by Saudi Arabia's Delta oil company (15 percent), Japan's Itochu Corporation and Inpex (7.22 percent each), the Turkmenistan government (7 percent), South Korea's Hyundai (5.54 percent), and Pakistan's Crescent Group (3.89 percent).[12] The pipeline is expected to cost $1.9 billion and have an annual capacity of 20 billion cubic meters. It is planned to run for 915 miles, from Turkmenistan's Dauletabad gas field to Multan, a city in central Pakistan. In March 1998, however, CENTGAS officials suggested that the project might fall through because international lenders were reluctant to make substantial investments in a project that ran through unstable Afghanistan. In August 1998, Unocal pulled out of CENTGAS in the wake of increasing US government dissatisfaction with the hard-line Taliban militia, which controls the territory in Afghanistan through which the pipeline will pass. Reports in early February 1999 that Unocal rival Bridas would purchase Unocal's CENTGAS shares, combined with reports of progress in Turkmenistan-sponsored peace talks between the warring Afghan factions, prompted Unocal to rejoin CENTGAS. The imposition of UN sanctions on Afghanistan in November 1999 and December 2000, as well as the continuing war there, have delayed this project indefinitely.

All of the factors just described have combined to provide various regional actors with an opportunity to engage in regional power projection, relatively unhindered by the superpower competition of the Cold War era that had limited such chances before. Nowhere else did the fall of the Soviet Union present such opportunities for power projection to neighboring countries that had long been stymied in this and other directions. Pakistan, blocked by South Asian behemoth and bitter regional rival India to the south, has never had an opportunity for trade and strategic depth like that which the opening of Central Asia presents. Similarly, Iran has been blocked in its efforts to project power into the Persian Gulf and Middle East because of its ethnic (Persian vs. Arab) and sectarian (Shia vs. Sunni) differences with its neighbors to the west and its staunch opposition to the United States since 1979. Turkey, too, has ethnic differences with its Middle Eastern neighbors, but more importantly, it finds its integration into and influence in Europe thwarted by its rivalry with Greece and the widespread Western European perception that Turkey is not a European country. Thus, all three regional middle powers see Central Asia as an area ripe with possibilities for their power expansion. Their competition may well be the defining characteristic of the region in the next decade.

Other actors have interests in this region as well, usually under the principle that "the enemy of my enemy is my friend." Most notably, Russia (and to a lesser extent the Ukraine) remains deeply interested in maintaining strong ties with its former satellite republics in Turkestan. Saudi Arabia has also gotten involved in the post–Cold War scramble for influence in Central Asia, primarily in support of Pakistan as a counterweight to its regional rival, Iran. Likewise, India has interests in spoiling Pakistani efforts at power projection into Central Asia, as does the United States with regard to Iran and, more recently, Pakistan. Finally, China has cross-border ethnic and religious ties with Kyrgyzstan and Kazakhstan, as well as a long-standing relationship with Pakistan.

In short, the recent independence of the five Central Asian republics has transformed the regional political and economic framework in at least five important ways. The renaissance of Islamic identity in these countries, in combination with regionwide ethnic, linguistic, and cultural heterogeneity, has provided established regional actors with motivation and opportunity to become engaged with the Central Asian states. The presence of significant oil and other mineral wealth in the new states, as well as opportunities for trade, investment, and market development, provides additional powerful incentives to draw regional actors toward Central Asia. Finally, the opportunity for power projection, strategic depth, and pan-ethnic projects—or the denial of some or all of these to rival countries—has led to a resurrection of the Great Game in the region. Not only states have been attracted to the region, however, but subnational and transnational actors, too. In the next section I consider all of these actors and examine the types of outside influences they have brought to the region.

Numerous outside actors have been involved in Afghanistan during the last two decades of the twentieth century, in three major ways. First, the Afghan War has provided superpowers, regional powers, and small neighboring countries alike the opportunity to engage in geostrategic maneuvering in the region. Many countries have provided support to one or more factions during the long Afghan conflict. Second, the war has turned Afghanistan into a humanitarian disaster zone, prompting many additional actors to provide relief assistance to the millions of Afghans affected by the violence. Third, as possibilities for intraregional trade and cooperation have emerged along with the Central Asian countries, new actors have appeared on the Afghan stage, motivated by a possibility of economic opportunity there that was previously nonexistent. I consider each of these means of interaction in turn.

The Afghan War began as a peasant rebellion; it could not have grown larger and continued without substantial support to both sides from outside actors. As a conflict that, at least in the 1980s, so clearly pitted opposing ideologies and allies, it attracted a great deal of attention from outside forces, of which there have been many: nation-states, international organizations, and nongovernmental organizations (NGOs).

The involvement and influence of actors has changed over time. Influential actors of the late 1970s are not necessarily important in Afghanistan today (indeed, the most important actor of that time, the Soviet Union, no longer exists). Likewise, some actors of importance in the late 1990s were unimportant two decades earlier (or did not even exist then, such as Uzbekistan, Tajikistan, and Turkmenistan). In general, the transition from one set of influential actors to another in Afghanistan occurred during the period beginning with the Soviet withdrawal in February 1989 and ending with the collapse of the Najibullah government in April 1992. Prior to the transition, seven national and international actors were of particular importance in relation to the Afghan War: the Soviet Union, the United States, Pakistan, Iran, China, Saudi Arabia, and the United Nations. After the transition, the roles of some of these actors changed dramatically, while new actors appeared. During the more recent period, six actors have been especially important: Pakistan, Iran, Saudi Arabia, Russia, the United States, and the United Nations.

The most important of all the outside actors was the Soviet Union, which propped up the Afghan communist government directly and indirectly from 1978 to 1992 and averaged 150,000 troops in Afghanistan from 1980 to 1989. More recently, the Soviet successor state Russia has aided various factions in the post-1992 civil war that has consumed Afghanistan. Pakistan, too, has had a critical influence on the conflict by providing sanctuary for over four million Afghan refugees and support for the mujahideen in the 1980s and early 1990s, and more recently by aiding the Taliban. The United States, through the covert assistance program of the Central Intelligence Agency (CIA), humanitarian aid, and bilateral aid to Pakistan in the 1980s, made it possible for Pakistan to stand firm against the Soviet threat. Iran absorbed 2.35 million Afghans during the 1980s but used them in the Iranian economy and the Iran-Iraq War rather than assisting them in their efforts to fight the Kabul regime. More recently, however, Iran has actively backed the northern Afghan minority groups in their struggle against the Taliban. China provided weapons and training to the mujahideen and diplomatic support for Pakistan during the Soviet phase of the Afghan War. Saudi Arabia provided money for the mujahideen and, more recently, for the Taliban, often at critical times.

Many other states provided some assistance to either the Afghan refugees, the mujahideen (or now Taliban), or the Pakistani government in connection with the Afghan crisis during the 1980s; these included the United Kingdom, France, West Germany, Belgium, Sweden, the Netherlands, Denmark, Norway, Italy, Kuwait, the Sudan, Canada, Australia, South Korea, and Japan. In particular, Egypt provided weapons and training for the mujahideen early in the Afghan War. Some states, primarily Soviet allies, assisted the communist government in Kabul; these included Vietnam, Bulgaria, Cuba, East Germany, Czechoslovakia, North Korea, India, and Ethiopia. Since the fall of the Soviet Union, former Soviet republics including Turkmenistan, Tajikistan, Uzbekistan, and Ukraine have also become embroiled in the Afghan conflict, primarily through military assistance or arms sales to various factions.

Finally, the United Nations has played a key role throughout the conflict, in various ways. The UN High Commissioner for Refugees (UNHCR), the World Food Program (WFP), and other UN organizations have led an international effort in relief for refugees and internally displaced persons, reconstruction and resettlement, and humanitarian assistance. Diego Cordovez, the special representative of the secretary-general during the mid-1980s, brokered the diplomatic negotiations that led to the Geneva accords of April 1988, which ended the period of active Soviet combat in Afghanistan. Subsequent peacemaking efforts have been less successful in settling the civil war, including the special mission to Afghanistan established by the UN General Assembly in December 1993 and headed by Mahmoud Mestiri (1993–1996) and Norbert Holl (1996–1997). In 1997 the secretary-general appointed Lakhdar Brahimi special envoy on Afghanistan, but Brahimi resigned in October 1999 in dismay at his inability to convince the Taliban and the Northern Alliance to stop fighting.[13] Veteran UN diplomat Francesc Vendrell was appointed Brahimi's successor in January 2000. Various other UN organizations, such as the UN Coordinator for Humanitarian and Economic Assistance Programs Relating to Afghanistan (UNCHEAP), UN Logistical and Transport Operations (UNILOG), the UN Good Offices Mission to Afghanistan and Pakistan (UNGOMAP), the UN Special Mission to Afghanistan (UNSMA), and the UN Office for the Coordination of Humanitarian Assistance to Afghanistan (UNOCHA), have focused on assessment of the ongoing battle in Afghanistan and postwar refugee resettlement and rebuilding there.

Many other international and nongovernmental organizations have also been involved with the Afghan refugees and mujahideen in various ways. Most of these organizations, such as the International Committee of the Red Cross, the League of Red Cross and Red Crescent Societies, and several hundred other NGOs, have been involved in assisting Afghan refugees in Pakistan and Iran, aiding internally displaced persons within Afghanistan, or providing resettlement and reconstruction support for repatriating refugees.

Looking more closely at the military and economic assistance provided by the first of three important outside actors—the USSR, Pakistan, and the United States—we have already seen that during stages two through five of the Afghan War the USSR was heavily committed in Afghanistan militarily, economically, politically, and diplomatically. Prior to 1978 the USSR was Afghanistan's most important trade partner, accounting for approximately 30 percent of Afghanistan's imports and exports.[14] It also was Afghanistan's largest source of foreign aid, primarily in loans at favorable rates.[15] During the 1980s the USSR dominated the Afghan economy so thoroughly that observers referred to the process as the "Sovietization" of the Afghan economy. By 1984, Soviet-Afghan trade was worth $1.1 billion, which represented 70–80 percent of all Afghan trade.[16] It continued to increase throughout the Soviet period in Afghanistan, ultimately tripling preinvasion levels.[17] The Soviets took natural gas from the Shiberghan fields (for example, 2.4 billion cubic feet in 1986, 50 percent of Afghanistan's total export value) and supplied essential commodities (including wheat) along with arms, machinery, and transportation equipment.[18] This economic relationship was designed to augment and support the Soviet war effort. From 1986 to 1989, numerous Afghan provinces signed individual agreements with Soviet republics and lower administrative units.

The Soviet Union also increased its foreign aid to Afghanistan in the 1980s to a level unprecedented for Third World countries. By 1986, the USSR had already disbursed $1.77 billion and intended to increase its aid during Afghanistan's 1986–1991 Five-Year Plan to 75 percent of Afghanistan's total economic aid. This included a "$150-million project to connect Kabul and several adjacent provinces with the Soviet power grid by 1991."[19]

The Soviet Union was the Kabul government's closest friend during the 1980s and early 1990s. It bolstered Afghanistan militarily and economically, and it championed the Kabul regime's cause diplomatically. In return, it was allowed a free hand politically and administratively in Afghanistan. Without the extensive, multifaceted involvement of the USSR in Afghanistan after the 1978 invasion, what began as a localized rebellion would never have become so protracted. And without the Soviet invasion, the introduction of a large modern army, and the resulting destruction, it is unlikely that the refugee crisis, the narcotics subculture, Kalashnikovization, or other Afghan and regional problems would ever have developed, at least to the magnitude described in chapter 4.

Pakistan played an important role as an outside actor beyond its position as host to four million Afghan refugees. It was the front-line state against the Soviet expansion into Afghanistan. Under the rule of Zia ul-Haq (1977–1988) for virtually all of the Soviet phase of the war, Pakistan cooperated with other outside actors in joint opposition to the Soviets. The extent of Pakistani military support to the mujahideen was not open for public discussion during the 1980s (unlike its humanitarian assistance program), but subsequently the nature and level of Pakistan's military involvement during this period has become clear.[20] Its more recent support for the Taliban has likewise been shrouded in secrecy and is just now becoming understood.[21]

Pakistan allowed the major resistance parties to operate from Peshawar and Quetta, where their offices and headquarters were located, from the late 1970s onward. Pakistan was also the conduit for most of the foreign military assistance received by the mujahideen.[22] Mujahideen arms depots and training camps, staffed in part by foreign trainers, were set up in Pakistani territory, although the extent of this activity was a closely held secret during the 1980s.[23] Pakistan provided a safe haven for the families of the fighters, a sanctuary for rest and relaxation, a training and resupply base, and a staging area for major operations. There is also evidence for the active involvement of Pakistani military and paramilitary units in the war,[24] just as there have been Pakistanis fighting more recently with the Taliban.[25] Diplomatically, Pakistan steadfastly opposed the Soviet presence in Afghanistan and the communist government in Kabul. After the Soviet invasion of Afghanistan, Pakistan also responded by strengthening its 450,000-man army, especially by upgrading its equipment.[26]

Pakistan's Inter-Services Intelligence Directorate (ISI) and the American CIA had joint responsibility for the multinational program of covert assistance to the mujahideen during the 1980s. Most of the necessary funds originated in the United States and in Saudi Arabia and other Persian Gulf states.[27] Most of the small arms supplied were purchased from China and Egypt. Training took place not only in Pakistan but also in China and Egypt, as well as in Iran and other Muslim states.[28] During the 1980s some weapons passed into Afghanistan through Iran, but most came through Pakistan. The CIA had responsibility for the arms until they reached Karachi, where the ISI took over.[29]

Weapons were transported from Karachi, Ormara, Pasni, and Gwadar to military bases near Islamabad and on to Peshawar, and by different routes from the ports directly to Quetta. In these centers the weapons were sorted and earmarked for distribution to the different mujahideen parties. They were then moved to mujahideen party arms depots near the Afghan border.[30] This border, with more than two hundred passes and crossing points, has long been one of the most permeable in the world, and weapons flowed into Afghanistan from five to ten major depots located from Chitral to Baluchistan.[31]

Unfortunately, the Pakistani arms pipeline proved to be a leaky conduit. The weapons had to pass through several hands in the Pakistani army and then through the mujahideen parties and intermediate commanders before they reached the combat mujahideen—all in a region that has traditionally relied on minor graft and bribery (baksheesh) to grease business relationships. Allegations of weapons being stolen or diverted were universal, with everyone blaming everyone else.

Corruption of the pipeline occurred on all levels, and weapons destined for use against the Soviets ended up in the hands of Pakistani soldiers or drug traffickers, were sold in the arms bazaars of the North-West Frontier Province (NWFP) and Federally Administered Tribal Areas

(FATA), or were stockpiled for later use.[32] Estimates of how much aid actually leaked ranged from 20 to 85 percent, but mujahideen combat commanders were vocal in their frustration at the lack of assistance.[33] The leakage of the weapons promoted the "Kalashnikovization" of both Pakistani and Afghan society, and families in the NWFP and FATA were known to upgrade their personal arsenals to include mortars, heavy machine guns, and even rocket launchers. Pakistan's domestic politics, always volatile, became more violent as a result.

Another product of this massive arms pipeline—the largest covert aid program by the CIA under the Reagan Doctrine—was the improvement for most of the 1980s of the previously strained relationship between the United States and Pakistan. By providing a counterweight to the Soviet role in Afghanistan, the US also played a critical role in the continuation of the conflict. Thus, the US and the USSR engaged in a superpower rivalry in Afghanistan of very high intensity.

Although US commitment to humanitarian assistance for the Afghan refugees was solid from the beginning, US policy over military aid to the mujahideen took longer to develop. For a combination of reasons, some of which are still unclear, the CIA was slow to involve the US in providing meaningful levels of support to the Afghan rebels. Partly, this delay was due to a belief that the mujahideen could not win, and also to fears by the Pakistani leadership that too much aid would expose their country to Soviet retaliation. Thus, for the first five years the program was extremely modest. President Jimmy Carter authorized $30 million in assistance within two weeks of the Soviet invasion,[34] although evidence suggests the CIA was already involved in resistance training prior to the invasion.[35] Despite President Ronald Reagan's interest in the aid program and his decision in the fall of 1982 to increase it qualitatively and quantitatively, through 1984 aid continued to consist primarily of small arms, including Soviet-made or copied assault rifles, machine guns, 82-mm mortars, and SAM-7 missiles, which allowed the US to deny supplying the guerrillas by maintaining that the weapons were captured.[36]

Covert aid gradually increased during the conflict. By the signing of the Geneva Accords in April 1988, the US government had spent over $2.0 billion, and greater than $1.0 billion more had come from Saudi Arabia.[37] Table 5.2 details the increases through the Soviet withdrawal in 1989.[38] Thereafter, American aid dropped almost immediately to $50 million per year through 1992, when it ceased altogether.

Quality improved over time, too. A limited number of Swiss Oerlikon 20-mm antiaircraft guns were bought and supplied to the mujahideen by the end of 1984, although twenty-nine of forty never made it all the way through the pipeline.[39] In 1985, Chinese-made 107-mm multibarreled rocket launchers were supplied. Finally, in September–October 1986, US Stinger missiles, along with US Redeye and British Blowpipe missiles, provided the mujahideen with their first effective antiaircraft weapons and changed the face of the war.[40] Subsequently, small quantities of Spanish 120-mm mortars and mine-clearing equipment were also supplied. This assistance was critical to the resistance, especially in 1986, when Soviet air power was winning the war.

The US also provided Pakistan with a massive infusion of aid after the Soviet invasion, although Carter's initial offer of $400 million ($200 million each for military and economic aid for 1980 and 1981) was derisively rejected by Zia as "peanuts." As Thomas Hammond noted: "It simply was not worth it to Zia to line up with the United States against the Soviet Union unless Washington gave evidence that it would be a generous and dependable ally."[41] Reagan gave such evidence, agreeing in September 1981 to a $3.2 billion aid package (50 percent military and 50 percent economic) over six years beginning in October

TABLE 5.2. US Covert Military Aid to Afghan Rebels during the 1980s

Year	Amount of aid
1980	$30 million
1981	$35 million
1982	$35–50 million
1983	$80 million
1984	$122 million
1985	$280 million
1986	$470–550 million
1987	$600 million
1988	$400 million
1989	$400–550 million

SOURCES: Robert Pear, "Arming Afghan Guerrillas: A Huge Effort Led by US," *New York Times*, 18 April 1988; David B. Ottaway, "US Widens Arms Shipments to Bolster Afghan Guerrillas," *Washington Post*, 21 September 1987; Ottaway, "Soviets, Afghan Rebels Pressure US on Arms," *Washington Post*, 2 October 1988; Carl Bernstein, "Arms for Afghanistan," *New Republic*, 18 July 1981, 8–10; Henry S. Bradsher, *Afghanistan and the Soviet Union*, 1985, 277–278; interview with Theodore Mataxis, field director, Committee for a Free Afghanistan, December 1989.

1982. Also, Pakistan was allowed to purchase forty F-16s for $1.1 billion.[42] Aid continued after this deal ended until 1990, when the 1985 Pressler Amendment, which required the US government to cease military and economic aid to Pakistan if it was "found" by the US president to "possess a nuclear explosive device," was finally invoked.[43] In 1994 President Bill Clinton temporarily waived the Pressler law in return for a Pakistani freeze on its nuclear program. The May and June 1998 Indian and Pakistani underground nuclear tests—the first public display of Pakistan's long-suspected nuclear capability—has further eroded US-Pakistani relations.

The three major outside actors during the 1980s (Pakistan supported by the US against the USSR) fought each other indirectly over Afghanistan, which provided the arena for their struggle. The Soviet Union used a full military occupation of Afghanistan, in conjunction with its political dominance over and overwhelmingly close economic relationship with the Kabul government, to project its influence south toward the warm waters of the Arabian Sea and Persian Gulf. In the process, the USSR became embroiled in a major war in Afghanistan that destroyed the country. Pakistan offered not only generous humanitarian assistance to the Afghan refugees but also military aid and training to the mujahideen—allowing its territory to be used as an arms pipeline—and diplomatic support for the resistance, in order to oppose the Soviet expansionist threat. Finally, the US provided more than $600 million in humanitarian aid to the refugees, more than $3 billion in covert aid to the mujahideen, more than $5 billion in bilateral aid to Pakistan, and diplomatic opposition to the Soviet presence in Afghanistan. The multinational aid effort led by the US and Pakistan gave the Afghan resistance the support it needed to continue to fight, thus creating a refugee-based insurgency along the Pakistan-Afghanistan border that protracted the Afghan War and ultimately led to the Soviet defeat there. For the US, the Afghan War was the cheapest and most significant of its Cold War victories.

With the Soviet withdrawal in 1989, the United States lost interest in Afghanistan, and American aid rapidly dried up. Likewise, with the dissolution of the Soviet Union by the beginning of 1992, another key actor disappeared from the Afghan stage. Pakistan remained extremely involved in Afghanistan, but other regional actors began to grow more involved as well. Iran increased its support of the Shia mujahideen parties, ultimately bringing them together in 1989 under a common banner as Hezb-i-Wahdat. Saudi Arabia supported Abdur Rasoul Sayyaf's

Ittehad-i-Islami in direct and bitter opposition to Hezb-i-Wahdat. Otherwise, the pattern of who supported whom became more complex as alliances within Afghanistan shifted during the 1990s. Generally, Uzbekistan supported Dostam's Uzbek militia, Tajikistan supported the Tajik-led Rabbani government and Jamiat-i-Islami, and Pakistan supported the various Pushtun-led parties, such as Hekmatyar's Hezb-i-Islami, until switching to the Taliban in 1994. By early 2000, the Taliban were supported militarily and financially by Pakistan, Saudi Arabia, the United Arab Emirates, and Ukraine. The northern minority groups were supported by Russia, Iran, India, Uzbekistan, and Tajikistan.

The second major way in which outside actors have influenced Afghanistan has been through the response of numerous states and several hundred nongovernmental organizations (NGOs) to the humanitarian crisis caused by the protracted Afghan War. This crisis was most consistently apparent in the Afghan refugee diaspora.

Afghanistan has produced the largest population of refugees and displaced persons in the world every year since 1981, despite the fact that their exact number was never precisely known. At the height of the refugee crisis, in 1990, Pakistan had 3.3 million registered Afghan refugees, but there were so many unregistered refugees that this number was probably 10 to 20 percent too low.[44] Thus, for most of the past two decades Pakistan had 3.3–4.0 million refugees, the largest refugee burden of any country in the world. These refugees were located in 344 refugee villages—70 percent in the NWFP and FATA, 25 percent in Baluchistan, and 5 percent in the Punjab.[45]

In 1990 there were also 2.94 million Afghan refugees in Iran, the second largest refugee population in the world. By 1998 there were still more than 1.5 million Afghan refugees in Iran—the world's largest refugee population for that year.[46] Only 3 percent of this population lived in camps—the majority were relatively self-sufficient unskilled laborers scattered throughout the country. For most of the Afghan conflict, however, Iran avoided international scrutiny of its relief efforts. The UNHCR was kept out completely until 1983 and since then has had only a minor role in Iran.[47]

There have also been more than 2 million internally displaced persons (IDPs) inside Afghanistan since the war began.[48] These people are not accorded refugee status because they did not cross an international border, but they suffer from the same problems of dislocation, culture shock, and uncertainty as do the "real" refugees. Afghanistan's IDP population was the third largest such group in the world in 1990.

At its peak, Afghanistan's combined international refugee population far exceeded any other group of refugees; indeed, in 1990 almost 42 percent of all refugees in the world were Afghan. Counting the internally displaced persons, 44 percent of Afghanistan's population was dislocated by 1990.[49] This massive and protracted refugee crisis provided an opportunity for the UN and many other actors to become involved in shaping Afghanistan through humanitarian assistance. Because this was done primarily through Pakistan, the following discussion of humanitarian assistance focuses on that country and the Afghan refugees there.

Today 1.2 million Afghan refugees still live in Pakistan, more than 2 million fewer than the nearly 3.3 million refugees who lived in 344 camps and villages in Pakistan at the beginning of the 1990s.[50] The vast majority of the refugees were located within 50 miles of the Afghan border in the North-West Frontier Province and Baluchistan. In 1987, approximately 2.2 million refugees lived in 250 camps in the NWFP's Settled Districts (Abbottabad, Bannu, Dera Ismail Khan, Kohat, Mansehra, Mardan, Peshawar I and II), Provincially Administered Tribal Districts (Chitral, Dir, and Swat), and Federally Administered Tribal Agencies (Bajaur, Malakand, Mohmand, Orakzai, Khyber, Kurram, North Waziristan, and South Waziristan), and there were an additional 400,000 unregistered refugees.[51] Baluchistan had 835,400 refugees in 73 camps in 7 districts, as well as 200,000 unregistered refugees.[52]

Afghan refugees in Pakistan came from every province and ethnic group in Afghanistan. The vast majority, however (estimated as high as 80 percent), were Pushtuns from southern and eastern Afghanistan, including people from all of the major tribes and subtribes. The predominantly Dari-speaking refugee population in Iran originated primarily in the three western provinces of Afghanistan.[53]

Most of these Pushtun refugees fled during the first two years after the Soviet invasion and remained refugees (and mujahideen) until 1992. Whereas refugee flows in 1980–1981 ran as high as 180,000 per month, they fell off to 15,000–20,000 per month in 1982–1985 and to 6,000–8,000 per month by 1987.[54] Repatriation began in earnest only after the fall of the Najibullah government in April 1992. In the six months immediately following that event, 1.2 million Afghans returned from Pakistan alone, while another 300,000 returned from Iran.[55]

Thus, Pakistan faced a massive refugee inflow in 1980 that did not ease until well into the 1990s. The response of Pakistan's government was to create an admirable framework for humanitarian assistance, in which numerous United Nations agencies and nongovernmental organizations also played vital roles. Refugees were encouraged to register with the Pakistani government and move into camps in order to simplify their receipt of relief goods as well as facilitate (and control) their involvement with Pakistani society. Refugees were not required to go to camps, however, nor were they prevented from moving freely throughout Pakistan and becoming involved in the local economy. Camp conditions were made tolerable (and therefore attractive) by the efforts of Pakistan's government, the UNHCR and WFP, numerous voluntary agencies, and bilateral assistance to Pakistan from the US and other states.

Conditions in the refugee camps were vastly different from living conditions in the refugees' home villages and towns in Afghanistan. Villages in Afghanistan often numbered no more than 100 families, whereas refugee camps in Pakistan averaged more than 1,000 families, with 7,000 to 10,000 people per camp.[56] The camps were frequently located in remote areas or spartan surroundings, and Afghans were unused to the sweltering heat of the Pakistani plains in the summer. Camp life produced vast cultural changes in the Afghan social framework.[57]

The Afghan population in the refugee camps comprised 24 percent men, 28 percent women, and 48 percent children.[58] Many of these children grew up with no knowledge of Afghanistan beyond the stories of their adult relatives, limited education or none at all, and no expectations for the future except more fighting. Thus, it is unsurprising that so many were drawn into the ranks of the factions struggling for power in Afghanistan after 1992, including the Taliban today. Fortunately, the vast international humanitarian effort limited sickness and hunger in the refugee population, but the widespread dislocation, coupled with the near genocidal policies of the USSR, had a severe impact on the Afghan population.

Afghan refugees received tents, some materials for the construction of mud dwellings, some clothing, cash maintenance allowances ($3.00 per month, infrequently paid), some cooking utensils, and kerosene oil to aid in their resettlement.[59] They also received a daily food basket containing 500 grams of wheat, 30 grams of edible oil, 20 grams of sugar, and 1.5 grams of tea, plus 25 liters of clean water per person. Other food items were supplied irregularly; indeed, shortfalls were common in the supply of all these items.[60] Nonetheless, refugee conditions in Pakistan, despite some serious problems, compared favorably with refugee conditions elsewhere during the 1980s and early 1990s.

The refugee problems in Pakistan were due primarily to the over-whelming size of the refugee population, its location along a volatile border, and its manipulation by various parties interested in its support. Although there was no widespread starvation or outbreak of disease, undernourishment and lack of inoculation did promote high susceptibility to illness. A comprehensive Pakistan-UNHCR program based on the "basic health unit" (BHU), designed to serve 15,000 refugees, provided medical services. By November 1985 there were 191 BHUs (133 Pakistan-UNHCR, 58 private voluntary agency) for 310 refugee camps. More than 20 hospitals and clinics, in addition to government hospitals, were available to the refugees by 1986. Nonetheless, there were still 12,117 refugees per physician and 8,014 per female health worker by 1986.[61]

Interviews that I conducted in refugee districts from northern Chitral to southern Baluchistan in 1986–1987 indicated similar refugee problems nationwide. Difficulty in supplying potable water was cited most frequently,[62] but people also mentioned overgrazing by the more than three million livestock brought by the refugees, deforestation for firewood, undercutting of local labor markets while prices were simultaneously driven up, and increased involvement in heroin smuggling and criminal activity—all of which combined to strain relations with the Pakistani host population.[63] Though the combined populations of the NWFP, Baluchistan, and the Federally Administered Tribal Agencies (FATA) outnumbered the refugees by a four-to-one ratio,[64] in certain areas such as Kurram Agency, refugees equaled or outnumbered the locals.[65] These demographics led to violence and internal unrest in these locales, often exacerbated by Soviet manipulation from Afghanistan during the 1980s.

Pakistan assumed an enormous burden in caring for the Afghan refugees, but its efforts were bolstered by substantial outside aid. In 1987 the overall daily expenditure for the upkeep of 3 million Afghan refugees was $1.13 million ($367 million per year).[66] Pakistan provided about 45 percent of this amount, the UNHCR provided 25 percent, the WFP about 25 percent, and voluntary agencies and direct bilateral assistance the rest.[67] Pakistan assisted the early refugees unilaterally; after the Soviet intervention, the UNHCR, WFP, and other organizations began to help Pakistan cope with the deluge of refugees that followed. A division of responsibility gradually developed whereby Pakistan emphasized village administration and transport of relief goods, the WFP operated in its traditional area of food provision, and the UNHCR coordinated international aid and supervised the implementation of relief efforts.

To best perform its comprehensive role, the UNHCR developed a multipurpose assistance plan and budget through which it attempted to supply a complete aid package. The general policy that guided UNHCR efforts emphasized refugee self-reliance, as is indicated by the reductions in funding over time for relief goods (tents and clothing) and increases in funding for income-generating activities, vocational and skills training, and education.

Also over time, the role of other intergovernmental organizations (IGOs) and NGOs in refugee relief and assistance grew. Among major IGOs, the International Labor Organization (ILO), World Health Organization (WHO), UN Development Program (UNDP), UN Children's Fund (UNICEF), and World Bank all engaged in assistance in their respective areas of specialization. NGO assistance also grew in size and importance. As Dupree and Dupree noted: "In 1987, the Pakistani government's official list of voluntary agencies included 85 organizations maintaining offices and/or programs in Pakistan."[68] These NGOs have come from many countries throughout Western Europe, North America, the Middle East, and Asia.

Although a surface examination of the relief effort emphasizes its multilateral characteristics, the United States provided a substantial portion of the funding, for it saw the Afghan crisis of the early 1980s as a golden opportunity to sting the Soviet Union at little cost to itself. Thus, the US provided the largest share of humanitarian assistance to maintain the refugees, who were critical to the refugee-based insurgency strategy.[69] For example, by 1982 the US was providing 30 percent of the UNHCR budget, 40 percent of the WFP budget, and 33 percent of the NGO budgets.[70] Frequent shortfalls were met by emergency pledges of food aid from the US. From 1980 through 1987, US contributions to Afghan relief totaled $534.8 million.[71] Beginning in 1985 the US began to provide limited humanitarian aid directly to Afghanistan through the resistance parties. Administered by the US Agency for International Development (USAID) and the US Information Agency (USIA), programs to provide aid in transportation, medicine, education, food, and agriculture were begun, as well as a media training program in 1987.[72] Overall during the 1980s, when military and economic assistance are included, Pakistan became the third largest recipient of US assistance (after Israel and Egypt), receiving more than $7.2 billion during the decade.[73] The close relationship that resulted between Pakistan and the US was opportunistic and somewhat artificial on both sides, as the suspension of that relationship in 1990 under the Pressler Amendment would demonstrate.[74]

Because the Afghan refugees provided the basis of the Afghan resistance movement, the international humanitarian assistance program to the refugees had the additional consequence of making the continued war possible during the 1980s. Refugees throughout Pakistan believed themselves to be involved in a joint undertaking to defeat the Kabul government. Participation in the economic life of Pakistan and residence in refugee villages were widely understood to be temporary measures for most Afghan refugees. Most were eager to return home, and many did so beginning in April 1992. But the Afghanistan they returned to had been altered, just as they themselves had been changed by their long national nightmare. The changing regional environment and situation in Afghanistan since 1992 has prompted new actors, often driven by new motivations, to appear in Afghanistan.

The new actors in Afghanistan today include subnational organizations, transnational corporations, and those formerly constituent parts of the Soviet Union that are now independent republics. Faced with the variety of challenges discussed earlier, some of which come out of Afghanistan, the newly emergent countries of Central Asia have been drawn into Afghan affairs. Their primary mode of involvement has been through providing support for factions involved in the Afghan fighting, although both Tajikistan government troops and Russian forces in Tajikistan have fought into northeastern Afghanistan, where opposition elements in the Tajikistan civil war periodically took refuge during the early and mid-1990s. Following the fall of northern Afghanistan to the Taliban in 1998, Islamist opposition fighters from Uzbekistan reportedly took refuge there, as did opposition elements from Kyrgyzstan in late 1999.

Subnational organizations have also become increasingly involved in Afghanistan in the last few years. Throughout the 1980s, the ISI and CIA played roles in Afghanistan, presumably carrying out the policy of the government with which each is affiliated. Since the Soviet withdrawal from Afghanistan, the ISI in particular has become more independent in its actions, to the point that, since mid-1997, it is no longer clear that its actions reflect Pakistani government policy (at least as that policy is articulated by the Pakistani Foreign Ministry). Some veteran analysts, however, believe that apparent differences between the ISI and the Foreign Ministry (for example, the August 1999 Foreign Ministry effort to negotiate between the Afghan belligerents in meetings in Dushanbe and Kandahar while the ISI-backed Taliban forces were engaged in an offensive against Afghanistan's United Front opposition) are merely a convenient mask covering widespread agreement within Pakistan's governing elite about Pakistan's policy toward Afghanistan.[75]

Certainly, many of the Pushtun officers involved in crafting the ISI's Afghanistan policy would favor having a friendly, Pushtun-led government in Afghanistan. But the situation is more complex than that. Numerous other subnational Pakistani actors play roles in Afghanistan, such that at any given moment several Pakistani policies, perhaps at cross purposes with each other, may be in effect in Afghanistan. For example, the Pakistani provincial governments, especially those of the NWFP and Baluchistan, often have different agendas from the federal government, especially since so many of the refugees have settled in those provinces and affected their economies. The Pakistani religious parties, especially the Jamiat-ul-Ulema-i-Islami (JUI), in whose madrasahs many of the present Taliban leaders were trained, and the Jamaat-i-Islami (JI), which long supported Gulbuddin Hekmatyar, also have goals they are trying to achieve through activities in Afghanistan.[76] The JUI and similar organizations have used their symbiosis with the Taliban to enhance their standing in Pakistan, especially in certain districts of Baluchistan, the FATA, and the NWFP. Some tribal groupings with cross-border ties, as well as Pakistani business interests (especially the trucking and narcotics industries), also pursue goals in Afghanistan. Even some private individuals have played roles in shaping Pakistan's multilayered Afghanistan policy, especially wealthy Gulf Arabs with fundamentalist religious agendas, whose financial support has often been critical in maintaining certain Afghan actors. In return, they gained access to weapons, training, and safe havens for certain groups of their own.

Most notable among these has been the renegade Saudi Arabian billionaire Osama bin Laden, who has allegedly financed militant Islamist activities in Saudi Arabia and elsewhere in the Middle East. He has resided in Taliban territory since at least early 1997.[77] In 1998 he allegedly supplied significant financial support for the successful Taliban offensive in northern Afghanistan, following his marriage to a daughter of Mullah Omar's. In August 1998 he sent teams to bomb US embassies in Kenya and Tanzania, in response to which the US fired cruise missiles from the Arabian Sea into Afghanistan at bin Laden's bases that same month. Since then, bin Laden has been the focus of intense pressure on the Taliban government, and for much of 1999 he lowered his profile by going into hiding within Afghanistan. Even UN economic sanctions on the Taliban, designed to force them to give up bin Laden and implemented in November 1999, did not work. New UN sanctions were implemented in December 2000, following an October 2000 attack on the USS *Cole* in the port of Aden, Yemen, that US intelligence officials alleged was carried out by men under bin Laden's direction. Fearing another retaliatory strike, bin Laden fled into the rugged hills of Uruzgan in November 2000. The Taliban's persistent refusal to give him up to Western authorities has made him a symbol for Pakistani and Afghan Islamists of their resistance to Western hegemony, while to the West he has become the "poster boy" for international terrorism.

The transnational actors have been the most recent to appear; they include corporations and other business interests drawn to the potential wealth of Central Asia. A good example of this kind of organization is the American oil company Unocal, which set up offices in Pakistan and Turkmenistan and put together a consortium to build a pipeline through western Afghanistan to carry Turkmenistan's natural gas south to Pakistan. Together with its rivals, primarily Bridas of Argentina, it demonstrates that the globalizing forces of the corporate world are coming to Central Asia, including the wasteland that is present-day Afghanistan.

In sum, numerous outside actors have shaped previously isolated Afghanistan over the past two decades. Both of the superpowers became deeply involved in the war in the 1980s, the Soviets as supporters of the Kabul regime and the US as patrons of the mujahideen. Other actors became involved as well—Pakistan, Iran, Saudi Arabia, China, and, to a lesser extent, Egypt and other Arab states, allies of either the USSR or the US, European neutrals, and the UN. Pakistan and Iran were the countries of first asylum, where their dissimilar foreign and refugee policies in the 1980s led to significant differences in their posture toward the Afghan refugee-warriors. Since 1992, new actors have appeared and begun to influence Afghanistan, including Turkmenistan, Uzbekistan, Tajikistan, other former Soviet republics, and various non-state actors, including large business interests.

Compelling evidence indicates the importance of outside actors to Afghanistan since 1978. Without them, the Afghan War could never have occurred and been maintained at such high intensity for so long. The war was and still is maintained by outside actors in several ways, but the most important were through Pakistan's willingness to host a refugee-based insurgency during 1978–1992 and its more recent patronage of the Taliban militia. From the beginning the resistance had to build from Pakistan because it lacked the strength to do so in Afghanistan, especially after the Islamist movement in Afghanistan initiated an unsuccessful revolt in the Panjshir Valley during 1975. As the Afghan War widened and intensified, the civilian population was increasingly targeted and the refugee population grew, especially during stage two. As this population increased, so did the refugee-based insurgency, putting the Soviets in the awkward position of successfully implementing one counterinsurgency strategy while simultaneously creating the conditions for a form of insurgency they could not defeat. The civilian supporters of the mujahideen became refugees, and it was among these refugees that the resistance found its support.

The insurgency had its roots before the war, but it truly developed after the war began. Several mechanisms promoted its development, but especially important was Pakistan's willingness to have its territory used as a staging, training, and supply area for the mujahideen. When contrasted with Iran's attitude toward the Afghan conflict, the importance of Pakistan's role becomes even clearer.

Only Pakistan and Iran were alternatives as countries of first asylum, and consequently, as the war raged throughout the 1980s, they came to house the world's largest refugee concentrations. For several reasons, however, Iran was not the destination for most of the refugees, nor was it to become the major staging area for the resistance.

Iran is a predominantly Shia Muslim country of Persians; the largely Sunni Pushtun, Tajik, and Uzbek Afghans tended to move south into Sunni Pakistan.[78] For the majority Pushtun tribes, there were strong ethnic relationships with the Pakistani Pushtuns. Peshawar has been a Pushtun city for centuries, and it naturally became the focal point of the resistance leadership. Furthermore, the Federally Administered Tribal Agencies were officially beyond Pakistani government control, so a foreign insurgency based in refugee camps there maintained a certain plausible deniability for Pakistan and its supporters. Meanwhile, Iran spent most of the Afghan-Soviet War engaged in its own war with Iraq (1980–1988); Afghans in Iran were frequently impressed into the service of this conflict rather than assisted in their own fight.[79] Finally, the animosity between Iran and the United States during the 1980s made direct US assistance to the mujahideen in Iran virtually impossible. Afghan Hazaras, Farsiwan, Aimaq, Qizilbash, and others from the western provinces took refuge in Iran, where they received only limited assistance. The remainder went south and east to Pakistan or moved into the large towns and cities or more remote rural areas of Afghanistan.

Thus, in the 1980s Pakistan became home to the world's greatest refugee population and, correspondingly, patron to the world's greatest refugee-based insurgency.[80] Not only was Pakistan the logical choice for most Afghan refugees by virtue of its proximity and cross-border ethnic ties with Afghanistan's Pushtun population, but it was also made inviting by Pakistan's Zia ul-Haq, who hoped to use the refugee-mujahideen population to pursue several interlocking foreign policy goals. First, on a national level Zia wished to use the refugee-mujahideen situation as a unifying issue, an excuse to maintain martial law, and a mechanism by which he could gradually extend his control into tribal areas. Regionally, he had to tie down the Soviets so that Pakistan would not feel pressure on two fronts simultaneously (Afghanistan and India), and he also hoped eventually to foster the creation of a more Islamist government in Afghanistan.[81] On a broader regional basis Zia wished to use the Afghan conflict to acquire political capital among the Arab states. Finally, on the highest geopolitical level, he intended to acquire US support in inevitable opposition to Soviet expansionism. The US was not only to supply and refit Pakistan's armed forces but also to provide a counterweight to the Soviet-Indian threat. In addition to these policy goals, the reality was that it would have been impossible for Pakistan to close its long and porous border with Afghanistan to the refugees, so Zia used the situation to Pakistan's advantage. Subsequent Pakistani governments, whether headed by Benazir Bhutto (1988–1990, 1993–1996), Nawaz Sharif (1990–1993, 1997–1999), or Pervaiz Musharraf (1999–present), have not been threatened by the Soviet army next door as Zia was, but their policy choices have been somewhat constrained by the decisions of the Zia era, and thus they, too, became involved in the Afghan imbroglio.

Without the intervention of the USSR in late 1979, the communist government in Kabul would have fallen in 1980. Without the sanctuary and arms pipeline provided by Pakistan, the assistance of the US and other countries, and the support of the refugees, the mujahideen would have been defeated by the mid-1980s. By 1985 the rebels were in complete disarray militarily, and though many observers have cited the introduction of the Stinger missile in 1986 as the reason the war turned around, if there had been no sanctuary in 1985 the mujahideen would have been doomed. The increased efforts of the Soviet-Kabul forces to interdict supply routes and strike across the border into Pakistan after 1985 demonstrates their understanding of the problem. The mujahideen could not have survived in the total absence of Pakistani sanctuary. The March 1983–March 1984 truce in the Panjshir Valley illustrates the problems faced by an active, internally based insurgency such as Massoud operated.[82] The more isolated, strategically insignificant resistance movements in the Hazarajat and Nuristan areas were also internally based, and they engaged the government forces far less frequently and intensively.

It is useful to recall the unsuccessful results of the abortive 1975 Panjshir uprising, the earlier Basmachi rebellion in Soviet Central Asia, and the Iraqi Kurdish rebellion of 1974–1975. The 1975 Panjshir Islamist uprising was doomed because the people were not united against the government and the rebels had insufficient training and weapons for such an undertaking. These problems were rectified in the Afghan-Soviet War. In the Basmachi case, the resistance lacked unity and outside assistance, and it also failed. The many other problems occupying the attention of the new Bolshevik government, as well as the rugged terrain and absence of high-technology weapons, made it possible for this conflict to drag on. Most telling of all was the Kurdish case of the mid-1970s. A low-intensity Kurdish resistance movement in Iraq intensified in 1974 with cross-border assistance from Iran and the CIA and sanctuary for the refugees in Iran. Iran and Iraq reached an agreement in 1975, Iranian aid to the Kurds was cut off and the border closed, and Iraq wiped out the resistance. These cases demonstrate the fragility of guerrilla resistance movements, especially those without sanctuary, outside assistance, and unity of purpose. It is possible that the Afghan insurgency could have continued in the absence of refugee-based support in Pakistan, but it is unlikely that it would have been the powerful force that ultimately drove the USSR to a political solution.

Since 1992, outside support has remained critical to the continuation of the war in Afghanistan. Without infusions of weapons, ammunition, and other necessary items, the Afghan factions would be unable to continue to fight, at least with any great intensity. Since 1998, the UN has belatedly increased its pressure on Afghanistan's neighbors to stop resupplying the Afghan factions, but they are all caught up in a geopolitical power struggle and have found it impossible to do so. In March 1998, Ahmed Rashid wrote that "both sides of the Afghan divide are preparing for a massive new round of fighting as arms supplies pour in from Russia, Iran, Tajikistan, Pakistan, and Saudi Arabia for their various proxies inside Afghanistan."[83] Words like these appear every spring; indeed, in 1999 the Taliban and Massoud stocked up until the snows melted in April and May, dickered at the conference table and fought some minor engagements until summer, and then engaged in heavy fighting from July to December, when the coming of winter forced a temporary halt to heavy hostilities. Over the winter they re-supplied their forces, to repeat the pattern in 2000. Clearly, Afghanistan's neighbors are not yet ready to turn away from the military solution there, and just as clearly, its central regional position means that so long as the country remains a bleeding wound—to borrow from Mikhail Gorbachev—it will drip on everyone in the region.

THE GEOPOLITICS OF CENTRALITY:
AFGHANISTAN'S POSITION IN ASIA

As in its days during ancient times as the home of the famous Silk Road to China, Afghanistan today finds itself again an Asian crossroads. Sharing borders with six other countries, it stands at the juncture between Central Asia and Russia to the north, Southwest Asia and the Middle East to the west, China to the east, and South Asia to the south. In the sense that the new Central Asian countries are still a part of the Russian civilization, Afghanistan also stands on the fault line of three civilizations (Islamic, Russian Orthodox, and Chinese) and very near to a fourth (Hindu).[84] Afghanistan's location has always been critical to its shape and existence, but as the country entered the third millennium CE, the way in which its central location is crucial appeared to be changing.

Five issues are most critical to the changing way in which Afghanistan's centrality is crucial. First, the overlapping of ethnolinguistic and religious identity groups, permeable national borders, and weak state governments throughout the region make possible ongoing ethnic conflict. This is especially problematic because no state in the region can easily curtail the sanctuary available to members of ethnolinguistic and religious groups that straddle its borders with another country. Pakistan's deep involvement in Afghanistan extends clearly from the inter-ethnic ties between Pushtun mujahideen and Taliban leaders, on one hand, and Pushtun military and intelligence commanders within the Pakistani army, on the other. Yet even if these official ties did not exist, the sanctuary and support available to Afghan Pushtuns in Pakistan's semiautonomous FATA and remote Baluchistan would draw Pakistan into the fray. Similarly, if to a lesser degree, Tajiks from both Afghanistan and Tajikistan have found succor in each other's countries throughout the 1990s. Uzbekistan has given aid to Afghanistan's northern Uzbek militia, and Iran has provided critical assistance to Afghanistan's Shia minority, especially the Hazara people of central Afghanistan. It is no exaggeration to say that without the continued involvement of neighboring countries, at the level of their governments as well as through nongovernmental personal and family ties, Afghanistan's long war could not have persisted.

Second, the resurgence of Islam as a force for political legitimacy and a foundation for political organization also has taken on regional connotations as it has appeared with varying degrees of success and virulence in every country in the area. The Islamic Renaissance Party (IRP), which was formed in southern Russia in 1990, exists in all the countries of Central Asia and has been especially significant so far in Tajikistan and Uzbekistan.[85] Other Islamic movements, such as the Wahabi movement in the Ferghana Valley and the Islamic Democratic Party in Uzbekistan, also pose challenges to the more secular governments of the new Central Asian republics.

The country that so far has been most affected by the growing Islamization of Afghanistan is Pakistan, which now has thousands of Pakistani Taliban veterans attempting to Islamize its political discourse and social life. Pakistan's involvement in Afghanistan in the late twentieth century has had myriad and far-reaching consequences for its own society. Most of those consequences are related to Pakistan's past role as host to the largest segment of the Afghan diaspora and its continued role as power broker to competing groups within Afghanistan. The Afghan refugees ruptured the flimsy social fabric of Pakistan and directly contributed to the Kalashnikovization of the country. By the early 1990s the leaky weapons pipeline and burgeoning drug culture had created a Pakistan rife with violence, crime, and corruption.

Increasingly, Pakistan's Islamist groups became not only frustrated with the government's failure to stem this Kalashnikovization but also acquainted with the tools of violence themselves. A complex interplay of Pakistani Islamist organizations and institutions gave rise to the Taliban and promoted a cross-border fertilization of Islamist ideology. The Islamization of Zia ul-Haq failed to take root in Pakistan, and the Islamist parties have never demonstrated much electoral clout there, but the rise of the Taliban gave Pakistani Islamism a shot in the arm that is regularly boosted with every wave of Pakistani Taliban who return from the battlefields of Afghanistan to spread the gospel at home. The most far-reaching consequence of Pakistan's long involvement in the Afghan War may yet prove to be its "Talibanization."

Although Islam has always played a significant role in Pakistan's polity and society, the surge in Islamist politics during the late 1990s known as Talibanization is a new and profoundly disturbing force in Pakistan's political life. For the first time, thousands of Pakistani youths have gone abroad to participate in a militant religious social movement. They return home having received weapons training and sometimes combat experience, ideological indoctrination, and a shared experience with other true believers in a grand jihad. Often they have developed or intensified a commitment to Islamize their own society. Like the "Arab Afghans" who returned from the jihad of the 1980s to challenge secular regimes in the Middle East, the Pakistani Taliban wish to apply the lessons they have learned on the battlefields of Afghanistan to Pakistan. There are now estimated to be eighty thousand to one hundred thousand Pakistani Taliban, who are viewed by the JUI and similar organizations as the foot soldiers in a crusade to change Pakistan forever.[86] Never has the JUI or JI (or smaller religious parties) played a significant role in national electoral politics in Pakistan, but they are becoming increasingly powerful in the border areas of Baluchistan, the FATA, and the NWFP, and national political leaders are paying attention.

The new militancy and vibrancy of Islamism in Pakistan has been most pronounced in the Pushtun areas that lie along the Afghan border, especially in the FATA. Under different names (Tehrik-i-Tulaba in Orakzai Agency, Tanzim Nifaz Shariat-i-Mohammadi in Bajaur Agency, Hizbul Mujahideen in Chitral and the Northern Areas), movements led by 'ulama connected with the same JUI madrasahs that imbued the Taliban with their ideology have sprung up throughout Pakistan's Pushtun areas. The leaders of these movements are imposing their interpretation of religious law on their areas, running for public office, and Islamizing society through the elimination of secular entertainment.[87] These border areas are especially vulnerable to Talibanization because of the large number of Pakistani Taliban they shelter and the ready access they have to weapons. The *Frontier Post*, for example, put it this way in the autumn of 1999:

> It is feared that in the case of failure or success of [the] Taliban movement in Afghanistan, their next destination would be Chitral. Hundreds of religious students from Chitral and Northern Areas are fighting along [with] the Taliban in Afghanistan and thousands of them have

received complete military training.... [T]hey struggle for the enforcement of complete Shariah in Chitral and Northern Areas.... The introduction of the Kalashnikov culture has further worsened the over all
situation.[88]

Talibanization has grown rapidly to have a nationwide impact in
Pakistan. Increasing pressure from Islamist groups led Prime Minister
Nawaz Sharif to declare on November 17, 1998, that Taliban justice was
needed in Pakistan. Legislation passed the lower house in 1998 (the
Shariat Bill) that would amend the constitution to make the sharia the
source of all law, which would complete the Islamization initiated by
Zia ul-Haq in the early 1980s. The Senate, where the opposition held
the majority, refused to pass the bill, but pressure from Islamist parties
grew throughout 1999. In August 1999 the Senate refused even to discuss a resolution to condemn the tribal practice of "honor killing."[89]
This was followed in September 1999 by inflammatory calls to arms,
such as when "Maulana Ajmal Qadri, the leader of a breakaway faction
of Jamiat-Ulema-e-Islam, or Party of Islamic Clerics, issued a religious
edict ... saying lawmakers opposing a constitutional amendment to
impose Islamic law here [Pakistan] deserve to die."[90]

The Talibanization of social discourse and policy in Pakistan represents a significant regional variation on the "blowback" phenomenon
often reported in Western press coverage of Afghanistan.[91] ("Blowback"
is a CIA term referring to the unanticipated and generally undesirable
consequences of an intelligence operation spilling back onto the country initiating the operation.) Talibanization in Pakistan has involved
narrowing access to public space for women, especially through honor
killings, forced veiling, and restrictions on their movement and activities, all of which fit the prevailing ideology of the Islamist groups there
as well as the Taliban in Afghanistan. It has prompted greater sectarian violence as Shias and Christians have been increasingly subjected
to attack by members of militant Sunni organizations. An especially
bloody period of such violence in early October 1999 led the Sharif government finally to attempt to rein in the Islamist organizations, sparking a series of events that culminated in the military coup that toppled
Sharif and placed General Pervaiz Musharraf in control of the government. Now it is Musharraf's turn to try to strike a balance between the
demands of the secular Western governments, which control desperately needed economic assistance, and the Islamist movements of Pakistan, which increasingly control the street there.

Talibanization has also led to the demonization of the West, especially the United States, as the enemy of Islam. This campaign reached an especially dangerous level in August 1999, when Maulana Fazlur Rehman, leader of the JUI, threatened to harm Americans in Pakistan if the US attacked Osama bin Laden. The US put increasing pressure on Pakistan during 1998–1999 to abandon the Taliban and bring its own religious right under control, even as Pakistani domestic forces pushed the Sharif and then Musharraf governments in the direction of greater confrontation with both India and the West. Talibanization combines the worst legacies of Pakistan's adventurist Afghan policy of the 1990s to create severe disorder in Pakistani politics and civil society. It narrows the parameters of public discourse and focuses attention on social policy when the country is wracked by entrenched corruption, record unemployment, and grinding poverty. It also harms Pakistan's relations with most of the rest of the world.

Afghanistan's centrality is crucial in a third way, as well—through the growing economic interconnections of the regional actors, with regard to both legitimate sources of trade, such as oil and natural gas, and illegitimate sources of trade, such as narcotics and weapons. Both types of industries are crucial to Afghanistan and the region in the new millennium. After two decades of war and most of a century as a rentier economy, Afghanistan is easily the least developed country in the region and thus is poorly positioned to benefit much in the short term from growing regional trade. Its location and potential for breeding regional instability, however, mean that its problems will need to be resolved if Pakistan is going to be able to engage in significant economic interactions with the former Soviet republics of Central Asia.

Fourth, just as permeable borders make possible the easy flow of people and economic goods throughout the region, they also make possible the spillover of conflict from one country to another, as from Afghanistan into Pakistan during the mid-1980s and from Tajikistan into Afghanistan and Uzbekistan in the early 1990s. Iran's mobilization of almost 250,000 troops along its border with Afghanistan in the fall of 1998, following the killing of its diplomats by Taliban forces during their capture of Mazar-i-Sharif, further illustrates the danger that continuing conflict in Afghanistan poses to regional stability. The Taliban's willingness to host Islamist militants from Chechnya, Kyrgyzstan, and Uzbekistan in 1999 also threatened peace in the region.

Finally, the fifth crucial new factor is the way the changing regional situation around Afghanistan in the aftermath of the Cold War and the collapse of the Soviet Union has sparked the geopolitical aspirations of regional actors. Various outside actors have meddled in Afghanistan, as we have seen, including especially the USSR, the US, and Pakistan during the 1980s (but also Iran, Saudi Arabia, and the United Nations). The dramatic changes in the international system during 1989–1992 altered the regional environment and the motivations of various actors toward Afghanistan. I conclude this chapter with a consideration of the more recent approach to Afghanistan of key actors during the 1990s.

Following the collapse of the Najibullah government, the Russians finally withdrew from Afghanistan, recalling their last diplomats and advisers from Kabul in August 1992. Nonetheless, for Russia, concerned about the possibility of Islamic fundamentalist movements in the former Central Asian republics, Afghanistan is still a problem. When the Taliban captured Kabul, Russia increased its supplies to the Northern Alliance forces while simultaneously increasing its diplomatic pressure on Pakistan to rein in the Taliban.[92] Taliban attacks and now victories in northern Afghanistan have seriously alarmed the Russians, who have responded by putting their twenty-five thousand troops in Tajikistan on alert, leading concerned Commonwealth of Independent States countries in military maneuvers, stepping up their flow of weapons and supplies to Massoud, openly accusing Pakistan of direct military activity in Afghanistan, blocking Taliban efforts to secure recognition at the UN, and leading the UN Security Council in imposing sanctions on the Taliban in December 2000.

After the Soviet withdrawal in 1989, the United States lost interest in Afghanistan. The independence of the Central Asian states, with their rich oil and gas fields, and the increased interest of Pakistan and Iran in Afghanistan partially revived American concern. Unocal's leadership during the mid-1990s of one of several competing consortiums negotiating to build a pipeline from Turkmenistan across western Afghanistan and into Pakistan gave rise to the speculation that the US was behind the Taliban movement. There was little hard evidence to support that claim, and early American interest in the Taliban declined and moved into hard opposition to the movement as the nature of its policies became clear.[93] The US government now seeks resolution of four outstanding issues with the Taliban as the price of American recognition and assistance. These issues are that the Taliban eliminate their support for terrorism, especially in the form of delivering up Osama bin Laden to American authorities, curtail the heroin traffic, modify their policies on women, and agree to a broad-based government that includes northern opposition figures.

Certainly Pakistan is behind the Taliban movement, because Pakistan needs a peaceful Afghanistan in order to compete with Iran and Turkey for a share of the riches of Central Asia. It also wants to minimize problems with the ethnic groups that overlap the countries' shared border. Pakistan believes a Pushtun-led government is needed in Kabul, and it had been attempting to install such a government since the Soviet withdrawal—finally succeeding with the Taliban takeover in September 1996. Thus, its relations with Afghanistan are complex, muddied by both the lack of clarity within its own government and factors such as drug trafficking and smuggling across the porous border. In late September 1998 Pakistan downgraded its diplomatic ties with the Taliban, although since then the Talibanization of Pakistan has threatened to destabilize that country as popular Pakistani support for the Taliban grew to its highest levels yet in 1999.

Iran, too, has aspirations toward Central Asia. It views the Taliban as a Pakistani militia that advances the anti-Iranian policy of both Saudi Arabia and the United States. Iran has traditionally supported the Shia factions in Afghanistan, which increased in power in the early 1990s. Throughout late 1996 and 1997 Iranian support for the Northern Alliance grew, which led to the Taliban's closing most of the western border and cutting off relations in early 1997. The Taliban's defeat in 1998 of most of Iran's proxies in northern Afghanistan and subsequent ethnic cleansing of the Afghan Shia there presented Iran with a difficult decision on Afghanistan—to accept its losses or to become more deeply and directly involved in the Afghan struggle. The killing of Iran's diplomats (reportedly executed in cold blood) by Taliban forces during the fall of Mazar-i-Sharif gave Iran the excuse to mobilize nearly 250,000 troops along its border with Afghanistan, where they engaged in some minor border clashes. The border was closed completely until November 1999, when a thaw in Iran-Taliban relations led to the reopening of the Islam Qala border post and the Iranian consulate in Herat. Despite inflamed rhetoric, Iran did not invade Afghanistan (reportedly, it could not afford to), but it has continued to supply the Northern Alliance and has maintained its enhanced border forces in place. A complicating factor for Iran's role is that the more moderate government led by Mohammad Khatami is now seeking to improve relations with the US.

During the earlier phase of the war, Saudi Arabia always focused its

aid on the most fundamentalist of the Sunni mujahideen parties, especially the organizations of Sayyaf and Hekmatyar.[94] Now Saudi Arabia
has become a backer of the Taliban, one of only three countries (along
with Pakistan and the United Arab Emirates) to recognize the Taliban
government.[95] Since August 1998, tensions over the continued sanctuary
provided by the Taliban for Saudi dissident Osama bin Laden has led
Saudi Arabia to expel the Taliban chargé d'affaires and to downgrade its
diplomatic ties with the Taliban regime.

Finally, the Central Asian republics have tended to allow their policies to follow their historical and cultural ties with the northern minorities of Afghanistan. Northern Afghanistan has 1.5 million Uzbeks, while
adjacent Uzbekistan has nearly 15 million, and the same international
border divides nearly 4 million Afghan Tajiks from nearly 5 million of
their cousins in Tajikistan. Although the issues are somewhat different
for each of the states that border Afghanistan, all are concerned to some
extent about the possibility of an ultimate Taliban victory in northern
Afghanistan. Until the Taliban successes in 2000 forced it to reconsider its position, Uzbekistan was the biggest Central Asian supporter of
the Northern Alliance, especially Dostam's forces, while Tajikistan was
initially more ambivalent toward Rabbani and Massoud because of
their earlier meddling in the Tajikistan civil war. Turkmenistan has had
the most cordial relations with the Taliban because the Saparmurad
Niyazov government still hopes to export its gas through Taliban-held
western Afghanistan.

Afghanistan has been and remains today a country that is significantly affected by its neighbors while affecting them significantly as
well. So far the war and the activities it has promoted, such as arms
trafficking and drug smuggling, have been the primary ways in which
Afghanistan and its neighbors have influenced each other. If geoeconomics increasingly pushes geopolitics off the stage, then growing pressure from outside actors to end the Afghan conflict may allow trade
to replace war as the primary way in which Afghanistan interacts with
its neighbors. The likelihood of this and other possibilities for Afghanistan's future is the subject of the last chapter.

6 / The Future of Afghanistan

The current situation in Afghanistan not only is one of the great tragedies of our day, made all the more poignant by the world's pronounced indifference, but also is profoundly threatening to the continued stability of many other countries. Since ancient times the land of Afghanistan has occupied a strategic point on the high road of Central Asia, and in the days of the Great Game it became the pivotal point between the expanding British and Russian empires. Even in recent years Afghanistan has played a critical role in shaping world events, for the Soviet withdrawal in 1989 opened the door to the Velvet Revolution in Eastern Europe and the end of the Cold War. The subsequent collapse of the Soviet Union into its constituent parts contributes to the analysis of Afghanistan's future, because the predominantly Muslim republics of the former Soviet Union that border Afghanistan on the north have now achieved independence, changing the regional equation dramatically.

Afghanistan spent much of the twentieth century as one of the poorest and least significant nations in the world, only to regain its nineteenth-century prominence as a Cold War battleground in the 1980s. That prominence came at a tremendous cost in death, destruction, and despair, affecting every Afghan and impinging deeply upon the national psyche. In the post–Cold War era, Afghanistan dropped off the front pages once again, only to reemerge with the rise of the Taliban. Sadly, that reemergence has not been positive, and many people

have now come to view Afghanistan as a land of drug traffickers, terrorists, and bizarre religious fundamentalists. Today, Afghanistan is
engaged in a great struggle to determine its national identity in a very
changed world. Few other countries face such tremendous threats to
their survival as national entities as the new millennium dawns.[1]

Never a strong state, Afghanistan was weakened to the point of
governmental collapse and national fragmentation by the long war.[2] In
addition to the widespread physical destruction it produced, the war
altered and transformed Afghanistan, adding some new factors to the
traditional divisions present there. Five of the most important of these
changes, as discussed in earlier chapters, were the development of new
political elites (mujahideen and Taliban) to replace the now-defunct
prewar elites, the proliferation of high-technology weaponry and concomitant cult of violence ("Kalashnikovization"), the growth of the narcotics traffic based on an opium-heroin economic sector, the increased
Islamization of Afghan society (now spilling over into Pakistan in the
form of "Talibanization"), and post–Cold War alterations to the region.[3]
These factors have combined with traditional centrifugal forces to pull
apart the Afghan state. These traditional forces include Afghanistan's
ethnolinguistic and religious divisions, its syncretic religious framework, its qawm-based social system, and its rugged geography. Also
important has been the historical process by which the Afghan state
developed as it overcame these centrifugal challenges and its location as
the "crossroads of Asia" to forge a national existence—if not a deeply
felt national identity—during the twentieth century. All of these factors, the traditional and the new, challenge the continued existence of
Afghanistan today and provide us with insight into both Afghanistan's
present and the possibilities for its future.

Afghanistan today is a country suffering from severe state failure. It
is not now, nor has it been for a long time, a country with a functioning, viable government and political system.[4] In the struggle over which
ideology best fits this Central Asian society (traditionalism, secularism,
or Islamism),[5] not only have the Afghan governments of recent decades
become casualties of the war there, but the whole notion of central
government itself has come under attack.[6] As Olivier Roy suggested,
in Afghanistan the struggle between state and society has been reborn,
with society resurgent and the state weakened to the point of collapse.[7]
Afghanistan's ascendant society, however, is not traditional but has been
altered, transformed, even perverted in the crucible of high-intensity
war and national destruction. Thus it is that young men with guns, who

derive their revenues primarily from heroin and smuggling but who legitimate their position in the name of Allah, have come to rule almost all of Afghanistan. That they rule bereft of most of the structures now held to be essential in most modern governments fits this country where the state has gone into decline.

Furthermore, the environment is excellent in Afghanistan today for continued political fragmentation. The destruction of the institutions and authority of the central government, constructed only with great difficulty over the last century, and the rise of an altered society—or the resurgence of traditional rural society[8]—have created a situation of great fluidity in Afghanistan. It has been argued that the Afghan state model forged by Abdur Rahman Khan, based on the predominance of the tribal Pushtuns and the preeminence of Kabuli authority, is now dead,[9] although the emergence of the Pushtun-dominated Taliban sug-gests otherwise. At the same time, the outcome of the war empowered new political elites while providing none with a clear advantage.[10] These new groups have significant stocks of military supplies and control a large share of the regional and world opium market.[11]

Perhaps most importantly, the rise of society over the state means the rise once again of the local community, or qawm. Afghans are now basing their identity on qawm and/or ethnicity, and Afghan national identity has become essentially a barren concept. Indeed, as the Afghan conflict has dragged on, it has become increasingly ethnicized as group alignments have become more heavily based on ethnicity, race, and linguistic or sectarian differences. This trend has reached a new and dangerous level since late 1998, when Taliban military successes in northern and central Afghanistan were followed by atrocities and mas-sacres that constituted nothing less than ethnic cleansing.[12] The unremit-ting commitment of the Taliban to a military solution in Afghanistan has even led some knowledgeable observers to suggest that the Taliban are bent on the "Pushtunization" of the whole country.[13] If so, then the subjugation of the northern minorities might be insufficient for Tali-ban purposes, and more permanent measures such as massacre, inter-nal relocation, and even genocide of these groups could be yet to come. Should such drastic policies be implemented, Afghanistan's national fragmentation will be complete, regardless of what borders remain on the maps and regardless of whether its shattered society finally enjoys a shaky peace.

Last, all of these internal developments have been occurring in a transformed international environment that has put Afghanistan in the middle of a rapidly changing region that enjoys limited big-power meddling. In light of the foregoing, can Afghanistan be reintegrated, and if so, how?

REQUIREMENTS FOR REINTEGRATION

To make Afghanistan a functioning state once again is a tall order, seemingly impossible in light of the recent atrocities coming on top of years of grinding war. At least three changes must occur for reintegration of the society and reconstruction of a functioning state to begin. First, widespread ethnic-based fighting must cease. Second, a reasonably legitimate government must be established. Third, normality must return to Afghanistan. Let us consider each of these in some detail, including what is necessary for the achievement of each.

As Afghanistan's protracted war has dragged on and the qawm has reemerged as the basis for identity and governance, conflict has occurred increasingly along ethnolinguistic and sectarian lines. In a country where the code of honor requires revenge killings, ethnic-based conflict can easily turn into ethnic cleansing. Given the spatial distribution of Afghanistan's ethnolinguistic groups within the broader region, neighboring states have found and continue to find it virtually impossible to avoid involvement in ethnic conflict in Afghanistan, at least by providing support to their Afghan client groups, thus driving the war on.

Obviously, the Afghan state cannot reassert itself, nor can there begin to be a reintegration of the Afghan nation, so long as various ethnic militias refuse to cede control over their local areas to a national government run (at least in part) by members of another ethnolinguistic, religious, or ideological group. An alternative arrangement would be for local communities to govern themselves, which would require at least the willingness of opposing ethnic-based militias to adopt a tolerant attitude toward the customs and culture of other groups.[14] Leaving aside for a moment the motivations of regional actors, for the vast majority of Afghans there is no longer any acceptable reason for the fighting to continue. It is now merely a power struggle between contending groups who offer Islamist explanations or geopolitical excuses for their continued unwillingness to cease fighting. The reality is that the battle is increasingly over ethnic identity and the regional aspirations of neighboring states. The ethnic foundation for the current power struggle has created a zero-sum game in Afghanistan. The Northern Alliance cannot lay down its arms when the outcome might be ethnic cleansing, nor can their patrons allow them to do so, and so the fighting continues.

Yet somehow the fighting must stop, at least long enough for the opposing sides to try out confidence-building measures that could lead to a lasting peace. Regardless of what agreements major powers may broker in Afghanistan, no ceasefire is likely to hold for long, because the Afghan fighters are too independent to be controlled even by their own leaders. For example, during talks in February–March 1999 in Ashkhabad, Turkmenistan, just as the opposing sides appeared to move closer to a possible agreement on power sharing in a coalition government, Taliban leaders cautioned that this did not mean that a ceasefire would necessarily follow. The fighting could be brought to a lower intensity, however, if neighboring countries would stop supplying and supporting their Afghan proxies with heavy weapons and ammunition. December 2000 UN Security Council Resolution 1333, which imposed sanctions on the Taliban, including their receipt of military supplies, represents the first meaningful effort to make this key step a reality It came on the verge of final victory for the Taliban, who were for the first time supported openly by Pakistan throughout 2000. It did not require supporters of the Northern Alliance to limit their supply of military equipment to Massoud's forces, and thus may prolong the war. Lowering the intensity of the conflict by reducing or eliminating the meddling of neighboring states must occur for Afghanistan to have a chance to rebuild.

Halting the fighting would slow or even stop the process of national fragmentation, but it would not by itself provide the basis for reintegration in Afghanistan. For that to occur, a legitimate government must be reestablished. For a government to be legitimate, its authority must be widely accepted, a far cry from what Afghanistan has had for the last twenty-five years. Legitimacy can best be established by appropriate representation of the entire population and/or by policy success. In the short run, legitimacy might also be claimed by a charismatic ruler, but there is no individual political actor currently on the Afghan scene who is acceptable to everyone who possesses substantial personal charisma. Only the former king, Zahir Shah, is ever mentioned in this context, and he has repeatedly refused to play anything other than an interim role in reestablishing a legitimate Afghan government (and in any event he is now in his mid-80s). All the other prominent Afghan leaders are unacceptable to at least one Afghan faction. Mullah Omar, for example, is rejected by the Northern Alliance; Ahmed Shah Massoud and Burhannudin Rabbani are rejected by the Taliban; and Gulbuddin Hekmatyar is rejected by both the Taliban and the Northern Alliance.

Thus, legitimacy will have to come either from the establishment of a government that represents all the people, in numbers that each group finds acceptable, or from successful governance by the group or groups that claim power, or both. The initial willingness among Kabulis to tolerate the Taliban is an example of the second case; they did so because the Taliban brought with them order and the implementation of Islamic law. The more recent chafing under their rule represents growing dissatisfaction with their overall policy failure. Given the size and depth of the ethnic divisions that exist in Afghanistan today, any government that does not include the major groups in sufficient numbers will not achieve policy success. A government in Afghanistan today can be legitimate only if it is based on the entire population. Gone are the days when the Pushtuns could dominate the northern minorities, especially the Hazara, simply on ethnic and religious grounds. A broad-based government heading a federal state with substantial provincial autonomy provides the best framework for achieving legitimacy. Again, this can be achieved only if outside actors pressure their Afghan clients to adopt a view of Afghan politics as a variable-sum game. Nazif Shahrani has emphasized the importance of community self-governance for Afghanistan, arguing that the Western state model never fit Afghanistan well and was perverted in its application there, and thus a return to a strong, centralized state is doomed to failure. He contends that "what is at issue is both the freedom of local communities to choose representatives to participate in the national political organs and institutions of the national state, and to act as free leaders of their communities, and, also the freedom of the communities themselves to be able to manage their own local affairs, instead of relinquishing that right to the central government to 'imprison' them again, as it was the case prior to the onset of the recent jihad."[15]

But even a broad-based government grounded on substantial autonomy for local communities will fail the legitimacy test if it is unable to tangibly improve people's material well-being. In short, a legitimate Afghan government must implement policies that revitalize economic and social life there and return Afghanistan to normalcy. The clock cannot be turned back to 1977; the long war has altered Afghanistan too profoundly for a return to the status quo ante bellum. Still, small-scale industrial production and legitimate commercial activity must begin again in Afghanistan, agriculture must shift its production away from opium monoculture, infrastructure must be rebuilt, and schools must be reopened. Government fosters all of these activities, and thus legitimacy is linked directly to government's provision of a solid business environment. People must come to believe that Afghanistan has a future in order for them to commit to rebuilding the Afghan nation.

As with the other two requirements for reintegration, the key to recreating normal conditions in Afghanistan is the role of outside actors. Most of the region wants a peaceful and stable Afghanistan, but to achieve the long-term stability that accompanies reintegration, these actors must not only cut off their Afghan client militias but also provide them with positive inducements for reintegration as well. No Afghan government will have any policy success or be able to rebuild the nation's shattered economy without outside support, so the role for outside actors of all sorts, but especially the United States, is crucial to the reintegration of Afghanistan.

Achieving the three conditions for reintegration of the Afghan state will be extremely difficult under current circumstances. Indeed, what can we predict for Afghanistan's future?

PROSPECTS FOR THE FUTURE OF AFGHANISTAN

After more than two decades of war, it is difficult to predict any positive future for Afghanistan. Nonetheless, we can consider a range of possible scenarios while exploring the interaction of factors that might make each one likely. Four scenarios seem possible: continued fragmentation, national disintegration, state reconstruction under a Pushtun-led government, and national reintegration under a broad-based government.[16] By fragmentation, I mean the continued de jure political unity of the existing state but de facto internal fragmentation into autonomous or semiautonomous regions (other examples include Sudan and Somalia). National disintegration is the political division of a country into two or more new states (for example, Pakistan, Czechoslovakia, Yugoslavia, USSR).

It is difficult to imagine a short-term future in Afghanistan that does not involve continued fighting among various contenders for power. Even the occasional reports of possible power-sharing agreements between the Taliban and the remnants of the northern forces, such as the tentative deal struck in Ashkhabad in March 1999, can give the seasoned observer of Afghanistan no more than the faintest glimmer of hope. Too often in the past, negotiations and agreements in principle have failed, and renewed fighting has prolonged the Afghan tragedy. If fighting does continue, then the most likely scenarios for Afghanistan's near future are national fragmentation and even disintegration into ethnic enclaves, perhaps affiliated with neighboring states.

A more hopeful model, based on the example of Abdur Rahman Khan at the end of the nineteenth century, might be that one strong-man or group will emerge from the current struggle for power in Afghanistan to reunite the country. No current contender, however, including the Taliban, seems to possess all the ingredients necessary to comprehensively defeat its major rivals. Although the Taliban have the upper hand at the moment in terms of military strength and the territory they control (90–97 percent of the country, depending on the source), they are more internally divided than at any other time since their emergence, and only a successful 1998 on the battlefield staved off the loss of their Pakistani support.[17] On-again, off-again efforts of the United Nations, regional powers, and even the generally uninterested United States to broker a deal that would halt the fighting continually founder on the belief by whichever faction is strongest at the moment that it can achieve its goals militarily. Thus, the apparent success of the February–March 1999 Ashkhabad negotiations, held under UN auspices, was merely a chimera, because both sides, especially the Taliban, moved almost immediately to the battlefield. Similarly, the UN's "Six Plus Two" negotiations in Tashkent and Kandahar in July 1999 produced a statement that bound neighboring countries from involvement in the Afghan conflict, but neutral observers within Afghanistan reported that the negotiations seemed merely to be delaying the Taliban's inevitable summer offensive. As expected, the offensive followed within days, and the heavy participation of Pakistanis on behalf of the Taliban made a mockery of the "Tashkent Declaration" that Pakistan had just signed. A prudent assessment of such peace negotiations suggests that they are no more likely to produce a lasting settlement than did the many previous attempts. In addition to the failed 1999 efforts, which ultimately led chief UN negotiator Lakhdar Brahimi to quit his post in utter frustration, each previous year has seen similar failures. For example, the April 1998 effort by US ambassador to the UN Bill Richardson produced a short-lived ceasefire and largely symbolic results that did nothing to prevent the Taliban's northern offensive in the summer of 1998.

Since the Afghan conflict moved into its Taliban phase, a clear pattern of conflictual and cooperative behavior has emerged. Fighting occurs from late spring to late fall; then the winter months and early spring

are used by the diplomats and political leaders for inconclusive negotiations while the military commanders use the time for extensive arms
buildups and training in expectation of another season of fighting
beginning with the late spring and summer. The 1999 negotiations in
Ashkhabad and especially Tashkent represented an effort to alter this
cyclical (and cynical) pattern by pushing negotiations into the prime
fighting period. Yet the major offensive still came, and smaller engagements occurred even during negotiations. In an atmosphere poisoned
by ethnic cleansing, atrocities, and human rights violations, and with
outside supporters continuing to provide necessary arms and supplies,
Afghan leaders will continue to view negotiations as merely another
tool of war, a way to buy time while troops prepare for battle. For semiautonomous local commanders on the front lines, with many scores
still to be settled, negotiations will have even less meaning. Thus, tragically, the war, now in its third decade, will continue grimly on.

The possibility of national disintegration appears to have lessened
somewhat in Afghanistan since the Taliban's gains in the minority areas
during the fall of 1998. Still, this scenario cannot be ruled out altogether,
because significant political fragmentation along ethnic-linguistic-
religious lines has already occurred that could provide the foundation
for long-term dominance of the periphery over the center. The increasing prevalence of ethnic-inspired atrocities exacerbates the likelihood
of this possibility. These atrocities include the May 1997 massacre by
northern forces of more than two thousand captured Taliban soldiers,
reprisal killings of civilians in Maimana and Qizalabad, the revenge
massacre of more than eight thousand northerners, not all of them
combatants, by the Taliban in 1998, and the July–September 1999 ethnic
cleansing by the Taliban of minority areas north of Kabul.

The Taliban are essentially a Pushtun group and are unpopular outside of the Pushtun areas. Even now, their hold on the captured northern and central provinces where national minorities are numerically
dominant is extremely tenuous, and they have lost some districts there
since October 1998. Massoud still controls the northeastern corner of
the country, which is largely populated by Tajiks. Dostam's Uzbek militia and some smaller Turkmen forces were shattered with the fall of
Mazar-i-Sharif in August 1998, as was the Hezb-i-Wahdat when Bamiyan
fell in September 1998. Smaller forces remain active in the northern
provinces even as non-Taliban leaders continue their efforts to produce
a political or military alliance that would pose a formidable challenge
to the Taliban. In January 1999, former interim president Sibghatullah

Mojaddidi and his fellow Sufi mujahideen leader Pir Sayed Ahmed Gailani announced the merger of their parties into the "Peace and National Unity Party" and committed this group to the principle of broad-based government. The Taliban quickly denounced this as the effort of Western stooges who merely sought access to power in Afghanistan.[18] In February 1999, former president Rabbani joined with Abdur Rasoul Sayyaf, Massoud, and surviving leaders of the northern and central ethnic minority communities to announce a new Afghan Leadership Council. This group, too, is committed to broad-based government, and the northern forces were represented in Ashkhabad under its banner. In November 1999 a loya jirga of prominent non-Taliban Afghans was held in Rome under the auspices of former king Zahir Shah.

Although the stalemate between the Taliban and the Northern Alliance was finally broken in 1998, the failure of the peace process and the survival of the northern forces on the battlefield in 1999 and 2000 (barely) could ultimately see Afghanistan partitioned into a Pushtun-Taliban south (supported by Pakistan and Saudi Arabia) and a Tajik-Uzbek-Hazara north (supported by Iran, Russia, India, Uzbekistan, Tajikistan, and Turkey).[19] In this scenario, Afghanistan's current international borders might or might not remain unchanged in the short run, but the reality would be a state divided.

Continued outside support for Afghan proxies is essential for either the disintegration or the fragmentation scenario to occur. Hence, the recent renewal of American and UN interest in resolving the Afghan conflict has been based on two important elements for success. First, the "Six Plus Two" formula of talks includes all of Afghanistan's neighbors—the six, Pakistan, Iran, Turkmenistan, Uzbekistan, Tajikistan, and China—plus the two major powers, Russia and the US. Second, the focus of calls for ending the Afghan conflict has begun to shift away from the Afghan factions and toward their supporters in other countries. Pakistan, especially, found itself increasingly at odds with the international community for continuing to maintain the Taliban and encouraging them to pursue a military solution in Afghanistan during 1999 and 2000. The forceful expression of Western dissatisfaction with Pakistan was communicated in both Washington and Islamabad during late 1998 and early 1999, and Pakistan was openly excoriated at the UN in the fall of 1999 in the wake of its obvious and extensive involvement in the Taliban's late summer offensive. The year 2000 brought a hardening of international attitudes toward Pakistan's increasingly open involvement in Afghanistan, culminating in the December UN Security Council Resolution imposing sanctions on the Taliban's receipt of military supplies and acetic anhydride (used in heroin production), the closure of their diplomatic missions, and a ban on the travel of their leaders abroad.[20] If Pakistan continues its military, logistic, financial, and diplomatic support for the Taliban, however, its regional rivals will continue to maintain enough support for the northern Afghans to allow them to survive. Thus, unless the Afghan rivals make real and lasting progress in future negotiations—which is unlikely under present circumstances—fighting will continue in Afghanistan, and it will continue along deeper ethnolinguistic-religious lines than at any point in the preceding two decades of combat (further limiting the possibility for peace negotiations to work).

A variation on the disintegration scenario, though it currently appears unlikely, could occur if the Taliban were to falter and lose significant ground, especially a city such as (in descending order of likelihood) Mazar-i-Sharif, Kabul, or Herat. The country would then be open for renewed fragmentation, especially in eastern and northwestern Afghanistan, which could pave the way for disintegration that would threaten Afghanistan's current territorial integrity. Cross-border ethnic ties (Tajiks, Uzbeks, and Turkomans with their Central Asian cousins; Farsiwan, Qizilbash, and Hazara with the Iranians; Pushtuns with the Pakistanis) could lead to the dismemberment of Afghanistan. In this scenario Afghanistan ceases to exist as its northern minorities turn toward the Central Asian republics, western Afghanistan falls under Iranian hegemony, and southern and eastern areas align with Pakistan.

If Afghanistan were to divide along ethnolinguistic lines, its constituent pieces might exist as independent or semi-independent states that would most likely continue to provide the basis for regional instability, or they might be joined to the relevant neighboring states. This latter possibility seems remote, though only in the context of recent world history, when international borders have been relatively sacrosanct. But over the last 250 years the world has seen substantial redrawing of maps, including those of the regions Afghanistan inhabits and borders. Of course, to redraw Afghanistan's map in such a way that the country itself ceases to exist, to the advantage of all of its immediate neighbors, could occur only if all the regional actors agreed, and probably in the face of substantial international opposition. Thus, on balance, the complete dismemberment of Afghanistan seems unlikely, but a partial dismemberment more possible. In any event, the overlapping ethnic groups and regional aspirations of Afghanistan's neighbors mean not only that disintegration cannot be ruled out entirely but also that the conflict that would bring it about is likely to continue.

The persistent support of outside actors leaves both sides convinced that a military struggle is still warranted, and so continued fragmentation is more likely in the short run than national disintegration. The continued fragmentation scenario is similar to the national disintegration scenario in that it, too, emphasizes the autonomy of various portions of the country at the expense of Kabul. Virtually all the key actors, domestic and regional, wish to maintain Afghanistan's current international borders, at least for the time being. Thus, the outside actors continue to arm their Afghan proxies in order to maintain enough battlefield parity to deny their opponents victory, while the ruggedness of the terrain and the long military experience of the combatants make outright victory elusive. Furthermore, the current struggle in Afghanistan occurs along ethnic lines, meaning that for the losers, the result could be extermination. Thus, the stakes are extremely high. The surviving non-Taliban forces approached both the 1999 peace negotiations and combat preparation with great seriousness of purpose, and they fought the 1999 and 2000 battles with grim determination.

Fighting and continued national fragmentation will drag on for as long as Afghanistan's neighbors continue to pursue regional interests defined purely in nationalistic terms. Sadly, although even in this scenario the vast majority of the country would not be a zone of conflict, scarce resources would continue to be devoted to the military struggle, thus delaying the reconstruction of infrastructure and rebuilding of the economy. This stagnation would undermine confidence in authorities above the local level and further retard the process of nation rebuilding in Afghanistan.

The two scenarios based on a reassertion of central government seem more likely in 2001 than at any other point during the preceding five years, if for no other reason than that the Taliban appear so close to winning. Thus, it is worth considering under what conditions Afghanistan could be made whole again, under either a Taliban government that controlled a peaceful country or a broad-based government built on local community autonomy.

The scenario that postulates a Pushtun-led government seemed especially promising in late 1998, in the wake of Taliban successes that left them in control of approximately 75–90 percent of the country. If they had been able to defeat Massoud and conquer northeastern Afghanistan in 1999, then they might have been able to impose a *pax Talibana* over the country. This scenario seemed likely in early 1999, but Massoud's ability to hang on over the course of the year made it clear that the Taliban would have to wait until the new century, at least, before declaring victory. Taliban combat successes in fall 2000 brought them to the brink of victory, but even a Taliban victory might fail to produce a Pushtun-led government, for several reasons.

First, no single group can succeed without a charismatic and capable leader who can, like Abdur Rahman a century earlier, forge a country out of the many groups within Afghanistan. To fit these criteria, the leader must be a Pushtun from an acceptable subtribe, which eliminates the country's most charismatic and capable leader, Ahmed Shah Massoud. Furthermore, the challenges to a modern-day nation builder far exceed those that confronted Abdur Rahman. It is not clear that Mullah Omar, the reclusive leader of the Taliban, has the necessary capabilities, despite his claim to be the Amir ul-Moemineen. Indeed, he may be no more than a figurehead; we know too little about the inner workings of the Taliban leadership to be certain.[21] It should also be noted that charismatic leaders are so significant to their movements that they become extremely attractive targets for assassination. Every major Afghan leader has had to face this threat, especially given the widespread availability of weapons and general situation of strife in the country. Mullah Omar narrowly escaped assassination by the explosion of a truck bomb next to his Kandahar compound on August 24, 1999, showing that at least someone believes him to be important enough to eliminate. Still, with or without Omar, it is clear that the Taliban government is not yet competent to manage even the routine tasks of governance. Perhaps with time, resources, and peace the Taliban will produce adequate administrators or give way to a more capable leadership, but it is more likely that they will be unable to coexist with or countenance a more modern government.

Furthermore, as the Taliban gained territory and expanded their movement, non-Kandahari Pushtuns and others joined them—for example, the important eastern Jadrani Pushtun commander Jalaluddin Haqqani. Leadership remains in the hands of the Kandahari Pushtuns, however, causing resentment and division within the Taliban ranks.[22] Even if the Taliban could gain control of the entire country, their movement would almost certainly fragment from within as Pushtun identity shifted back to its normal clan and subtribe level.[23] Indeed, the fragmentation of the Taliban appears already to have begun, with the fall 1998–winter 1999 purge of former Khalqi communist members of the Taliban movement. Other signs of the instability of the Taliban movement include the growing number of incidents of lawlessness in which Taliban members are alleged to be involved, the reported split in early 1999 between Osama bin Laden and his Taliban hosts, and the defection of some local Pushtun commanders and their forces back to their earlier leaders throughout 1999 (such as some northern Pushtuns affiliated with Hekmatyar).

Nonetheless, the Taliban are still the most potent military force in Afghanistan as the war settles into its third decade. This is evinced by their sweeping successes in Afghanistan's northern provinces in 1998, their powerful offensive north of Kabul in July–August 1999, and their ability to mount a second grinding attack north of Kabul following their punishing setback at the hands of Massoud's lightning counter-attack in early August 1999, and their almost total victory in northeastern Afghanistan in fall 2000. And if anything, their northern rivals have so far proved to be even more fractious. Indeed, if the recent Taliban victories in the north were due in large measure to active Pakistani involvement and bin Laden's money, it also helped that the northern opposition was torn by dissent and susceptible to bribery. Yet for the Taliban to finish conquering all of Afghanistan, the outside supporters of Massoud and his colleagues would have to cut off their supplies, too, an unlikely prospect so long as Pakistan continues to aid the Taliban. Moreover, both the ethnicity and the ideology of the Taliban make this solution unacceptable to at least half of the countries participating in the "Six Plus Two" framework of negotiations.

Thus we are left with the fourth scenario, which envisions a national coalition government headed by new elites—a "broad-based govern-ment" in the current lexicon of Afghanistan watchers. Throughout the 1990s the prospects for this scenario were always dismal, but recent changes in the geopolitical framework in which Afghanistan exists may have given the scenario life at last. The March 14, 1999, announcement from the Ashkhabad talks of an agreement in principle from both sides to a coalition government composed of both Taliban and non-Taliban leaders appeared promising, even if the Taliban almost immediately backed away from the bargain. Still, the diplomatic progress of early 1999 reflected at least three significant changes in the geopolitical fac-tors affecting Afghanistan. First, increased pressure on Pakistan by the United States, especially after Pakistan's nuclear tests in May 1998 and the US embassy bombings in August 1998, forced some elements within the Pakistani government to push the Taliban away from continued military conflict. Second, Iran's mobilization of troops along the Afghan border in the fall of 1998 led it to reassess its ability and willingness to regionalize the Afghan conflict, and it, too, has sought a diplomatic solution since then. Third, the Afghan actors themselves have grown increasingly aware of the fragility of their coalitions of support—not just the currently weak northern forces but even the Taliban, who have suffered defections, localized resistance to their edicts, and even uprisings. Thus, all the major actors have at the very least significant internal factions that favor a resolution of the conflict.

Nonetheless, a note of caution is warranted. All the actors, especially the Taliban, also have significant factions that remain committed to a military solution, and after many failed agreements and conferences during the past twenty years, no one has much confidence that a negotiated settlement will last.[24] After all, until the Ashkhabad negotiations in early 1999, the UN effort had produced nothing and was taken seriously by few Afghan leaders. Of course, subsequent events in 1999 demonstrated that the Ashkhabad negotiations were themselves meaningless. Hard-line elements within the Taliban still insisted on implementing their interpretation of Islam throughout the country, while the northern minorities insisted on local autonomy. With both conditions apparently non-negotiable, it was difficult to see on what foundation a broad-based government might be established.

In the long run, however, a broad-based government that includes all the major groups and actors, adequately represented and with sufficient guarantees of local autonomy, is probably the only solution to Afghanistan's crisis. It was clear to me in the summer of 1997, as I talked to people from all walks of life throughout Afghanistan, that two changes would have to take place for any progress to be made. First and foremost, the US would have to take a leading, active, and determined role in securing a settlement in Afghanistan. Second, and thought by most people to be possible only if the first change were to occur, neighboring countries would have to agree to a "negative symmetry" arrangement in supplying arms to their respective Afghan clients. That is, all outside patrons would agree to cut off supplies of weapons and war materiel to their clients, leaving them at existing levels, with no effort to adjust for perceived imbalances (which would be positive symmetry, the arrangement provided for in UN Security Council Resolution 1333). With military capability frozen, continued warfare might cease to be an attractive option to the combatants. Only then, local observers felt, might the intransigence of both sides be softened enough, as their material capability to harm each other declined, for real negotiations about Afghanistan's future to begin.

On the eve of the fighting season of 1999, it appeared that the key political actors had finally considered these two critical changes seriously. The United States appeared to have reengaged itself in Afghanistan, especially through visits by leading State Department officials to Pakistan in late 1998.[25] The Ashkhabad negotiations had the full backing of the United States, as did the subsequent Tashkent meeting. The initial progress made in both sets of negotiations, along with growing international pressure for cutting off arms supplies to the Afghan factions, seemed to be another promising development. The Taliban offensive in the late summer of 1999, however (with blatant Pakistani support), the subsequent military coup in Pakistan, and the continued support of other countries for Massoud's forces all proved that optimism to be premature. The moribund diplomatic efforts of 2000, followed by the Taliban victory in Takhar during the fall of the year, further suggested that the Taliban leadership and their Pakistani patrons were still committed to a military solution. Moreover, Afghanistan's protracted war remains a back-burner issue for most Western powers, meaning that the new century will likely bring continued fighting and fragmentation.

Unless a meaningful and lasting peace can be crafted for Afghanistan in the near future, its continued fragmentation in an age of reawakening ethnic nationalism and religious fundamentalism may prove a dangerous mixture for peace and stability in this region. Afghanistan has long been the linchpin of Asia, connecting the cultures and peoples of Central, South, and Southwest Asia. Failure to put Afghanistan back together again may delay development in these regions for years to come and will certainly mean decades of continued neglect for Afghanistan. It is difficult for the actors currently involved, however, to see beyond their immediate, narrow self-interests, and so this interminable conflict drags on. It appears that a "new Great Game" has been born.[26]

AFGHANISTAN: LESSONS FROM A FAILED STATE

Drawing to a close, it is perhaps worthwhile to consider Afghanistan in a broader context. Does it, as a weak state in a region undergoing dramatic post–Cold War change, provide any lessons for policymakers and others interested in the future of the state? In the first chapter, I identified certain characteristics of weak states and hypothesized that weak states are more prone to state failure than strong states. In much of the rest of this book I have argued that Afghanistan possesses all of the characteristics of weak states and that the impact of protracted, high-intensity war has activated those characteristics to destroy the Afghan state. What does state failure mean for the future of states infected by it, and what does it mean for their neighbors? Weak states are more likely to face political fragmentation, and in turn their fragmentation may prove destabilizing to their neighbors, to the extent that the neighbors are also weak states or to the extent that conditions allow internal instability in the weak state to spill over into neighboring countries.

The Afghan case suggests that certain characteristics of weak states are especially important in explaining their propensity for various state failure dysfunctions, including political disintegration, fragmentation, and collapse, or government failure even as the state and society continue to exist and even appear to function (as, for example, in Kenya and Nigeria at present). After all, not all weak states fall apart. These characteristics can be divided into four broad variables: state strength, population stability, socioeconomic well-being, and geostrategic position. These variables may have different dimensions, or subvariables. Each of the variables, along with its subvariables and its hypothesized relationship with state failure, is summarized in Table 6.1.

Numerous countries today appear to be candidates for state failure,[27] and the Soviet Union, Yugoslavia, Czechoslovakia, and Ethiopia have all recently experienced actual political disintegration. Other countries have suffered internal political fragmentation or government collapse. Afghanistan is a very strong candidate for state failure, as we have seen.[28] Prior to concluding this analysis of Afghanistan's problems with state failure, however, two additional points should be made.

First, state failure is not only a political phenomenon, a mere exercise in changing borders on maps. Subtler and harder-to-measure forms of social, cultural, and economic failure and dysfunction can occur within or aside from the existing political framework. Indeed, it is possible that a country might have an apparently strong and stable government and yet still be a good candidate for state failure, if these other forms of failure were more influential. This is an important area worthy of further inquiry, not least because such social, cultural, and economic pathologies may presage full-blown state failure. State collapse, as described by Robert Kaplan and by William Zartman,[29] occurs when governments fail to address significant social and economic problems, and it is especially prevalent among weak developing states.

TABLE 6.1 Variables Correlated with State Failure

Variable	Subvariables	Hypothesized Relationship with State Failure
Strength of the state	(1) Political institutionalization: establishment of stable and mature political institutions (2) Political penetration: acceptance of government throughout country	The stronger the state, the less likely state failure.
Stability of the population	(1) Population homogeneity: ethnic, linguistic, and religious divisions (2) Population mobility: fluidity of population changes	The more stable the population, the less likely state failure.
Economic well-being of society	(1) Economic and social development: general standard of living (2) Resource problems: presence/absence of key economic or natural resources	The stronger the economy, the less likely state failure.
Geostrategic position of the state	(1) Involvement of outside actors: interference of neighbors or big powers (2) Location: geostrategic value of country to major powers	The greater the state's geostrategic value, the less likely state failure.

Second, there is the question of significance. Outside of Afghanistan and the surrounding region, who cares whether Afghanistan falls apart? Why, from the point of view of the major powers, is the political failure of a marginal developing state a threat to regional security or world order? Should this phenomenon, even if the threat is fully realized, alter the existing national security doctrines or policies of great powers such as the United States? The answer to the last question is yes. Third World state failure is a threat to security—perhaps the most important security issue facing the world early in the twenty-first century. This is because the Hobbesian man is reemerging, and he is fighting with others over a range of issues and on a variety of battlefields that are untraditional.[30] What happens when drug lords get tactical nuclear weapons? When crime organizations take over local governments? When terrorists strike anywhere, everywhere, against anyone, confident that a major force of integration (the international media, such as CNN) will cover it? While wars between major powers with large conventional forces are becoming less common, new security threats are emerging. If liberal democracy is indeed the ideology and form of government of Fukuyama's Last Man,[31] and if pacific relationships among democracies are the norm,[32] then the transitional countries of the former Second and Third Worlds will provide the security threats of the next century.[33] With the proliferation of high-technology weapons (including weapons of mass destruction) throughout the world and the growing gulf between the "have" and "have-not" states,[34] the political failure of the less-developed countries will produce the next serious threats to the interests and security of the developed countries.

Today, an important distinction is also to be made between First World (developed) and Third World (developing) states—the former are more influenced at the moment by integration, the latter by fragmentation. Former Second World (communist) countries and newly industrializing countries are pulled by both forces. It is not just a question of whether governments hold onto their territory, but whether governments increasingly become meaningless or at least less meaningful actors within their society, and which factors (integration or fragmentation) constrain their sovereignty.[35]

Thus, states that are candidates for failure are found primarily in the Second and Third Worlds—including much of Africa, Asia, and Eastern Europe. The phenomenon has been most obvious so far in the former Soviet Union (now divided into fifteen independent states and counting), the former Yugoslavia (five states and counting), the former

Czechoslovakia (two states), and the former Ethiopia (two states). It is also appearing in virulent form in Afghanistan, India, Pakistan, Somalia, Sri Lanka, Sudan, and throughout sub-Saharan Africa.

The current situation in Afghanistan provides an excellent empirical case study of a weak state facing serious state failure, perhaps even national disintegration, in the post–Cold War era. It does so in part because the country's political fragmentation fits the variables thought to explain the failure of weak states quite well. Afghanistan's political status today can be considered in terms of the four variables thought to impact upon state failure: state strength, population stability, economic well-being, and geostrategic position.

First, I hypothesize that the stronger the state, the less likely is its probability of state failure. The variable of state strength can be divided into two subvariables: political institutionalization and political penetration. In Afghanistan's case, political institutions have always been tenuous, and their control over a rugged and inhospitable countryside has always been questionable. The Afghan War destroyed Afghanistan's civil society and disrupted its traditional mechanisms for local policy-making. It attempted to replace the national elite and political institutions with others alien and unacceptable to the Afghan people. For the last twenty years, Afghanistan has had little political institutionalization or political penetration, as might be expected in a country undergoing national civil war. But throughout its modern history, Afghanistan's political development has always been weak.[36] The current civil war, reassertion of local loyalties to the qawm, and de facto division of the country are all compelling evidence for the weakness of the state in Afghanistan.[37] As of early 2001, the Taliban controlled 90 to 97 percent of the country, but their government was recognized by only three other countries (Pakistan, Saudi Arabia, and the United Arab Emirates), two of which (Pakistan and Saudi Arabia) recently downgraded diplomatic relations under Western pressure. Massoud's Tajik fighters still operate in the northeast, as do smaller units of Hazaras, Uzbeks, Turkmen, and northern Pushtuns in some northern and central districts. Much of Afghanistan exists with little connection to any central or regional government, and de facto local autonomy is the norm—the qawm triumphant.

Second, I hypothesize that population stability is correlated with lower likelihood of state failure. Population stability consists of high population homogeneity and low population mobility. Afghanistan has had just the opposite, especially during the past two decades. It has deep and enduring ethnic-linguistic-religious cleavages, and its major ethnic groups overlap into bordering states, prompting the meddling of neighbors and the possibility of irredentism. Afghanistan's population has also been among the most mobile in the world, with approximately 50 percent displacement (refugees and internally displaced persons) by the early 1990s, high mortality, and rapid population growth.

Third, I hypothesize that the stronger the economy, the less likely is state failure. This variable also has two dimensions: economic-social development and resource problems. Afghanistan was always one of the poorest countries in the world, but during the last two decades of war it has been ravaged and further impoverished. It is one of the bottom ten countries in every major indicator of social and economic development. It has never had an abundance of natural resources of consequence, except for the natural gas fields of Shiberghan in the north-central part of the country, which were tapped heavily by the Soviets during the 1980s. Afghanistan has no significant natural resources or technical expertise today with which to develop, except for its burgeoning production of opium and heroin for the illicit European and Pakistani market. Moreover, armed groups who have contributed to the breakdown of central governmental authority control this narcotics production and traffic.

Finally, I hypothesize that the greater the geostrategic value of a state, the less its likelihood of state failure. This is because of the involvement of outside actors and the location of the state. Afghanistan has been the recipient of significant attention from the outside world, but this attention exacerbates existing cleavages and provokes further fragmentation of the country. Afghanistan's very existence is a product of its days as an imperial buffer state, a role that was reprised when it became the last great Cold War battlefield in the 1980s. In the wake of the Cold War, Afghanistan's location has become significant again as the hub of Central Asia, the state through which economic traffic must eventually flow if the region is to become economically integrated. Having a stable Afghanistan is good for business, but although this goal is important to regional powers, it has so far failed to arouse the United States or Russia to significant efforts to prevent Afghanistan's failure as a state or to help it reintegrate.

What will be the future of Afghanistan? The Afghan experience since 1978 demonstrates that war and political violence can be extremely harmful to national development, even leading to the disintegration of the state. More than two centuries of slow and painful progress toward the development of a viable Afghan state that was an important part of Afghan society were destroyed in just a few years of intense conflict. It is unclear how this damage will be repaired. Afghanistan has been shattered, and so far there has been no element in Afghan society or the post–Cold War world order with sufficient interest, power, and political will to put it back together again.

Afghanistan in 2001 provides us with a good example of a weak state that has suffered from state failure in the post–Cold War era. Sadly for Afghanistan, the underlying foundation for the failure of its political institutions and for its national fragmentation consists of seemingly intractable problems, meaning that it may be well into the twenty-first century before a strong and stable government is again in place in Kabul, and even longer before significant reconstruction can return Afghanistan to twentieth-century levels of development. Sadly for people throughout the developing world, there are more weak states like Afghanistan out there, potential candidates for state failure, with all the suffering and misery that usually accompany that process. If these states fail, then the new millennium may begin with a wave of state destruction, reconfiguration, and transformation. The cartographers will be busy for years to come.

Appendix
Major Actors in Modern Afghan History

The following are brief sketches of some of the major organizations and persons of importance in Afghanistan during the last twenty-five years of the twentieth century.

ORGANIZATIONS

Harakat-i Inqilab-i Islami (Movement of the Islamic Revolution). One of the seven major mujahideen parties based in Peshawar during the 1980s, this was one of three "moderate" parties and was headed by Maulavi Mohammad Nabi Mohammadi. It acquired a large following in the early 1980s, especially in the south and among madrasah teachers and students. Many of the Taliban leaders had affiliations with this party.

Harakat-i Islami (Islamic Movement). Sheikh Asif Mohseni led this Shia group during the 1980s. It received support from both the Hazara and the Qizilibash populations.

Hezb-i-Islami (Islamic Party, Hekmatyar faction). One of the seven major mujahideen parties based in Peshawar during the 1980s, this was one of four "fundamentalist" parties and was headed by Engineer Gulbuddin Hekmatyar. It received support from the Ghilzai and smaller Pushtun tribes and enjoyed the lion's share of support from the

Pakistani government until Pakistan switched its support to the Taliban in 1994. Hekmatyar's Hezb-i-Islami was driven from the battlefield by the Taliban in 1995 and 1996, although some Hekmatyar commanders fight on in northern Afghanistan, reportedly opportunistically switching sides for money.

Hezb-i-Islami (Islamic Party, Khalis faction). One of the seven major mujahideen parties based in Peshawar during the 1980s, this was one of four "fundamentalist" parties and was headed by Maulavi Yunus Khalis. It was smaller, more localized, and more moderate than the Hekmatyar faction. Its support came primarily from eastern Afghanistan. Some of its commanders fight with the Taliban now.

Hezb-i-Wahdat (Unity Party). The major Shia resistance parties were pushed into creating this umbrella organization by Iran in 1989. During the subsequent decade, Wahdat became a major player in Afghanistan's internal power struggle, operating from its home base in the Hazarajat. Hezb-i-Wahdat splintered in 1998 after the Taliban victories in Mazar-i-Sharif and Bamiyan.

Ittehad-i Islami Bara-yi Azadi Afghanistan (Islamic Union for the Freedom of Afghanistan). One of the seven major mujahideen parties based in Peshawar during the 1980s, this was one of four "fundamentalist" parties. It was headed by Abdur Rasoul Sayyaf and drew heavily on Saudi sources of funding. After the fall of the Najibullah government, Ittehad fought aqainst the Shia Hezb-i-Wahdat but joined the Northern Alliance against the Taliban following their takeover of Kabul in 1996.

Jamiat-i-Islami (Islamic Society). One of the seven major mujahideen parties based in Peshawar during the 1980s, this was one of four "fundamentalist" parties and was headed by Professor Burhanuddin Rabbani. Unlike the other Peshawar resistance parties, Jamiat was composed primarily of northern minorities and had the war's most famous commanders in Ahmed Shah Massoud of the Panjshir Valley and Ismail Khan of Herat. Rabbani became acting president in the summer of 1992, following the fall of Najibullah and the short stint in office of Sibghatullah Mojaddidi, and thereafter he refused to give up the position. Jamiat fought against other mujahideen groups over control of Kabul from 1992 until 1995. Since being driven into northeastern

Afghanistan in 1996, it has fought under various umbrella labels (Northern Alliance, United Front) against the Taliban.

Jebha-i-Milli Nejat (National Liberation Front, or NLF). One of the seven major mujahideen parties based in Peshawar during the 1980s, this was one of three "moderate" parties and was headed by Professor Sibghatullah Mojaddidi. He drew on his traditional family and Naqshbandiyya Sufi linkages to create this rather small party. It plays no combat role in Afghanistan today.

Mahaz-i-Milli Islami-yi Afghanistan (National Islamic Front of Afghanistan, or NIFA). One of the seven major mujahideen parties based in Peshawar during the 1980s, this was one of three "moderate" parties and was headed by Pir Sayed Ahmed Gailani. He drew on his traditional family and Qadiriyya Sufi linkages to create this rather small party. It plays no combat role in Afghanistan today.

People's Democratic Party of Afghanistan (PDPA). This was Afghanistan's communist party, formed in 1965. Divided into two bitterly opposed factions, Khalq (Masses) and Parcham (Banner), it ruled Afghanistan from 1978 to 1992, the last two years after changing its name to Hezb-i Watan. Led by Nur Mohammad Taraki and Hafizullah Amin, Khalq ruled in 1978–1979. After the Soviet invasion, Babrak Karmal took over until 1986, followed by his fellow Parchami Najibullah until 1992.

Sazman-i Nasr-i Islam-yi Afghanistan (Islamic Victory Organization of Afghanistan). A Khomeinist Hazara group.

Shura-i-Inqilab-i Ittefaq-i Islami Afghanistan (Revolutionary Council of the Islamic Union of Afghanistan). Headed by the Hazara religious leader Sheikh Sayed Ali Beheshti, this organization controlled the Hazarajat from 1979 to 1982.

Taliban (religious students). This Islamist movement of former mujahideen, madrasah teachers, and religious students appeared in southwestern Afghanistan in 1994 and by 2001 controlled 90 to 97 percent of Afghanistan. It is headed by the reclusive Mullah Omar Akhund.

Hezb-i Watan (Homeland). Name for the PDPA from 1990 to 1992.

INDIVIDUALS

Amin, Hafizullah (1929–1979). Khalqi communist president of Afghanistan in late 1979, he was assassinated by Soviet special forces during the 1979 Soviet Christmas invasion. Amin was a Kharruti Ghilzai from Paghman.

Daoud, Mohammad (1909–1973). President of Afghanistan (1973–1978) after overthrowing his cousin, King Zahir Shah. Previously prime minister (1953–1963). Daoud and his family were all killed during the Saur Revolution.

Dostam, Abdul Rashid. Head of the northern Uzbek militia and a semi-autonomous warlord during 1992–1997. Dostam is a Jowzjani Uzbek general whose militia served the PDPA until its defection in early 1992 caused the PDPA government to fall.

Gailani, Pir Sayed Ahmed. Head of the Qadiriyya Sufi order and of NIFA, married to a daughter of King Habibullah.

Hekmatyar, Gulbuddin. Head of a faction of Hezb-i Islami and an active leader in Islamist politics since his school days in the late 1960s and early 1970s. Hekmatyar is a Kharruti Ghilzai.

Karmal, Babrak (1929–1998). Parchami communist president of Afghanistan (1979–1986). Karmal's ethnic background was unclear, but probably he was Ghilzai Pushtun.

Khalis, Maulavi Yunus. Head of a smaller faction of Hezb-i Islami that had strong support during the 1980s and early 1990s in eastern Afghanistan.

Massoud, Ahmed Shah. Nicknamed "Lion of the Panjshir," this legendary commander fought with Jamiat during the 1980s and was Rabbani's defense minister. He is now the military head of the Northern Alliance of forces that provides the Taliban with their stiffest remaining opposition. Massoud is a Tajik from the Panjshir Valley.

Mohammadi, Maulavi Mohammad Nabi. Head of Harakat-i Inqilab-i Islami during the 1980s, Mohammadi is a Pushtun from Logar who now supports the Taliban. He was a member of parliament in the 1960s.

Mojaddidi, Sibghatullah. Head of the Naqshbandiyya Sufi order and the NLF; formerly a professor of theology who was educated at Al-Azhar University in Egypt. He is a Pushtun who has often been a compromise choice as leader of the squabbling mujahideen governments. He was the first post-Najibullah president for two months in 1992.

Najibullah (1947–1996). An Ahmadzai Ghilzai, Najibullah was president of Afghanistan from 1986 to 1992. Prior to that, he headed the dreaded state intelligence agency, KhAD, from 1980 to 1986. Following the mujahideen takeover in 1992, Najibullah took refuge in the United Nations compound in Kabul, where he stayed until the Taliban took over Kabul in 1996. Their first action was to take him from the compound and execute him for "crimes against the Afghan people."

Omar Akhund, Mullah. Considered by his followers to be Amir ul-Moemineen (Commander of the Faithful), Omar is the reclusive head of the Taliban. A commander with Nabi Mohammadi's Harakat during the 1980s, Omar is a Hotaki Ghilzai Pushtun from the Kandahar area.

Rabbani, Burhanuddin. Head of the Jamiat organization during the 1980s jihad, Rabbani became president of Afghanistan in 1992 and refused to give up the job. He was ousted in 1996 when the Taliban gained control of Kabul, but he is still recognized as the head of state by many countries. He is a Tajik from Badakhshan who was educated at Al Azhar University in Egypt and became a professor of theology at Kabul University before the war.

Sayyaf, Abdur Rasoul. A Kharruti Pushtun like both Hekmatyar and Hafizullah Amin, Sayyaf heads the Ittehad-i Islami. He had strong ties to the Arab supporters of the mujahideen during the 1980s and early 1990s, but very few Afghan mujahideen or commanders affiliated with him.

Taraki, Nur Mohammad (1917–1979). An early leader of the PDPA, Taraki became president of Afghanistan following the Saur Revolution in 1978. His former student Hafizullah Amin, however, had him purged and executed in 1979.

Zahir Shah. King of Afghanistan from 1933 to 1973, he was overthrown in a bloodless coup by his cousin Mohammad Daoud while traveling abroad. Since 1973 he has lived in Italy.

Notes

PREFACE

1. See, for example Olivier Roy, "The New Political Elite of Afghanistan," in Myron Weiner and Ali Banuazizi, eds., *The Politics of Social Transformation in Afghanistan, Iran, and Pakistan* (Syracuse, NY: Syracuse University Press, 1994), 72–100; and Olivier Roy, "Has Islamism a Future in Afghanistan?" in William Maley, ed., *Fundamentalism Reborn? Afghanistan and the Taliban* (Washington Square, NY: New York University Press, 1998), 199–211.

2. Three recent works that adopt this perspective are Asta Olesen, *Islam and Politics in Afghanistan* (Surrey, UK: Curzon Press, 1995); Bernt Glatzer, "Is Afghanistan on the Brink of Ethnic and Tribal Disintegration?" in Maley, *Fundamentalism*, 167–181; and Ralph H. Magnus and Eden Naby, *Afghanistan: Mullah, Marx, and Mujahid* (Boulder, CO: Westview, 1998).

3. M. Nazif Shahrani, "The Future of the State and the Structure of Community Governance in Afghanistan," in Maley, *Fundamentalism*, 212–242.

4. Good examples of his work from this perspective include Barnett R. Rubin, "Political Elites in Afghanistan: Rentier State Building, Rentier State Wrecking," *International Journal of Middle East Studies* 24, no. 1, February 1992, 77–99; Rubin, *The Fragmentation of Afghanistan* (New Haven, CT: Yale University Press, 1995); and Rubin, "The Political Economy of War and Peace in Afghanistan," Online Center for Afghan Studies, www.afghan-politics.org, 21 June 1999.

5. Rentier states are those that rely heavily on rents for their revenues, rather than on a mixture of rents and taxes or on taxes alone. Economic rent is the difference between the market price of a good or resource and the opportunity cost of its production. For example, oil may cost $2.00 per barrel

to produce and sell for $20.00 per barrel; the difference between the figures is rent. See Hazem Beblawi and Giancomo Luciani, eds., *The Rentier State* (New York: Croom Helm, 1987).

6. See Roy, "New Political Elite," 72–100. Also see Olivier Roy, *Afghanistan: From Holy War to Civil War* (Princeton, NJ: Darwin Press, 1995).

7. Barnett R. Rubin, "Redistribution and the State in Afghanistan: The Red Revolution Turns Green," in Weiner and Banuazizi, *Politics of Social Transformation*, 187–227. See also Rubin, "Political Elites," 77–99; Rubin, *Fragmentation of Afghanistan*; Rubin, "Political Economy."

8. Rubin, "Redistribution," 202.

9. See among others, Richard S. Newell and Nancy Peabody Newell, *The Struggle for Afghanistan* (Ithaca, NY: Cornell University Press, 1981); Anthony Hyman, *Afghanistan under Soviet Domination, 1964–1983* (London: Macmillan, 1984); M. Nazif Shahrani and Robert L. Canfield, eds., *Revolutions and Rebellions in Afghanistan* (Berkeley: University of California, Institute of International Studies, 1984); Henry S. Bradsher, *Afghanistan and the Soviet Union* (Durham, NC: Duke University Press, 1985); Edward Girardet, *Afghanistan: The Soviet War* (New York: St. Martin's, 1985); J. Bruce Amstutz, *Afghanistan: The First Five Years of Soviet Occupation* (Washington, DC: National Defense University, 1986); Rosanne Klass, ed., *Afghanistan: The Great Game Revisited* (New York: Freedom House, 1987); Milan Hauner and Robert L. Canfield, eds., *Afghanistan and the Soviet Union: Collision and Transformation* (Boulder, CO: Westview Press, 1989); George Arney, *Afghanistan* (London: Mandarin, 1990); Mark Urban, *War in Afghanistan*, 2d ed. (New York: St. Martin's, 1991); Mohammad Yousaf and Mark Atkin, *The Bear Trap* (Lahore, Pakistan: Jang Publishers, 1992); and Mark Galeotti, *Afghanistan: The Soviet Union's Last War* (London: Frank Cass, 1995).

10. The Afghan War inspired quite a few contributions to the genre of "combat reportage," perhaps because of the danger and rigors imposed by the location and nature of the conflict. Some representative samples of this work include Sandy Gall, *Behind Russian Lines* (London: Sidgwick and Jackson, 1983); Gall, *Afghanistan: Agony of a Nation* (London: Bodley Head, 1988); Nigel Ryan, *A Hitch or Two in Afghanistan: A Journey behind Russian Lines* (London: Weidenfeld and Nicolson, 1983); Mike Martin, *Afghanistan: Inside a Rebel Stronghold* (Poole, Dorset, UK: Blandford Press, 1984); Geoffrey Moorhouse, *To the Frontier* (New York: Holt, Rinehart and Winston, 1984); Richard Reeves, *Passage to Peshawar* (New York: Simon and Schuster, 1984); Peregrine Hodson, *Under a Sickle Moon: A Journey through Afghanistan* (London: Hutchinson, 1986); Arthur Bonner, *Among the Afghans* (Durham, NC: Duke University Press, 1987); Jan Goodwin, *Caught in the Crossfire* (New York: E. P. Dutton, 1987); Doris Lessing, *The Wind Blows Away Our Words* (London: Pan Books,

1987); P. J. O'Rourke, "Bizarre Bazaar," *Rolling Stone*, 20 April 1989, 87–92, 109; and Robert D. Kaplan, *Soldiers of God* (Boston: Houghton Mifflin, 1990).

11. Grant M. Farr and John G. Merriam, eds., *Afghan Resistance: The Politics of Survival* (Boulder, CO: Westview, 1987); Amin Saikal and William Maley, eds., *The Soviet Withdrawal from Afghanistan* (Cambridge: Cambridge University Press, 1989); Riaz M. Khan, *Untying the Afghan Knot* (Durham, NC: Duke University Press, 1991); Diego Cordovez and Selig S. Harrison, *Out of Afghanistan: The Inside Story of the Soviet Withdrawal* (New York: Oxford University Press, 1995); Barnett R. Rubin, *The Search for Peace in Afghanistan* (New Haven, CT: Yale University Press, 1995); William Maley, "The UN in Afghanistan: 'Doing Its Best' or 'Failure of a Mission'?" in Maley, *Fundamentalism*, 182–198.

12. Rasul Baksh Rais, *War without Winners* (Karachi: Oxford University Press, 1994); Maley, *Fundamentalism;* Peter Marsden, *The Taliban: War, Religion, and the New Order in Afghanistan* (London: Zed, 1998); Ahmed Rashid, *Taliban: Militant Islam, Oil, and Fundamentalism in Central Asia* (New Haven: Yale University Press, 2000).

13. Magnus and Naby, *Afghanistan.*

CHAPTER 1. AFGHANISTAN IN THE POST–COLD WAR WORLD

1. John F. Burns, "Afghans: Now They Blame America," *New York Times Magazine*, 4 February 1990, 27; Larry P. Goodson, "Afghanistan," *Collier's Encyclopedia* (Moscow: Open Society Institute, 1999, in Russian).

2. United States Committee for Refugees, *World Refugee Survey* (New York: American Council for Nationalities Service, 1992), 32.

3. Robert D. Kaplan, "Afghanistan: Postmortem," *Atlantic Monthly*, April 1989, 26.

4. S. B. Majrooh and S. M. Y. Elmi, *The Sovietization of Afghanistan* (Peshawar, Pakistan: Frontier Limited, 1986); United Nations Co-Ordinator for Humanitarian and Economic Assistance Programs Relating to Afghanistan (UNCHEAP), *First Consolidated Report*, Geneva, September 1988, chs. 8–10.

5. David Wilkinson, "Unipolarity without Hegemony," *International Studies Review* 1, no. 2, Summer 1999, 141–172.

6. Tonya Langford, "Things Fall Apart: State Failure and the Politics of Intervention," *International Studies Review* 1, no. 1, Spring 1999, 59–79.

7. Thomas L. Friedman, *The Lexus and the Olive Tree* (New York: Farrar Strauss Giroux, 1999); Benjamin R. Barber, *Jihad v. McWorld* (New York: Times Books, 1995).

8. See Joel S. Migdal, *Strong Societies and Weak States* (Princeton, NJ: Princeton University Press, 1988), chapter 1.

9. There were exceptions, of course, such as the splitting of Pakistan and Bangladesh in 1971, but the overwhelming number of former colonies achieved independence and found themselves locked into their spatial and political positions within an international system that was already in place.

10. Samuel P. Huntington has advanced the controversial thesis that civilizations will be the source of post–Cold War conflict and that countries like Afghanistan that straddle civilizational "fault lines" will be at the center of much warfare in the near future. See Huntington, *The Clash of Civilizations and the Remaking of World Order* (New York: Simon and Schuster, 1996).

11. For a classic treatment of this subject, see Gabriel A. Almond and James S. Coleman, eds., *The Politics of the Developing Areas* (Princeton, NJ: Princeton University Press, 1960).

12. Robert E. Gamer, *The Developing Nations: A Comparative Perspective*, 2d ed. (Dubuque, IA: Wm. C. Brown, 1988).

13. John Spanier, *American Foreign Policy since World War II*, 12th ed. (Washington, DC: Congressional Quarterly, 1991), esp. chapter 10; Bruce D. Porter, *The USSR in Third World Conflicts* (Cambridge: Cambridge University Press, 1984).

14. Monte Palmer, *Dilemmas of Political Development*, 4th ed. (Itasca, IL: F. E. Peacock, 1989); Michael P. Todaro, *Economic Development in the Third World*, 4th ed. (London: Longman, 1993).

15. Charles Tilly, *Coercion, Capital, and European States*, AD *990–1990* (Cambridge, MA: Blackwell, 1990).

16. Robert D. Kaplan, "The Coming Anarchy," *Atlantic Monthly*, February 1994, 63.

17. Migdal, *Strong Societies*, 4.

18. Magnus and Naby, *Afghanistan*.

19. Olivier Roy, *Islam and Resistance in Afghanistan*, 1st ed. (Cambridge: Cambridge University Press, 1986).

20. Andre Singer, *Guardians of the North-West Frontier* (Amsterdam: Time-Life Books, 1982), 15.

21. W. B. Fisher, "Afghanistan: Physical and Social Geography," *Middle East and North Africa Yearbook 1990* (London: Europa Publications, 1990); Syed Abdul Quddus, *The Pathans* (Lahore, Pakistan: Ferozsons, 1987), 78–79; Louis Dupree, *Afghanistan* (Princeton, NJ: Princeton University Press, 1973); Olaf Caroe, *The Pathans* (Karachi: Oxford University Press, 1958);

22. Dupree, *Afghanistan*, 126; Quddus, *Pathans*, 67–76; Singer, *Guardians*, 46–59.

23. Quddus, *Pathans*, 101.

24. *Ibid.*, 103–104; Dupree, *Afghanistan*, 278.

25. Quddus, *Pathans*, 101–106; Dupree, *Afghanistan;* Caroe, *Pathans*. Afghan specialists emphasize this unique form of self-government. The jirga system is touted as the method by which the fractious contenders for power in Afghanistan today can achieve a common program for Afghanistan's future, and it is still the mechanism by which local decision-making occurs. An incident that occurred near my house on the outskirts of Peshawar in January 1987 illustrates its continued vitality. A jirga of elders had settled a case in Pakistan's Khyber Agency concerning the construction of a road. When they went to deliver the verdict to the person affected, he opened fire, killing five tribal elders. The sense of outrage thereafter was intense, not only because of the crime but also because it symbolically represented the rejection of the tribal will. The killer became an outlaw in the truest sense of the word, having rejected both the government and his tribe.

26. Richard F. Nyrop and Donald M. Seekins, eds., *Afghanistan: A Country Study* (Washington, DC: Foreign Area Studies, American University, 1986); Dupree, *Afghanistan;* Robert L. Canfield, "Ethnic, Regional, and Sectarian Alignments in Afghanistan," in Ali Banuazizi and Myron Weiner, eds., *The State, Religion, and Ethnic Politics: Afghanistan, Iran, and Pakistan* (Syracuse, NY: Syracuse University Press, 1986), 75–103; Hassan Poladi, *The Hazaras* (Stockton, CA: Moghul Press, 1989).

27. Dupree, *Afghanistan*, 57.

28. Olesen, *Islam and Politics;* Roy, *Islam and Resistance*, 1986; Ashraf Ghani, "Islam and State-Building in a Tribal Society: Afghanistan, 1880–1901," *Modern Asian Studies* 12, no. 2, 1978, 269–284.

29. Dupree, *Afghanistan*, especially chapter 8.

30. Olesen, *Islam and Politics*, 44–48.

31. *Ibid.*, 1995.

32. Dupree, *Afghanistan;* Roy, *Islam and Resistance*, 1986. Olesen, *Islam and Politics*, especially chapter 2, argues, to the contrary, that Islam has been the most important force in Afghanistan for centuries, especially through providing the only accepted basis for education until the twentieth century.

33. Dupree, *Afghanistan*, 104.

34. Quddus, *Pathans*, 91.

35. Magnus and Naby, *Afghanistan*.

36. Roy, "Has Islamism a Future?" 202.

37. Dupree, *Afghanistan*, 183–192; Roy, *Islam and Resistance in Afghanistan*, 2d ed. (Cambridge: Cambridge University Press, 1990), 242; Quddus, *Pathans*.

38. Quddus, *Pathans*, 101.

39. Shahrani and Canfield, *Revolutions and Rebellions;* Hafizullah Emadi,

"The State and Rural-Based Rebellion in Afghanistan," *Central Asian Survey* 15, no. 2, 1996, 201–211.

40. Roy, *Islam and Resistance*, 1990, 19.

41. Barnett R. Rubin, "Afghanistan: Back to Feudalism," *Current History* 88, no. 542, December 1989, 421–424, 444–446; Roy, *Islam and Resistance*, 1990, 23.

42. Jolanta Sierakowska-Dyndo, "The State in Afghanistan's Political and Economic System on the Eve of the April 1978 Coup," *Central Asian Survey* 9, no. 4, 1990, 85–86.

43. Roy, *Islam and Resistance*, 1986.

44. Fisher, "Afghanistan: Physical and Social Geography," 269.

45. Vartan Gregorian, *The Emergence of Modern Afghanistan* (Stanford, CA: Stanford University Press, 1969); Hasan Kawun Kakar, *Government and Society in Afghanistan* (Austin: University of Texas Press, 1979).

46. Olivier Roy used the term "Talibanization" at the annual meeting of the Middle East Studies Association in Chicago, Illinois, in December 1998. See also Larry P. Goodson, "Foreign Policy Gone Awry: The Kalashnikovization and Talibanization of Pakistan," in Craig Baxter and Charles H. Kennedy, eds. *Pakistan 2000* (New York: Lexington Books, 2000); and Ahmed Rashid, "The Taliban: Exporting Extremism," *Foreign Affairs* 78, no. 6, November–December 1999, 22–35.

CHAPTER 2. HISTORICAL FACTORS SHAPING MODERN AFGHANISTAN

1. Ludwig Adamec, *Afghanistan, 1900–1923* (Berkeley: University of California Press, 1967); Leon B. Poullada, *Reform and Rebellion in Afghanistan, 1919–1929* (Ithaca, NY: Cornell University Press, 1973). Afghanistan is sometimes considered to date to 1749, when Ahmed Shah Durrani achieved the ascendancy of the Durrani (Abdali) tribe over the Ghilzai Pushtun and subsequently extended his empire east to Lahore, south to the Arabian Sea, west into Persia, and north to the Amu Darya River.

2. Dupree, *Afghanistan*, 260.

3. *Ibid.*, 260–268. This evidence appears in the Mundigak IV phase near present-day Kandahar.

4. W. K. Fraser-Tytler, *Afghanistan: A Study of Political Developments in Central and Southern Asia*, 3d ed. (London: Oxford University Press, 1967), 17; Dupree, *Afghanistan*, 1272. Although there is some scholarly debate, it is generally thought that the first references to Afghanistan by its ancient name Aryana appear in the *Avesta*, the scriptures of Zarathustra (Zoroaster).

5. Frank L. Holt, *Alexander the Great and Bactria* (Leiden: E. J. Brill, 1988).

6. Dupree, *Afghanistan;* Caroe, *Pathans;* Quddus, *Pathans.*

7. Holt, *Alexander the Great,* 53.

8. Dupree, *Afghanistan,* 278, cites Arrian's account.

9. Holt, *Alexander the Great,* 77–81; S. Enders Wimbush and Alex Alexiev, "Soviet Central Asian Soldiers in Afghanistan," *Conflict* 4, nos. 2–4, 1983, 325–338; Alexander Alexiev, *Inside the Soviet Army in Afghanistan* (Santa Monica, CA: RAND Corporation, R-3627-A, May 1988).

10. Dupree, *Afghanistan,* 330.

11. Holt, *Alexander the Great,* 70–86; J. L. Lee, *The 'Ancient Supremacy': Bukhara, Afghanistan and the Battle for Balkh, 1731–1901* (Leiden: E. J. Brill, 1996).

12. The interplay of forces is vividly captured in Dupree, *Afghanistan,* chapter 16, which recounts the spread of Islam and the ascendancy of the Durrani Pushtuns in Afghanistan.

13. *Ibid.,* 248–251.

14. Vincent A. Smith, *The Oxford History of India,* 4th ed., ed. Percival Spear (Karachi: Oxford University Press, 1983).

15. Dupree, *Afghanistan,* 322.

16. *Ibid.,* 355.

17. The Great Game was able to occur because of the decline of the Safavid Persian empire and the Ottoman Turkish empire, which left the competition in Central Asia to the expanding British and Russian empires.

18. To even begin to outline the complexities of this situation would fill volumes. Useful sources include Lee, *Ancient Supremacy;* Edward Allworth, ed., *Central Asia: 120 Years of Russian Rule* (Durham, NC: Duke University Press, 1989); Dupree, *Afghanistan;* and Caroe, *Pathans.*

19. Dupree, *Afghanistan,* 321; Lee, *Ancient Supremacy;* Abdur Rahman Khan, *The Life of Abdur Rahman, Amir of Afghanistan,* ed. Mir Munshi Sultan Mahomed Khan, 2 vols. (Karachi: Oxford University Press, 1980; first published in 1900).

20. For a different perspective, see Lee, *Ancient Supremacy.*

21. Caroe, *Pathans.* Also see Evelyn Howell, *Mizh* (Karachi: Oxford University Press, 1979), which is one of the best of many books on the Pushtun tribes by British officers and political agents who served on the North-West Frontier.

22. Quddus, *Pathans,* 27–30.

23. *Ibid.,* 27–28.

24. As described in chapter 1, Afghanistan has been saddled with borders that divide ethnic groups. The Durand Line, for example, which has separated Afghanistan and northwestern India (now Pakistan) since 1893, was designed to divide ethnic groups, especially the Pushtun tribes. See Nyrop and Seekins,

Afghanistan: A Country Study, 37–38. The solution of the ethnic groups divided by the Durand Line has been to ignore it, and they travel between the two countries with impunity.

25. Dupree, *Afghanistan,* 58–64.

26. *Ibid.,* 343.

27. Afghanistan's weak central government persisted throughout the twentieth century. Even the bloody "Iron Amir," Abdur Rahman Khan (ruled 1880–1901), who centralized governmental authority, could not truly control Afghanistan. See Gregorian, *Emergence of Modern Afghanistan;* Kakar, *Government and Society.*

28. Gregorian, *Emergence of Modern Afghanistan,* 132–134; Kakar, *Government and Society,* 123–135. There are still pockets of Ghilzai and other Pushtuns in northern Afghanistan today.

29. The *muwajib* (allowances or payments) system is described in Caroe, *Pathans,* 349–350. In addition to the official documents now maintained in the India Office Library, British National Archives, London, numerous other accounts detailing government-tribal relations exist from the British period in India.

30. Gregorian, *Emergence of Modern Afghanistan.*

31. Galeotti, *Afghanistan: Soviet Union's Last War,* provides a nice summation of the multiple reasons for the Soviet invasion.

32. Dupree, *Afghanistan,* 363.

33. See Fraser-Tytler, *Afghanistan,* 128.

34. Lee, *Ancient Supremacy.*

35. Amstutz, *Afghanistan: The First Five Years,* 4.

36. *Ibid.,* 5.

37. *Ibid.;* Rosanne Klass, "The Great Game Revisited," in Klass, *Afghanistan: The Great Game Revisited,* 1–4; Abdur Rahman Khan, *Life of Abdur Rahman.*

38. Numerous books recount the events of this "signal catastrophe," including accounts by several of the European survivors. See, for example, Vincent Eyre, *Journal of an Afghanistan Prisoner* (London: Routledge and Kegan Paul, 1976; first published London, 1843); Lady Florentia Sale, *A Journal of the Disasters in Affghanistan, 1841–1842* (London: John Murray, 1843); Patrick Macrory, *Signal Catastrophe* (London: Hodder and Stoughton, 1966); J. A. Norris, *The First Afghan War, 1838–1842* (Cambridge: Cambridge University Press, 1967); T. A. Heathcote, *The Afghan Wars* (London: Osprey, 1980); and John H. Waller, *Beyond the Khyber Pass.* (Austin: University of Texas Press, 1990).

39. Dupree, *Afghanistan,* 399.

40. Smith, *Oxford History of India;* W. Habberton, *Anglo-Russian Relations concerning Afghanistan: 1837–1907* (Urbana: University of Illinois Press, 1937); Richard A. Pierce, *Russian Central Asia 1867–1917: A Study in Colonial Rule* (Berkeley: University of California Press, 1960).

41. Dupree, *Afghanistan,* 401–402.

42. *Ibid.,* 405.

43. Gregorian, *Emergence of Modern Afghanistan,* 108–118.

44. Sir Percy Sykes, *History of Afghanistan,* 2 vols. (London: Macmillan, 1940); Dupree, *Afghanistan,* 406–413.

45. Abdur Rahman Khan, *Life of Abdur Rahman;* Kakar, *Government and Society,* 123–135; Gregorian, *Emergence of Modern Afghanistan,* 132–134.

46. Kakar, *Government and Society.*

47. As quoted in Donald N. Wilber, *Afghanistan,* 2d ed. (New Haven, CT: Yale University Press, 1962, 19).

48. Dupree, *Afghanistan,* 419.

49. Abdur Rahman Khan, *Life of Abdur Rahman.*

50. *Ibid.*; Gregorian, *Emergence of Modern Afghanistan,* 158–160; Fraser-Tytler, *Afghanistan,* 189. See Caroe, *Pathans,* for an opposing view.

51. Dupree, *Afghanistan,* 425.

52. Adamec, *Afghanistan,* 183.

53. Dupree, *Afghanistan,* 425.

54. Kakar, *Government and Society,* 108–113, discusses the role of the irregular forces under Abdur Rahman.

55. As autonomous regions for the Pushtun tribes, Pakistan's Federally Administered Tribal Agencies (or Areas) demonstrate the continued viability of this contention. During my period in Peshawar in 1986–1987, even government efforts to close down the heroin factories in the Tribal Agencies failed, despite the use of the army supported by tanks.

56. When British efforts to bribe or cow the tribes into submission or acquiescence failed and violence occurred, retribution followed, as virtually all students of Anglo-Afghan relations have noted. The Soviet Union used similar punitive tactics in its Afghan war.

57. David Isby, *Russia's War in Afghanistan* (London: Osprey Publishing, 1986), 6–8; Urban, *War in Afghanistan,* 1991.

58. From my house in Peshawar, it was possible to hear and see the fighting in the nearby Khyber Tribal Agency during the campaign to clean out the heroin labs in 1986–1987. The subsequent explosive growth of the drug business, both quantitatively and qualitatively, has been an unfortunate by-product of the war in Afghanistan. Judging from observations and confidential interviews

in both Afghanistan and Pakistan over the past twelve years, I do not believe the government of Pakistan or the competing governments in Afghanistan currently possess the political will to close down the drug business.

59. See note 31. Also see Singer, *Guardians,* 16–18.

60. Caroe, *Pathans;* J. W. Spain, *The Way of the Pathans* (London: Robert Hale, 1962).

61. Mike Edwards, "When the Moguls Ruled," *National Geographic* 167, no. 4, April 1985, 462–493.

62. Virtually any weapon can be bought in Darra Adam Khel, or in similar villages, in the Tribal Areas today. In one of my trips to Darra in 1987, I purchased a British Lee Enfield bayonet dating from 1917, which was confiscated by Pakistani authorities at the Peshawar airport as I left Pakistan. See Singer's description of Darra in *Guardians,* 60–71.

63. My observations of mujahideen training in Pakistan in 1987 confirmed their reputation for accuracy and expertise with weapons. Introduction of the Stinger missiles and, to a lesser extent, Chinese multibarreled rocket launchers and mortars turned the course of the war.

64. Anonymous comments in a group interview at the Refugee District Administration Headquarters, Bannu, North-West Frontier Province, Pakistan, 28 June 1987.

65. Nyrop and Seekins, *Afghanistan: A Country Study,* 288; Dupree, *Afghanistan,* 83–89, 127.

66. Nyrop and Seekins, *Afghanistan: A Country Study,* 289.

67. Louis Dupree, "Post-Withdrawal Afghanistan: Light at the End of the Tunnel," in Saikal and Maley, *Soviet Withdrawal,* 30–31; Thomas T. Hammond, *Red Flag over Afghanistan* (Boulder, CO: Westview, 1984); Shahrani and Canfield, *Revolutions and Rebellions.*

68. Nyrop and Seekins, *Afghanistan: A Country Study,* 288–294.

69. Adamec, *Afghanistan;* Ludwig W. Adamec, *Afghanistan's Foreign Affairs to the Mid-Twentieth Century* (Tucson: University of Arizona Press, 1974); Gregorian, *Emergence of Modern Afghanistan;* Poullada, *Reform and Rebellion.*

70. The Brest-Litovsk Treaty (March 1918) extricated the new Soviet Union from World War I, but the civil war between Reds and Whites (and various ethnic nationalists) continued in South Russia, the Ukraine, Siberia, and Turkestan until 1920.

71. Rosanne Klass, "Afghanistan: The Accords," *Foreign Affairs* 66, no. 5, Summer 1988, 922–945; Yossef Bodansky, "Soviet Military Involvement in Afghanistan," in Klass, *Afghanistan: The Great Game Revisited,* 229–285.

72. Khan Marwat Fazal-ur-Rahim, *The Basmachi Movement in Soviet Central*

Asia (Peshawar, Pakistan: Emjay Book International, 1985); Elizabeth E. Bacon, *Central Asians under Russian Rule: A Study in Culture Change* (Ithaca, NY: Cornell University Press, 1966); Klass, "Great Game Revisited," 1–29.

73. "A Letter from a Soviet Ambassador," in Klass, *Afghanistan: The Great Game Revisited*, 32.

74. *Ibid.*, 33; Adamec, *Afghanistan*, 188–191.

75. Hélène Carrère d'Encausse, "Civil War and New Governments," in Allworth, *Central Asia*, 225; "Letter from a Soviet Ambassador," 33.

76. Fazal-ur-Rahim, *Basmachi Movement*, 37–39.

77. "Letter from a Soviet Ambassador," 34.

78. Dupree, *Afghanistan*, 448, refers to the reconquest of the "Tsarist Central Asian Empire."

79. Fazal-ur-Rahim, *Basmachi Movement*, 13–16, also chapter 4 and the biographical sketches of the "Young Turks" in the Basmachi revolt. D'Encausse, "Civil War," 230–231, notes that in the early stages of the Central Asian independence movement (1918–1929), British troops posed a serious danger to Soviet consolidation.

80. Adamec, *Afghanistan's Foreign Affairs*, 67; Gregorian, *Emergence of Modern Afghanistan*, 261–262.

81. "Letter from a Soviet Ambassador," 31–32.

82. Fazal-ur-Rahim, *Basmachi Movement*, 27–28, 39, 111–112; d'Encausse, "Civil War," 224–253. See also John Anderson, *The International Politics of Central Asia* (Manchester, UK: Manchester University Press, 1997).

83. Alexandre Bennigsen, "The Soviet Union and Muslim Guerrilla Wars, 1920–1981: Lessons for Afghanistan," *Conflict* 4, nos. 2–4, 1983, 301–324, in setting forth a model for Soviet success against Muslim guerrilla movements, did not emphasize famine as a weapon. See also d'Encausse, "Civil War," 224–253.

84. Poullada, *Reform and Rebellion*.

85. Robert D. McChesney, *Kabul under Siege: Fayz Muhammad's Account of the 1929 Uprising* (Princeton, NJ: Markus Wiener, 1999).

86. Dupree, *Afghanistan*, 448; Fazal-ur-Rahim, *Basmachi Movement*.

87. Dupree, *Afghanistan*, 448.

88. D'Encausse, "Civil War," 251–253.

89. Fazal-ur-Rahim, *Basmachi Movement*, 112.

90. Dupree, *Afghanistan*, 460.

91. *Ibid.*, 460–461; Fazal-ur-Rahim, *Basmachi Movement*, 138.

92. D'Encausse, "Civil War," 224–253.

93. Fazal-ur-Rahim, *Basmachi Movement*, 143–144.

94. These incursions have been widely reported, especially since 1986, and

are discussed in greater detail in chapter 3. See, for example, Amstutz, *Afghanistan: The First Five Years*, 134.

95. Gregorian, *Emergence of Modern Afghanistan*; Dupree, *Afghanistan*; Adamec, *Afghanistan's Foreign Affairs*; Nyrop and Seekins, *Afghanistan: A Country Study*.

96. Gregorian, *Emergence of Modern Afghanistan*, 231.

97. Dupree, *Afghanistan*, 443.

98. See Adamec, *Afghanistan*, 188–191, for the full text.

99. Dupree, *Afghanistan*, 448.

100. Amstutz, *Afghanistan: The First Five Years*, 12.

101. Dupree, *Afghanistan*, 451.

102. Amstutz, *Afghanistan: The First Five Years*, 14.

103. *Ibid.*, 15–17.

104. *Ibid.*, 16–17.

105. Gregorian, *Emergence of Modern Afghanistan*, 333. See also Dupree, *Afghanistan*, 471–474, on entrepreneurial economic activities in northern Afghanistan during the 1930s.

106. Dupree, *Afghanistan*, 478.

107. Although Nadir Shah's successor, Zahir Shah, reigned from 1933, his uncles Mohammad Hashim (prime minister 1933–1946) and Shah Mahmud (prime minister 1946–1953) actually ruled Afghanistan until his cousin, Mohammad Daoud, took power in a bloodless coup in 1953. Daoud then ruled until 1963, when he resigned under pressure from the king. Thus, Zahir Shah reigned for thirty years before he ruled Afghanistan.

108. Amstutz, *Afghanistan: The First Five Years*, 15.

109. The Pushtunistan issue was revived in 1961, ultimately leading to the resignation of Mohammad Daoud as prime minister. See Dupree, *Afghanistan*, 538–558. More recently, it has been reported that the Taliban's maps for "Greater Afghanistan" also lay claim to the Pushtun areas of Pakistan (interview with Liz Spencer, deputy director of the Agency Coordinating Body for Afghan Refugees [ACBAR], Peshawar, Pakistan, June 1997).

110. Leon B. Poullada, "The Road to Crisis, 1919–1980," in Klass, *Afghanistan: The Great Game Revisited*, 40; M. Siddieq Noorzoy, "Long-Term Soviet Economic Interests and Policies in Afghanistan," in Klass, *Afghanistan: The Great Game Revisited*, 74–75.

111. Poullada, "Road to Crisis," 39–43.

112. Noorzoy, "Long-Term Soviet Economic Interests," 76–77.

113. *Ibid.*, 77.

114. Poullada, "Road to Crisis," 46.

115. *Ibid.,* 44–46.

116. Dupree, *Afghanistan,* 499; Poullada, "Road to Crisis," 45.

117. Bradsher, *Afghanistan and the Soviet Union,* 25, 28; Amstutz, *Afghanistan: The First Five Years,* 22.

118. Bradsher, *Afghanistan and the Soviet Union,* 28.

119. Poullada, "Road to Crisis," 46.

120. Bradsher, *Afghanistan and the Soviet Union,* especially chapter 4, devotes considerable attention to the second Daoud period (1973–1978). See also Hammond, *Red Flag over Afghanistan.*

121. Bradsher, *Afghanistan and the Soviet Union,* 72–81.

122. Anthony Arnold, *Afghanistan's Two-Party Communism: Parcham and Khalq* (Stanford, CA: Hoover Institution Press, 1983).

123. Amstutz, *Afghanistan: The First Five Years,* 31.

124. Sources differ on the figures. Amstutz, *Afghanistan: The First Five Years,* 167–169, suggests eighty thousand troops by late January 1980. Joseph J. Collins, *The Soviet Invasion of Afghanistan* (Lexington, MA.: Lexington Books, 1985), 79, has eighty-five thousand Soviet troops by March 1980. The actual initial invasion force numbered five thousand men.

CHAPTER 3. MODERN WAR IN AFGHANISTAN

1. Larry Goodson, "The Impact of Arms Proliferation on the Resolution of Regional Conflict: The Drug Culture and 'Kalashnikovization' of Afghanistan," paper presented at the annual meeting of the American Political Science Association, Chicago, September 1992.

2. Dupree, "Post-Withdrawal Afghanistan," 30; Shahrani and Canfield, *Revolutions and Rebellions.*

3. Bradsher, *Afghanistan and the Soviet Union,* 72.

4. Bradsher, *Afghanistan and the Soviet Union.*

5. Newell and Newell, *Struggle for Afghanistan,* 72–75.

6. *Ibid.,* 76, 84.

7. *Ibid.,* 85.

8. The splintering of the Afghan resistance movement is best documented in Roy, *Islam and Resistance,* 1986, 76–79, and chapter 7.

9. Amstutz, *Afghanistan: The First Five Years,* 130; Bradsher, *Afghanistan and the Soviet Union,* 101.

10. Newell and Newell, *Struggle for Afghanistan,* 86.

11. Amstutz, *Afghanistan: The First Five Years,* 180–181. Isby, *Russia's War in Afghanistan,* 18, suggests an even lower troop strength of twenty thousand by the end of 1980.

12. Interviews with survivors in Kerala refugee camp in Bajaur Agency, Federally Administered Tribal Areas, Pakistan, in July 1987. Hyman, *Afghanistan under Soviet Domination*, 126–127, recounts the tale of the Kerala massacre.

13. Bradsher, *Afghanistan and the Soviet Union*, 101.

14. Galeotti, *Afghanistan: Soviet Union's Last War*, 7–10. See also Anthony Arnold, *Afghanistan: The Soviet Invasion in Perspective* (Stanford, CA: Hoover Institution Press, 1981); and Abdul Samad Ghaus, *The Fall of Afghanistan* (Washington, DC: Pergamon-Brassey's International Defense Publishers, 1988).

15. M. Hassan Kakar, *Afghanistan: The Soviet Invasion and the Afghan Response, 1979–1982* (Berkeley: University of California Press, 1995), 39.

16. *Ibid.*

17. Bradsher, *Afghanistan and the Soviet Union*, 163–164, 178; Kakar, *Afghanistan: The Soviet Invasion*, chapter 1.

18. Bradsher, *Afghanistan and the Soviet Union*, 179.

19. Kakar, *Afghanistan: The Soviet Invasion*, 26–27.

20. Amstutz, *Afghanistan: The First Five Years*, 130; Mark Urban, *War in Afghanistan*, 1st ed. (New York: St. Martin's, 1988); Tom Rogers, *The Soviet Withdrawal from Afghanistan: Analysis and Chronology* (Westport, CT: Greenwood, 1992). The monthly *Afghanistan Report* published by the Institute of Strategic Studies, Islamabad, Pakistan, is excellent but did not begin until March 1984.

21. Amstutz, *Afghanistan: The First Five Years*, 132.

22. Louis Dupree coined the term "rubbleization" in "Soviet Intervention in Afghanistan: A New Ball Game," a paper delivered at the annual meeting of the American Political Science Association, New Orleans, 1985.

23. US Committee for Refugees, *World Refugee Survey*, 1991. Significant repatriation following the fall of the Najibullah government in 1992 probably dropped the total number of Afghan refugees to less than the long-standing Palestinian refugee population by the late 1990s.

24. Edward Girardet, "Migratory Genocide," *New Republic*, 4 March 1985, 14. See also Dupree, "Soviet Intervention."

25. Yousaf and Atkin, *Bear Trap*.

26. Rubin, *Fragmentation of Afghanistan*, 215; Roy, *Islam and Resistance*, 1990.

27. Rubin, *Fragmentation of Afghanistan*, 216.

28. *Ibid.*, 211.

29. Roy, *Islam and Resistance*, 1986.

30. Rubin, *Fragmentation of Afghanistan*, 212. See also Marsden, *Taliban*.

31. Abdur Rashid, "The Afghan Resistance: Its Background, Its Nature, and the Problem of Unity," in Klass, *Afghanistan: The Great Game Revisited*, 203–227; Rosanne Klass, "Who's Who in the Afghanistan Resistance," in Klass, *Afghanistan: The Great Game Revisited*, 427–437.

32. Robert L. Canfield, "Afghanistan: The Trajectory of Internal Alignments," *Middle East Journal* 43, no. 4, Autumn 1989, 635–648.

33. Girardet, *Afghanistan: The Soviet War,* 136–138; Kakar, *Afghanistan: The Soviet Invasion,* 70–71.

34. Amstutz, *Afghanistan: The First Five Years,* 284–290.

35. US Department of State, *Afghanistan: Eight Years of Soviet Occupation* (Washington, D.C.: Bureau of Public Affairs, Special Report no. 173, December 1987), 14–17.

36. *Ibid.,* 17. Also, US Department of State, *Soviet Influence on Afghan Youth* (Washington, DC: Bureau of Public Affairs, Special Report no. 139, February 1986).

37. Amstutz, *Afghanistan: The First Five Years,* 295–297.

38. Hyman, *Afghanistan under Soviet Domination.*

39. Amstutz, *Afghanistan: The First Five Years,* 133; Isby, *Russia's War in Afghanistan,* 5–7; Urban, *War in Afghanistan,* 1988, 118–119, 124–125, 137–138.

40. Isby, *Russia's War in Afghanistan,* 7–8; Urban, *War in Afghanistan,* 1988, 144–148, 155.

41. Isby, *Russia's War in Afghanistan,* 7–8; Urban, *War in Afghanistan,* 1988, 151–153, 156–157.

42. Amstutz, *Afghanistan: The First Five Years,* 133; Isby, *Russia's War in Afghanistan,* 8. This approach caused "rubbleization" and "migratory genocide."

43. Isby, *Russia's War in Afghanistan,* 6; Urban, *War in Afghanistan,* 1988, 63–164, 168–169, 174–180.

44. Data compiled from *Afghanistan Report* (Islamabad, Pakistan: Institute of Strategic Studies), nos. 8 (November 1984) and 19–43.

45. *Ibid.,* nos. 22–26.

46. *Ibid.,* nos. 23–25; also, my interview with Jallaluddin Haqqani in June 1987 in Miran Shah, North Waziristan, Federally Administered Tribal Areas, Pakistan, reported in my article "Jallaluddin Haqqani: Portrait of a Mujahideen Commander," *Free Afghanistan Report,* special edition, January–February 1988, 4–5; Urban, *War in Afghanistan,* 1988, 190–194.

47. On the Geneva talks, see Cordovez and Harrison, *Out of Afghanistan;* Khan, *Untying the Afghan Knot;* Selig S. Harrison, "Inside the Afghan Talks," *Foreign Policy* 72, Fall 1988, 31–60; and Nyrop and Seekins, *Afghanistan: A Country Study,* 253–255.

48. The secret police of the DRA were known for much of the war by their acronym, KhAD, standing for Khadamat-i Ittila'at-i Dawlati and meaning State Information Service. After Najibullah became president, he gave the KhAD ministerial status, changing its name to Wizarat-i Amaniyyat-i Dawlati (WAD). See Rubin, *Fragmentation of Afghanistan,* 132–134.

49. The statement about widespread support for the mujahideen is based on my observations along the Afghan border and inside Afghanistan, September 1986–August 1987. International support for the mujahideen was demonstrated in annual UN votes calling for the withdrawal of forces from Afghanistan, which passed with increasing margins every year from 1979 to 1988.

50. *Afghanistan Report*, nos. 22–34, and my observations during this period.

51. US Department of State, *Afghanistan: Eight Years of Soviet Occupation*, 21.

52. Richard Mackenzie, "Afghan Rebels Never Say Die," *Insight*, three-part story, 25 January 1988, 8–16.

53. Many air losses are due to mechanical failure, pilot error, etc. Analysis of data on air losses from issues of *Afghanistan Report* indicates no appreciable immediate increase after the introduction of Stinger missiles, but other accounts report very high levels of accuracy and lethality that led to increased air losses. For example, David Isby, "Flares over Afghanistan," *Soldier of Fortune*, November 1987, 40, stated that "U.S. government sources report that 68 percent of all Stinger firings yield destroyed Soviet aircraft." I have heard accuracy rates as high as 80 percent hits per firings, but because these cannot be independently verified, I accept the confidential report of a Western military advisor in Peshawar in June 1987 that the claims are grossly exaggerated. Still, the Stinger missiles certainly led to dramatic changes in Soviet air strategy. For example, I observed bombing runs on mujahideen positions at Jaji in Paktia Province in July 1987 in which the pilots came in far too high to drop their bombs accurately. For more on the impact of the Stingers, see Michael Getler, "US Stingers Boost Afghan Rebels' Performance and Morale," *Washington Post*, 14 October 1987; Michael Mecham, "US Credits Afghan Resistance with Thwarting Soviet Air Power," *Aviation Week and Space Technology*, 13 July 1987, 26–27; Edward Girardet, "Afghan Fighters Slowly Erode Soviet Control," *Christian Science Monitor*, 13 December 1987, 7–8.

54. *Afghanistan Report*, 1986, nos. 22–34.

55. *Ibid.*, nos. 22–43.

56. Rogers, *Soviet Withdrawal*.

57. According to Rubin, Karmal "was a Persian-speaking Kabuli of Kashmiri descent, although he sometimes claimed some Pashtun ancestry" (*Fragmentation of Afghanistan*, 126). Klass suggested that he might have been of Tajik origin (Rosanne Klass, "Who's Who in the DRA and the PDPA: A Selected List," in Klass, *Afghanistan: The Great Game Revisited*, 442), whereas Adamec suggested that he was at least partially of Ghilzai Pushtun descent (Ludwig Adamec, *Historical Dictionary of Afghanistan* [Metuchen, NJ: Scarecrow, 1991], 136).

58. Among other things, these steps included a new constitution in November 1987 in which the Democratic Republic of Afghanistan reverted to its earlier name, the Republic of Afghanistan. See Rubin, *Fragmentation of Afghanistan*.

59. Cordovez and Harrison, *Out of Afghanistan;* Khan, *Untying the Afghan Knot;* United Nations, *The Geneva Accords: Agreements on the Settlement of the Situation relating to Afghanistan* (New York: UN Department of Public Information, July 1988); William Maley, "The Geneva Accords of April 1988," in Saikal and Maley, *Soviet Withdrawal,* 12–28.

60. Yousaf and Atkin, *Bear Trap,* 235.

61. Ted Mataxis, "Perestroika and Glasnost—Not in Afghanistan," *Free Afghanistan Report,* February 1990, 3.

62. *Ibid.*

63. Rubin, *Search for Peace.*

64. Theodore L. Eliot, Jr., "Afghanistan in 1990," *Asian Survey* 31, no. 2, February 1991, 125–133.

65. Rais, *War without Winners,* 125.

66. Anwar-ul-Haq Ahady, "Saudi Arabia, Iran and the Conflict in Afghanistan," in Maley, *Fundamentalism,* 117–134.

67. Salamat Ali, "A Peace on Paper," *Far Eastern Economic Review,* 18 March 1993, 22.

68. Alam Payind, "Evolving Alternative Views on the Future of Afghanistan," *Asian Survey* 33, no. 9, September 1993, 923–931.

69. Radek Sikorski, "Afghanistan Revisited," *National Review,* 23 August 1993, 40–42; also, my interviews and personal observation, Kabul, July 1997.

70. Rubin, *Fragmentation of Afghanistan.*

71. Confidential interviews, Peshawar, Pakistan, July 1992.

72. See, for example, Foreign Broadcast Information Service, Near East Section, vol. 93, transcript no. 135, 16 July 1993.

73. Shah M. Tarzi, "Afghanistan in 1992," *Asian Survey* 33, no. 2, February 1993, 165–174.

74. Ralph H. Magnus, "Afghanistan in 1996: Year of the Taliban," *Asian Survey* 37, no. 2, February 1997, 111.

75. Ahmed Rashid, "Divisions Multiply," *Far Eastern Economic Review,* 31 July 1997, 20–21.

76. Trevor Fishlock, "Fire of the Taliban Threatens to Ignite Oil Region," *Electronic Telegraph,* Issue 1178, 16 August 1998; Raja Asghar, "Pakistan Urges World to Recognize Afghan Taleban," *Reuters,* 15 August 1998.

77. Anthony Davis, "How the Taliban Became a Military Force," in Maley, *Fundamentalism,* 43–71.

78. Ahmed Rashid, "Pakistan and the Taliban," in Maley, *Fundamentalism,* 72–89.

79. Anthony Hyman, "Russia, Central Asia and the Taliban," in Maley, *Fundamentalism,* 104–116. Also see Larry Goodson, "Afghanistan," *Jane's Sentinel Security Assessment, South Asia* (Coulsdon, UK: Jane's Information Group, 1999).

80. Goodson, "Afghanistan," *Jane's*, 1999, 3.

81. *Ibid.*

82. *Ibid.*

83. Rashid, "The Taliban: Exporting Extremism."

84. "Pakistani Army Moves against Prime Minister after Military Chief Sacked," *CNN*, 12 October 1999; "Pakistan TV: Government Dismissed," *Associated Press*, 12 October 1999. Both articles found at Afghanistan Online, www.afghan-web.com. See also Goodson, "Foreign Policy Gone Awry."

85. Goodson, "Afghanistan," *Jane's*, 1999, 3.

86. Figures for Taliban and Northern Alliance forces are taken from Goodson, "Afghanistan," *Jane's*, 1999, 32, 35. Much higher figures of 80,000 Taliban fighters, 65,000 Shura-I-Nazar troops, 65,000 Jumbush militia, and nearly 50,000 Shia soldiers were provided in an interview with Lieutenant Colonel Kevin Logan, UN Special Mission to Afghanistan, July 1997, Islamabad, Pakistan.

87. Rashid, "Pakistan and the Taliban," in Maley, *Fundamentalism.*

88. For an alternative point of view, see an earlier version of this chapter published as "Periodicity and Intensity in the Afghan War," *Central Asian Survey* 17, no. 3, 1998, 471–488.

89. Larry Goodson, "Mustaqbal Afghanistan Bayn Al Siraa' Al Erqi Wal Tafattut Al Siyasi" [The Future of Afghanistan: Ethnic Conflict and Political Fragmentation], in Ibrahim Arafat, ed., *Al Qadiyah Al Afghaniyah Wa Inikasatiha Al Iqlimiyah Wal Dawliyah* [The Case of Afghanistan: Its Regional and International Implications] (Center for Asian Studies, Cairo University, 1999), 301–318; Goodson, "Periodicity and Intensity"; Larry Goodson, "Scenarios for the Future of the Afghan State," *Middle East Affairs Journal* 2, no. 1, Spring–Summer 1994, 32–48.

90. *The World Almanac and Book of Facts 2000* (Mahwah, NJ: World Almanac Books, 1999), 768. See also Rashid 2000, which gives the infant mortality rate as 163 per 1000.

CHAPTER 4. IMPACT OF THE WAR ON AFGHAN STATE AND SOCIETY

1. Several journalists with experience covering the Vietnam War told me in Peshawar in 1986–1987 that the differences were quite significant. In Afghanistan, unlike Vietnam, a journalist could not get on a helicopter and fly to a forward base or area of combat, watch for a bit, and fly back at nightfall to enjoy the comforts of the rear area. To cover Afghanistan, journalists frequently had to hike in, sometimes traveling for days, always aware that the Soviets were deliberately targeting Western journalists in order to discourage their coverage of the conflict. Conditions were little better during the 1990s. For parallels with the Vietnam War, see David Chaffetz, *Afghanistan, Russia's Vietnam?* (Special

Paper no. 4, Afghanistan Council of the Asia Society, New York, 1979).

2. Barnett R. Rubin, "The Fragmentation of Afghanistan," *Foreign Affairs* 68, no. 5, Winter 1989–1990, 150–168; United States Committee for Refugees, *World Refugee Survey,* 1987, 1990, 1991.

3. UN High Commissioner for Refugees, *Refugees* 2, no. 108, 1997, 7.

4. Noor Ahmed Khalidi, "Afghanistan: Demographic Consequences of War, 1978–1987," *Central Asian Survey* 10, no. 3, 1991, 106.

5. Marek Sliwinski, "Afghanistan: The Decimation of a People," *Orbis* 33, no. 1, 1989, 39–56.

6. M. Siddieq Noorzoy, "Some Observations on and Assessment of the Population Losses in Afghanistan," *WUFA, Journal of the Writers Union of Free Afghanistan* 3, no. 3, 1988, 6–14.

7. Khalidi, "Afghanistan: Demographic Consequences," 109.

8. Interviews, Pakistan and Afghanistan, July 1997.

9. Interview with Lieutenant Colonel Kevin Logan, UN Special Mission to Afghanistan, July 1997, Islamabad, Pakistan.

10. Human Rights Watch, *Afghanistan: The Massacre in Mazar-i Sharif* 10, no. 7, November 1998, at www.hrw.org.

11. Rais, *War without Winners,* 20.

12. Interviews, Pakistan and Afghanistan, July 1997.

13. UNHCR, *Refugees,* 1997, 3–10.

14. Rubin, "Fragmentation of Afghanistan," 150–168.

15. Larry Goodson, "Refugee-Based Insurgency: The Afghan Case" (Ph.D. dissertation, University of North Carolina, 1990).

16. Interview with Sarah Russell, information officer, UN Office for the Co-ordination of Humanitarian Assistance to Afghanistan, Islamabad, Pakistan, July 1997. Also, Goodson, "Afghanistan," *Jane's,* 1999, 8.

17. Rubin, "Political Economy."

18. Interviews, Herat, Afghanistan, July 1997.

19. Goodson, "Afghanistan," *Jane's,* 1999.

20. "United Nations Seeks Afghanistan Aid," *United Press International,* 3 December 1996.

21. Kaplan, *Soldiers of God;* Urban, *War in Afghanistan,* 1991; Marvin G. Weinbaum, "Pakistan and Afghanistan: The Strategic Relationship," *Asian Survey* 31, no. 6, June 1991, 496–511; Yousaf and Atkin, *Bear Trap;* Ikramul Haq, "Pak-Afghan Drug Trade in Historical Perspective," *Asian Survey* 36, no. 10, October 1996, 945–963.

22. Dupree, "Soviet Intervention"; Roy, *Islam and Resistance,* 1990.

23. UNCHEAP, *First Consolidated Report,* 1988, chapter 8. See Antonio

Giustozzi, *War, Politics and Society in Afghanistan, 1978–1992* (Washington, D.C.: Georgetown University Press, 2000) for more on militias.

24. Shah M. Tarzi, "Politics of the Afghan Resistance Movement," *Asian Survey* 31, no. 6, June 1991, 483.

25. Roy, *Islam and Resistance*, 1990; Magnus and Naby, *Afghanistan*.

26. Marvin G. Weinbaum, "The Politics of Afghan Resettlement and Rehabilitation," *Asian Survey* 29, no. 3, March 1989, 287–307; Weinbaum, "Pakistan and Afghanistan," 496–511; Marvin G. Weinbaum, "War and Peace in Afghanistan: The Pakistani Role," *Middle East Journal* 45, no. 1, Winter 1991, 71–85; Magnus and Naby, *Afghanistan*.

27. Interviews in Herat and Kabul, Afghanistan, and Peshawar, Pakistan, July 1997. See also Rashid, *Taliban*.

28. Isby, *Russia's War in Afghanistan*; Urban, *War in Afghanistan*, 1991.

29. UNCHEAP, *First Consolidated Report*, September 1988.

30. Weinbaum, "Politics of Afghan Resettlement."

31. For example, see Aimal Khan, "Dacoities on Rise in Taliban-Ruled Areas," *Frontier Post*, 5 October 1999.

32. Gilles Dorronsoro and Chantal Lobato, "The Militia in Afghanistan," *Central Asian Survey* 8, no. 4, 1989; Kristian Berg Harpviken, "Transcending Traditionalism: The Emergence of Non-State Military Formations in Afghanistan," *Journal of Peace Research* 34, no. 3, 1997, 271–287; Giustozzi, *War, Politics and Society in Afghanistan*, esp. Part IV.

33. Rubin, *Fragmentation of Afghanistan*, 161–164.

34. Rubin, "Political Economy"; Goodson, "Afghanistan," *Jane's*, 1999.

35. "Alarming Opium Production Rise in Afghanistan Worries UN," *NNI*, 11 September 1999 (found at Afghanistan Online, www.afghan-web.com).

36. Christopher S. Wren, "Afghanistan's Opium Output Drops Sharply, UN Survey Shows," *New York Times*, 27 September 1998, 11.

37. US Department of State, *International Narcotics Control Strategy Report* (Washington, D.C.: Bureau of Public Affairs, 1997).

38. Nathan Associates, Inc.–Louis Berger International, Inc., "Afghanistan Studies Project: Report of the Opium Subsector Survey," Unpublished manuscript, August 1992; interview with James Magnor, US Drug Enforcement Administration official, 23 July 1992, Islamabad.

39. "UN: 120 Per Cent Increase in Production of Raw Opium in Afghanistan for 1999," *M2 Communications*, 13 September 1999 (found at Afghanistan Online, www.afghan-web.com).

40. Nathan Associates–Louis Berger, "Afghanistan Studies Project"; "Alarming Opium Production Rise."

41. Interview with journalist Rahimullah Yusufzai, Peshawar, Pakistan, 28 July 1992.

42. Nathan Associates–Louis Berger, "Afghanistan Studies Project"; Doris Buddenberg, *Illicit Drugs and Drug Policies in Pakistan* (United Nations Research Institute for Social Development, 1996).

43. US Department of State, *International Narcotics Control Strategy Report*, 1997, 1998, 1999. The decline in opium production reported for 1998 was attributed not to Taliban efforts to curtail production but to poor growing conditions.

44. US Department of State, *International Narcotics Control Strategy Report*, 1997; Rashid, "The Taliban: Exporting Extremism."

45. Roy, "New Political Elite," 72–100.

46. Larry Goodson, "The Culture of Fragmentation in Afghanistan," *Alif: Journal of Comparative Poetics* 18, Spring 1998, 269–289; Goodson, "Impact of Arms Proliferation."

47. Roy, "New Political Elite," 75–78.

48. Maley, *Fundamentalism*; Marsden, *Taliban*.

49. Roy, *Afghanistan*, 31–32.

50. Olesen, *Islam and Politics*; Magnus and Naby, *Afghanistan*.

51. Roy, *Islam and Resistance*, 1986.

52. Olesen, *Islam and Politics*; Kakar, *Government and Society*.

53. Rashid, *Taliban*; Rashid, "The Taliban: Exporting Extremism"; Maley, *Fundamentalism*; Marsden, *Taliban*; Larry Goodson, "Clash of Communities in Afghanistan: The Taliban and Their Impact on National Unity," paper presented at the annual meeting of the Middle East Studies Association, Chicago, December 1998; Rameen Moshref, *The Taliban* (New York: Afghanistan Forum, Occasional Paper no. 35, 1997); Magnus, "Afghanistan in 1996."

54. Rashid, "The Taliban: Exporting Extremism."

55. There is some contention over the ethnic composition of the Taliban leadership. Barnett Rubin claims that the inner leadership is not especially representative of the traditional Durrani hierarchy, whereas others, such as Ahmed Rashid, Anthony Davis, and Rameen Moshref, see more Durrani representation in the movement's leadership. Regardless of the ethnicity of the top leaders, the core of the Taliban's followers and public support is found among the Durrani tribes of Afghanistan's southwest. See Barnett R. Rubin, "Testimony on the Situation in Afghanistan," United States Senate, Committee on Foreign Relations, 8 October 1998; Rashid, "Pakistan and the Taliban," in Maley, *Fundamentalism*, 72–89; Davis, "How the Taliban Became a Military Force," in Maley, *Fundamentalism*, 43–71; and Moshref, *Taliban*.

56. Anwar-ul-Haq Ahady, "The Decline of the Pashtuns in Afghanistan," *Asian Survey* 35, no. 7, July 1995, 621–635; Rubin, *Fragmentation of Afghanistan.*

57. Rashid, "Divisions Multiply."

58. The Deobandi school refers to the conservative Islamic madrasah founded in 1867 in the Indian town of Deoband. Since then, this school has flourished, and affiliated madrasahs have spread throughout South Asia, especially in the frontier areas of Pakistan, where they have had great influence among the Afghan diaspora. As Rashid, "The Taliban: Exporting Extremism," notes, however, these madrasahs have corrupted the more tolerant teachings of the Deobandi school. For more on the Deobandi school, see Barbara D. Metcalf, *Islamic Revival in British India: Deoband, 1860–1900* (Princeton, NJ: Princeton University Press, 1982).

59. Olesen, *Islam and Politics.*

60. William Maley, "Introduction: Interpreting the Taliban," in Maley, *Fundamentalism,* 16–23.

61. Davis, "How the Taliban Became a Military Force," 43 71.

62. Confidential interviews, Herat and Kandahar, Afghanistan, July 1997.

63. Interviews with former president Sibghatullah Mojaddidi and his son, Abdullah Mojaddidi, Peshawar, Pakistan, July 1997; Ahady, "Saudi Arabia," 117–134.

64. Interview with Mullah Bismullah Akhund, Ministry of Foreign Affairs official and Supreme Shura member, Herat, Afghanistan, 17 July 1997.

65. Interview with Maulavi Wakil Ahmed, spokesman for Mullah Omar and Inner Shura member, Kandahar, Afghanistan, 22 July 1997.

66. Davis, "How the Taliban Became a Military Force," 43–71; Ahmed Rashid, "Pakistan and the Taliban," *The Nation,* 4-part article, April 1998

67. Rashid, "Pakistan and the Taliban," in Maley, *Fundamentalism,* 76–77.

68. *Ibid.,* 78.

69. *Ibid.*; also Rashid, "The Taliban: Exporting Extremism."

70. Davis, "How the Taliban Became a Military Force," 43–71; Rashid, "Pakistan and the Taliban," in Maley, *Fundamentalism,* 72–89.

71. Davis, "How the Taliban Became a Military Force," 43–54.

72. *Ibid.*; interviews in Islamabad and Peshawar, Pakistan, and Kabul, Afghanistan, July 1997.

73. Davis, "How the Taliban Became a Military Force," 43–71.

74. See "Afghan Northern Alliance Says Attacked by Pakistan," *Reuters,* 31 July 1998; "Taliban Tightens Grip on Northern Afghanistan," *AFP,* 11 August 1998 (found at Afghanistan Online, www.afghan-web.com).

75. These allegations were widely reported in the international media and received quite a lot of attention at the United Nations. See, for example, "UN

Chief Urges Afghanistan's Neighbours to Stay Out of Fight," *AFP*, 6 August 1999 (found at Afghanistan Online, www.afghan-web.com).

76. Davis, "How the Taliban Became a Military Force," 67–70.

77. Goodson, "Afghanistan," *Jane's*, 1999, 32.

78. Khalq (Masses) and Parcham (Banner) were rival factions of the People's Democratic Party of Afghanistan (PDPA), which ruled the country during its communist period from 1978 to 1992 (although the party was renamed Hizb-i-Watan, or Fatherland Party, in 1990). The Khalq faction was dominant from 1978 until the end of 1979, when the Soviet Union invaded and placed the Parcham faction in power, where it remained until the fall of the Najibullah government in 1992.

79. Rashid, "Pakistan and the Taliban," in Maley, *Fundamentalism*, 87.

80. *Ibid.*, 85.

81. *Ibid.*, 82–84.

82. *Ibid.*, 82–84.

83. Unocal has been the major promoter of a plan to build a $2-billion, 1,500-kilometer pipeline to carry natural gas from Turkmenistan to Pakistan across western Afghanistan. In 1997 it formed and led the Central Asia Gas Pipeline Ltd. Consortium (CENTGAS), composed of oil companies and the Turkmenistan government. In 1998, Unocal increased its share in the consortium to more than 54 percent, but by 1999 it had pulled out of the plan because it had become clear that the US government would not recognize the Taliban regime as the government of Afghanistan.

84. Goodson, "Afghanistan," *Jane's*, 1999, 5; Rubin, "Political Economy."

85. Rashid, "Pakistan and the Taliban," in Maley, *Fundamentalism*, 88; see also Rubin, "Political Economy."

86. Davis, "How the Taliban Became a Military Force," 68–70.

87. Rashid, "Pakistan and the Taliban," in Maley, *Fundamentalism*, 87.

88. Davis, "How the Taliban Became a Military Force," 69, suggested that the Taliban were "pre-eminently a military organization rather than a political movement."

89. The exact number of members is unclear. Various numbers have been reported over time, but this body has gradually expanded to include representatives of groups that have joined the Taliban as their ranks swelled beyond the original Kandahari core.

90. Marsden, *Taliban*, 31, reports that Omar was affiliated with Yunus Khalis's Hezb-i Islami, which may also be correct, because many Harakat members left for other parties during the war. Still, Rahimullah Yusufzai has interviewed Omar and reports his background as being in Harakat (interview, Peshawar, Pakistan, 10 July 1997).

91. Interview with journalist Rahimullah Yusufzai, Peshawar, Pakistan, 10 July 1997.

92. Interviews with Supreme Shura members, Herat and Kandahar, Afghanistan, July 1997.

93. Interviews in Herat and Kandahar, Afghanistan, July 1997. For details of the Taliban leadership, see Mohammed Zahid, "Taliban: Ring of Leadership," *Frontier Post*, 24 February 1995; and Goodson, "Afghanistan," *Jane's*, 1999, 5. Rumors in late 1998 of the purge of acting president Maulavi Mohammad Rabbani ultimately proved to be unfounded. However, there was a purge of the Taliban movement in September 1998, primarily of members with ties to the Khalq communists. See "Taliban Arrest Dozens of Alleged Coup Plotters," *AFP*, 23 October 1998.

94. Interview with Maulavi Wakil Ahmed, spokesman for Mullah Omar and Inner Shura member, Kandahar, Afghanistan, 22 July 1997.

95. Tim Johnston, "Taliban Fire Civil Servants," *Reuters*, 4 November 1997.

96. Confidential interviews, Kabul, Afghanistan, July 1997.

97. US Department of State, *Afghanistan: Human Rights Practices* (Washington, DC: Bureau of Democracy, Human Rights, and Labor, 1996).

98. Interview with Maulavi Wakil Ahmed, 22 July 1997.

99. Davis, "How the Taliban Became a Military Force," 69, reported that the Taliban had "a functioning brigade and divisional structure" by late 1996, but my interviews in July 1997 led me to believe that the military structure was still somewhat fluid then.

100. Rubin, "Political Economy"; Rashid, "The Taliban: Exporting Extremism."

101. Anders Fänge, "Afghanistan after April 1992: A Struggle for State and Ethnicity," *Central Asian Survey* 14, no. 1, 1995, 17–24.

102. Interviews, Herat and Kabul, Afghanistan, July 1997.

103. This has been documented in many journalistic accounts, as well as in the reports of numerous human rights organizations and in confidential interviews I conducted in Kabul, Afghanistan, in July 1997. Among published sources, see, for example, Physicians for Human Rights, *The Taliban's War on Women: A Health and Human Rights Crisis in Afghanistan* (Boston: Physicians for Human Rights, 1998); Caitriona Palmer, "The Taliban's War on Women," *Lancet* 352, no. 9129, 29 August 1998, 734–735; "Taleban Say 225 Women Punished for Improper Dress," *Reuters*, 5 December 1996; and US Department of State, *Afghanistan: Human Rights Practices*, 1996, 1997, 1998.

104. US Department of State, *Afghanistan: Human Rights Practices*, 1996–98.

105. Interviews, Kabul, Afghanistan, July 1997.

106. Confidential interview, Kabul, Afghanistan, 24 July 1997.

107. Physicians for Human Rights, *The Taliban's War on Women*, 65. See also

Rashid, *Taliban*, 218; Larry P. Goodson, "Perverting Islam: Taliban Social Policy Toward Women," presented at the 34th Annual Meeting of the Middle East Studies Association, Orlando, FL, November 16–19, 2000.

108. Physicians for Human Rights, *The Taliban's War on Women*, 70.

109. Rashid, *Taliban*, 107; also Physicians for Human Rights, *The Taliban's War on Women*, 70.

110. Physicians for Human Rights, *The Taliban's War on Women*, 49–50.

111. Magnus and Naby, *Afghanistan*.

112. Interview with journalist Sarah Horner, Islamabad, Pakistan, July 1997.

113. Human Rights Watch, *Afghanistan: The Massacre in Mazar-i Sharif* 10, no. 7, November 1998; United Nations General Assembly, *Situation of Human Rights in Afghanistan* (New York: Report of the Economic and Social Council, A/53/539, 26 October 1998).

114. Interviews, Herat, Afghanistan, July 1997.

115. Sayed Salahuddin, "Aid Agencies' Exit Means Hardship for Kabul," *Reuters*, 23 July 1998.

116. Interview with World Food Program representative, Kabul, Afghanistan, July 1997; Goodson, "Afghanistan," *Jane's Sentinel Security Assessment, South Asia* (Coulsdon, UK: Jane's Information Group, 2000).

117. "Afghan Taleban Ban Selected Banknotes," *Reuters*, 4 December 1996; Goodson, "Afghanistan," *Jane's*, 2000.

118. Unocal pulled out of the consortium and pipeline deal in August 1998, opening the door to rival Bridas of Argentina. In February 1999 it was rumored that Unocal was reconsidering withdrawing from the CENTGAS project.

119. "Turkmen Gas Pipe Might Help Afghan Peace," *Reuters*, 6 April 1998; Sayed Salahuddin, "Afghan Rivals Said to Agree on Gas Pipeline Plan," *Reuters*, 22 May 1998.

120. Numerous accounts of these punishments have been recorded. For example, see US Department of State, *Afghanistan: Human Rights Practices*, 1996, 1997, 1998.

121. Interviews, Kabul and Herat, Afghanistan, July 1997.

122. Rashid, "Divisions Multiply."

123. Ahmed Rashid, "Massive Arms Supplies Reach All Afghan Factions," *The Nation*, 15 March 1998.

124. Rehmat Shah Afridi, "Taliban: The Beginning of the End," *Frontier Post*, 11 May 1998.

125. Roy, *Afghanistan*.

126. Magnus and Naby, *Afghanistan*.

127. The military-led government of General Pervaiz Musharraf, after coming to power in October 1999, moved quickly to distance itself from the Taliban,

prompting the resumption of Taliban-Iranian ties. For background on Pakistan's policy toward the Taliban, see Rashid, "Pakistan and the Taliban," in Maley, *Fundamentalism*, 72–89.

128. Roy, *Islam and Resistance*, 1986.

129. Rubin, *Fragmentation of Afghanistan*; Rais, *War without Winners*.

130. Taliban policies toward entertainment and culture have been well documented by numerous journalists and outside organizations. See, for example, US Department of State, *Afghanistan: Human Rights Practices*, 1997, 1998; "Taliban Smash Televisions in Kabul," *Associated Press*, 1 August 1998; Ranjan Roy, "City Crackdown," *Associated Press*, 9 December 1996; Ranjan Roy, "Afghans Want Entertainment," *Associated Press*, 7 December 1996.

131. "Taliban Make Bonfire of Hindi Movies," *AFP*, 8 December 1996.

132. Magnus and Naby, *Afghanistan*; Majrooh and Elmi, *Sovietization*.

133. United Nations Development Program, *Human Development Report 1996* (New York: Oxford University Press, 1996).

134. United Nations Children's Fund, "Statistics," www.unicef.org, updated 1 December 1999.

135. US Department of State, *Afghanistan: Human Rights Practices*, 1997, 1998.

136. Hyman, *Afghanistan under Soviet Domination*; Kakar, *Afghanistan: The Soviet Invasion*.

137. Confidential interview, Herat, Afghanistan, 19 July 1997.

138. Ahmed Rashid, "Crime of the Century," *Far Eastern Economic Review*, 21 September 1995, 60–62.

139. Christopher Thomas, "Lost Forever: A Nation's Heritage Looted by Its Own People," *London Times*, 22 October 1996.

140. "Kabul's Past," *Los Angeles Times*, 14 November 1996.

141. Paul Clammer, personal communication, 24 November 1999.

142. Interview with Jon Rothenberg, UNHCR official, Herat, Afghanistan, July 1997.

143. For more on *buzkashi*, see G. Whitney Azoy, *Buzkashi: Game and Power in Afghanistan* (Philadelphia: University of Pennsylvania Press, 1982).

144. Glatzer, "Is Afghanistan on the Brink?" 180.

CHAPTER 5. AFGHANISTAN AND THE CHANGING REGIONAL ENVIRONMENT

1. Daniel C. Diller, ed., *Russia and the Independent States* (Washington, DC: Congressional Quarterly, 1993).

2. *Ibid.*

3. *Ibid.*, 157.

4. Mehrdad Haghayeghi, *Islam and Politics in Central Asia* (New York: St. Martin's, 1995); *World Almanac*, 1999, 1998.

5. David E. Twining, *The New Eurasia* (Westport, CT: Praeger, 1993), 147.

6. Ahmed Rashid, *The Resurgence of Central Asia* (Karachi: Oxford University Press, 1994); Gregory Gleason, *The Central Asian States* (Boulder, CO: Westview, 1997).

7. Twining, *New Eurasia*, 153.

8. *Ibid.*, 166.

9. *Ibid.*, 21.

10. Rashid, *Resurgence*, 201.

11. Marat Gurt, "Afghan News: Oil, Gas, and Others," *Reuters*, 25 October 1997.

12. Sebastian Alison, "US Firm Unocal Gloomy on Turkmen Pipeline Project," *Reuters*, 11 March 1998.

13. Maley, "The UN in Afghanistan," 182–198.

14. Dupree, *Afghanistan*, 627.

15. Rubin, *Fragmentation of Afghanistan*.

16. US Department of State, *Afghanistan: Six Years of Soviet Occupation* (Washington, DC: Bureau of Public Affairs, Special Report no. 135, 1985), 11. Also see Nake M. Kamrany, *The Six Stages in the Sovietization of Afghanistan* (Boulder, CO: Economic Institute for Research and Education, 1983); and Alam Payind, "Soviet-Afghan Relations from Cooperation to Occupation," *International Journal of Middle Eastern Studies* 21, 1989, 107–128.

17. US Department of State, *Afghanistan: Seven Years of Soviet Occupation* (Washington, DC: Bureau of Public Affairs, Special Report no. 155, 1986), 15.

18. US Department of State, *Afghanistan: Eight Years of Soviet Occupation*, 16.

19. *Ibid.*, 17.

20. Yousaf and Atkin, *Bear Trap;* Mohammad Yousaf, *Silent Soldier: The Man behind the Afghan Jehad* (Lahore, Pakistan: Jang Publishers, 1991).

21. Rashid, "Pakistan and the Taliban," in Maley, *Fundamentalism*, 72–89.

22. This conduit role was widely reported by the mid-1980s. See, for example, Tim Weiner, "Leaks in Afghan Arms Pipeline Cost CIA Millions," *News and Observer*, 28 February 1988; James Rupert, "Afghanistan: The New Battlefields," *Washington Post*, five-part series, 12–16 January 1986; John G. Merriam, "Arms Shipments to the Afghan Resistance," in Farr and Merriam, *Afghan Resistance*, 71–102; and Amstutz, *Afghanistan: The First Five Years*, 202–213.

23. Yousaf and Atkin, *Bear Trap;* Bradsher, *Afghanistan and the Soviet Union*, 276–277. I visited mujahideen training camps and arms depots near Peshawar, Chitral, Parachinar, and Miran Shah in 1987.

24. On the basis of confidential interviews in Pakistan (December 1986– April 1987), I believe that Pakistani soldiers fought in Afghanistan, but not in

large numbers. However, many Pakistani Pushtuns from the Federally Administered Tribal Agencies, NWFP, and Baluchistan fought in Afghanistan. See also Yousaf and Atkin, *Bear Trap;* Bradsher, *Afghanistan and the Soviet Union.*

25. The direct involvement of Pakistani "volunteers" in combat in Afghanistan has been widely reported since 1996. For example, see Anthony Davis, "The Not So Hidden Hand," *Asiaweek,* 25 November 1996; Goodson, "Afghanistan," *Jane's,* 1999, 3, 32. Also, see note 74, chapter 3, and notes 72–73, chapter 4.

26. *The Military Balance 1989–1990* (London: International Institute for Strategic Studies, 1989); Richard F. Nyrop, ed., *Pakistan: A Country Study* (Washington, DC: Foreign Area Studies, American University, 1984).

27. Bradsher, *Afghanistan and the Soviet Union;* Girardet, *Afghanistan: The Soviet War;* David B. Ottaway, "Soviets, Afghan Rebels Pressure US on Arms," *Washington Post,* 2 October 1988; Robert Pear, "Arming Afghan Guerrillas: A Huge Effort Led by US," *New York Times,* 18 April 1988.

28. For example, I interviewed a mujahid instructor near Chitral in June 1987 who said he had received training in China. Also, Amstutz, *Afghanistan: The First Five Years,* 206–214, and Bradsher, *Afghanistan and the Soviet Union,* 277–278, mention the possibility of mujahideen training in Egypt, Iran, and other states.

29. Girardet, *Afghanistan: The Soviet War;* Yousaf and Atkin, *Bear Trap;* Weiner, "Leaks in Afghan Arms Pipeline."

30. I observed the transport and unloading of weapons in Peshawar, Kurram Agency, and North Waziristan Agency during 1987.

31. Major arms depots included sites I visited or learned of near Chitral, Peshawar, Miran Shah, Parachinar, and Quetta. Also see Yousaf and Atkin, *Bear Trap.*

32. Numerous sources report the leakage and diversion of weapons: for example, Edward Girardet, "Corrupt Officials Reap Spoils of Afghan War," *Christian Science Monitor,* 7 September 1988. I saw an enormous diversity and quantity of arms available for sale in the arms bazaars in the Tribal Areas near Peshawar in 1986–1987. Especially prevalent were millions of rounds of Chinese-made 7.62-mm ammunition for the Kalashnikov assault rifle.

33. Girardet, "Corrupt Officials Reap Spoils"; Rupert, "Afghanistan: New Battlefields." Confidential interviews in Pakistan and Afghanistan in 1987.

34. Bradsher, *Afghanistan and the Soviet Union,* 277; Carl Bernstein, "Arms for Afghanistan," *New Republic,* 18 July 1981, 8–10.

35. Pear, "Arming Afghan Guerrillas."

36. *Ibid.;* David B. Ottaway, "US Widens Arms Shipments to Bolster Afghan Guerrillas," *Washington Post,* 21 September 1987.

37. Pear, "Arming Afghan Guerrillas"; Ottaway, "US Widens Arms Shipments"; Ottaway, "Soviets, Afghan Rebels."

38. Pear, "Arming Afghan Guerrillas"; Ottaway, "US Widens Arms Shipments"; Ottaway, "Soviets, Afghan Rebels." Also, Bernstein, "Arms for Afghanistan"; Bradsher, *Afghanistan and the Soviet Union,* 277–278; interview with Theodore Mataxis, field director, Committee for a Free Afghanistan, December 1989.

39. Weiner, "Leaks in Afghan Arms Pipeline," reports the disappearance of 70 percent of the Oerlikons. I located several Oerlikons in a Pakistani military installation in Kurram Agency in 1987. I appreciate the confidential interview given to me by the Washington-based arms merchant who arranged the Oerlikon deal (26 March 1988 in Durham, NC).

40. Pear, "Arming Afghan Guerrillas"; Ottaway, "US Widens Arms Shipments"; Ottaway, "Soviets, Afghan Rebels."

41. Hammond, *Red Flag over Afghanistan,* 218.

42. Bradsher, *Afghanistan and the Soviet Union,* 198.

43. Devin T. Hagerty, "Kashmir and the Nuclear Question," in Kennedy and Rais, *Pakistan 1995,* 168.

44. UNHCR, *Refugees,* 1997; US Committee for Refugees, *World Refugee Survey,* 1989, 1992. See also note 23, chapter 3.

45. United Nations High Commissioner for Refugees, "Fact Sheet: Pakistan," vol. 2, no. 2, October 1988; Said Azhar, "Three Million Uprooted Afghans in Pakistan" (Islamabad: Chief Commissionerate for Afghan Refugees, 15 February 1987).

46. UNHCR, *Refugees,* 1997; US Committee for Refugees, *World Refugee Survey,* 1999.

47. United Nations High Commissioner for Refugees, "Fact Sheet: Iran," vol. 2, no. 2, October 1988. A small percentage of the total number of Afghan refugees (fewer than 5 percent), relocated farther afield, primarily in the United States, Canada, and Europe. Most of these people were better educated and/or had higher social status than the average Afghan refugee and were less likely to be repatriated to Afghanistan when peace made it safe to return.

48. US Committee for Refugees, *World Refugee Survey,* 1992.

49. US Committee for Refugees, *World Refugee Survey,* 1991.

50. UNHCR, *Refugees,* 1997; US Committee for Refugees, *World Refugee Survey,* 1989.

51. Interviews with Sajida Shah, UNHCR public information officer: NWFP, in Peshawar, 25 March 1987; Ahmed Zeb Khan, chief protocol officer, Commissionerate for Afghan Refugees: NWFP, Peshawar, February–March 1987; and Khan Khattak, commissioner for Afghan refugees: NWFP, Peshawar, 6 June 1987.

52. Interview with commissioner for Afghan refugees: Baluchistan, Quetta, 23 April 1987; also, US Committee for Refugees, *World Refugee Survey,* 1989, 79.

53. Amstutz, *Afghanistan: The First Five Years,* 226.

54. The Chief and Provincial Commissionerates for Afghan Refugees in Pakistan kept monthly totals of newly arrived Afghan refugees. See, for example, Azhar, "Three Million Uprooted Afghans."

55. UNHCR, *Refugees,* 1997, 6.

56. These figures are based on primary data collected from the Chief and Provincial Commissionerates for Afghan Refugees' monthly totals during 1987, updated with similar data collected in 1992 and 1997. See also Amstutz, *Afghanistan: The First Five Years,* 228. These figures do not take into account that some massive camps, such as Kacha Gari and Nasir Bagh near Peshawar, are divided into several camp-sized subsections.

57. Louis Dupree, "Cultural Changes among the Mujahidin and Muhajerin," in Bo Huldt and Erland Jansson, eds., *The Tragedy of Afghanistan* (London. Croom Helm, 1988), 20–37; David B. Edwards, "Marginality and Migration: Cultural Dimensions of the Afghan Refugee Problem," *International Migration Review* 20, no. 2, Summer 1986, 313–325.

58. Azhar, "Three Million Uprooted Afghans."

59. Pakistan, Chief Commissioner for Afghan Refugees, *Handbook on Management of Afghan Refugees in Pakistan,* revised edition (Islamabad: States and Frontier Regions Division, 1984), chapter 4; Shah Zaman, *Humanitarian Assistance Programme for Afghan Refugees in North West Frontier Province, Pakistan* (Peshawar, Pakistan: Afghan Refugee Commissionerate, January 1987); Hasan-Askari Rizvi, "Afghan Refugees in Pakistan: Influx, Humanitarian Assistance, and Implications," *Pakistan Horizon* 37, no. 1, Spring 1984, 59; Allen K. Jones, *Afghan Refugees: Five Years Later* (US Committee for Refugees Issue Paper, American Council for Nationalities Service, January 1985), 9. I never interviewed anyone who had received his cash allowance.

60. Interviews with Kevin J. Lyonnette, UNHCR chief of mission: Pakistan, Islamabad, 15 April 1987; and Said Azhar, chief commissioner for Afghan refugees, Islamabad, 10 March 1987.

61. Jeral Ahtone et al., eds., *Operations Manual for Afghan Refugee Health Programme in Pakistan* (Islamabad: United Nations High Commissioner for Refugees and Chief Commissionerate Afghan Refugees, Government of Pakistan, 1986).

62. Interview with Mohammad Javed Khan, agency administrator for Afghan refugees, North Waziristan Agency, Miran Shah, Pakistan, 29 June 1987. Insufficient potable water was cited by most refugee officials as a problem.

63. US Committee for Refugees, *World Refugee Survey,* 1988.

64. Nyrop, *Pakistan: A Country Study,* 314.

65. There were 377,000 Afghan refugees and 250,000 indigenous Pakistanis

in Kurram Agency in late June 1987 (based on primary data collected in interviews in Parachinar, Pakistan, in June 1987).

66. Azhar, "Three Million Uprooted Afghans," 113.

67. Rizvi, "Afghan Refugees in Pakistan," 49.

68. Louis Dupree and Nancy Hatch Dupree, "Afghan Refugees in Pakistan," US Committee for Refugees, *World Refugee Survey*, 1988, 18.

69. The dramatic decline of US humanitarian assistance for the Afghans during the 1990s was perhaps a manifestation of "donor fatigue," but it also represented the decline of the refugees in importance to US geopolitical strategy in South Asia. The Pressler Amendment was invoked in 1990, causing US aid to Pakistan to dry up dramatically, including much of the assistance connected with the Afghan exile population. This amendment required the US government to cease military and economic aid to Pakistan if the US president could not certify that Pakistan did not have a nuclear bomb.

70. United Nations High Commissioner for Refugees, *Report on UNHCR Assistance Activities in 1983–84 and Proposed Voluntary Funds, Programmes and Budget for 1985* (Geneva, 1984), 387; US Committee for Refugees, *World Refugee Survey*, 1983; Jones, *Afghan Refugees*, 12; World Food Program data collected in an interview with John Moore, World Food Program director: NWFP, Peshawar, 11 June 1987; US Department of State, *Afghanistan: Eight Years of Soviet Occupation*. Also US Department of State, Special Reports 155 (1986), 135 (1985), 120 (1984), 112 (1983), 106 (1982), 86 and 79 (1981).

71. US Committee for Refugees, *World Refugee Survey*, 1988.

72. Edward Girardet, "US Humanitarian Aid under Fire," *Christian Science Monitor*, 8 December 1987; numerous interviews, Peshawar, 1987.

73. Weinbaum, "War and Peace in Afghanistan," 72.

74. Hagerty, "Kashmir and the Nuclear Question," 167–168.

75. Marvin Weinbaum, personal communication, 16 January 1999.

76. Rashid, "Pakistan and the Taliban," in Maley, *Fundamentalism*, 74–76.

77. Zaheeruddin Abdullah, "Taliban Army Hosts Billionaire," *Associated Press*, 5 March 1997.

78. UNHCR, *Refugees*, 1997.

79. UNHCR, *Refugees*, 1990; UNHCR, "Fact Sheet: Iran," October 1988.

80. Goodson, "Refugee-Based Insurgency."

81. Richard P. Cronin, "Pakistani Capabilities to Meet the Soviet Threat from Afghanistan," in Theodore L. Eliot, Jr., and Robert L. Pfaltzgraff, Jr., eds., *The Red Army on Pakistan's Border* (Washington, DC: Pergamon-Brassey's International Defense Publishers, 1986), 19–43; S. M. Burke and Lawrence Ziring, *Pakistan's Foreign Policy*, 2d ed. (Karachi: Oxford University Press, 1990), 443–455.

82. Isby, *Russia's War in Afghanistan*, 7; Urban, *War in Afghanistan*, 1988, 118–119.

83. Rashid, "Massive Arms Supplies."

84. Huntington, *Clash of Civilizations.* Also see Ali Banuazizi and Myron Weiner, eds., *The New Geopolitics of Central Asia and Its Borderlands* (Bloomington: Indiana University Press, 1994).

85. Haghayeghi, *Islam and Politics;* Rashid, *Resurgence;* Ludmilla Polonskaya and Alexei Malashenko, *Islam in Central Asia* (Reading, UK: Ithaca Press, 1994).

86. Rashid, "The Taliban: Exporting Extremism."

87. Rahimullah Yusufzai, "Pakistani Taliban at Work," *The News,* 21 December 1998.

88. "The Talibanisation of Chitral," *Frontier Post,* 7 September 1999 (found at Afghanistan Online, www.afghan-web.com).

89. "Shame," *Friday Times* (Pakistan), 13–19 August 1999 (found at Afghanistan Online, www.afghan-web.com).

90. Kathy Gannon, "Religious Extremist Threatens to Murder Lawmakers," *Associated Press,* 19 September 1999 (found at Afghanistan Online, www.afghan-web.com).

91. See Tim Weiner, "Blowback from the Afghan Battlefield," *New York Times Magazine,* 13 March 1994, 52–55.

92. Zalmay Khalilzad, "Anarchy in Afghanistan," *Journal of International Affairs* 51, no. 1, Summer 1997, 50–51.

93. Richard Mackenzie, "The United States and the Taliban," in Maley, *Fundamentalism,* 90–103.

94. Interviews, Peshawar, Pakistan, July 1992.

95. Ahady, "Saudi Arabia," 117–134.

CHAPTER 6. THE FUTURE OF AFGHANISTAN

1. William Maley, "The Dynamics of Regime Transition in Afghanistan," *Central Asian Survey* 16, no. 2, 1997, 167–184.

2. Rubin, *Fragmentation of Afghanistan.*

3. Roy, "New Political Elite"; Yousaf and Atkin, *Bear Trap;* Goodson, "Impact of Arms Proliferation"; Urban, *War in Afghanistan,* 1991; Weinbaum, "Pakistan and Afghanistan"; Kaplan, *Soldiers of God.*

4. Maley, "Dynamics of Regime Transition."

5. See Magnus and Naby, *Afghanistan.*

6. Shahrani, "Future of the State," 212–242.

7. See Roy's *Afghanistan* and *Islam and Resistance,* 1990.

8. Roy, *Afghanistan.*

9. Shahrani, "Future of the State," 212–242; Fänge, "Afghanistan after April 1992."

10. Roy, "New Political Elite," 72–100.

11. Fänge, "Afghanistan after April 1992."

12. See note 107, chapter 4.

13. David Champagne presented this analysis in commentary during a panel session at the annual meeting of the Middle East Studies Association in Chicago, December 1998.

14. Shahrani, "Future of the State," 212–242.

15. *Ibid.*, 238.

16. Goodson, "Mustaqbal Afghanistan" and "Scenarios for the Future."

17. Rashid, "Pakistan and the Taliban," *The Nation.*

18. "Taliban Denounce Mediatory Efforts," *Dawn,* 11 January 1999.

19. The possibility of a partition of Afghanistan into ethnic enclaves has been discussed for more than a decade, but preexisting regional political borders have so far proved more potent than ethnicity. Since the rise of the Taliban, however, Afghanistan's internal conflict has become increasingly virulent, with ethnicity, religion, and race dividing the combatants and providing the basis for atrocities and ethnic cleansing. What long-term impact this will have on Afghanistan's internal solidarity or the relations of its ethnic groups with their cultural cousins in neighboring countries is yet unclear. See Glatzer, "Is Afghanistan on the Brink?" 167–181; Shahrani, "Future of the State," 212–242; Rashid, "The Taliban: Exporting Extremism"; and Rashid, "Pakistan and the Taliban," *The Nation.*

20. The UN Security Council finally became the scene for open condemnation of Pakistani support following the Taliban's 1999 summer offensive, and the sanctions imposed by the UN against the Taliban must in some measure be meant as a message to the Pakistani government. See United Nations Security Council, *Resolution 1267 on the Situation in Afghanistan,* adopted 15 October 1999, and *Resolution 1333 on the Situation in Afghanistan,* adopted 19 December 2000.

21. Francoise Chipaux, "The Man behind the Taliban," (*Le Monde*) *World Press Review* 46, no. 2, February 1999, 31; Moshref, *Taliban;* Marsden, *Taliban.*

22. Rashid, "Divisions Multiply," 21.

23. Interviews, Peshawar and Islamabad, Pakistan, and Kabul, Afghanistan, July 1997.

24. Khalilzad, "Anarchy in Afghanistan," *Journal of International Affairs,* 1997, 55.

25. Interview with analysts at the Bureau of Intelligence and Research, South Asia, US State Department, Washington, DC, 10 December 1998.

26. M. E. Ahrari, *The New Great Game in Muslim Central Asia* (Washington, DC: Institute for National Strategic Studies, McNair Paper no. 47, 1996); M. E.

Ahrari, "The Dynamics of the New Great Game in Muslim Central Asia," *Central Asian Survey* 13, no. 4, 1994, 525–539.

27. Daniel C. Esty et al., *Working Papers: State Failure Task Force Report* (McLean, VA: Science Applications International Corporation, 30 November 1995); Daniel C. Esty et al., *State Failure Task Force Report: Phase 2 Findings* (McLean, VA: Science Applications International Corporation, 31 July 1998); Larry Goodson, "The Future of the State: Creating an Index of State Fragmentation Likelihood," *Proceedings of the Fifth Annual American University in Cairo Research Conference*, Summer 1998, 310–325.

28. Rubin, *Fragmentation of Afghanistan*.

29. I. William Zartman, ed., *Collapsed States* (Boulder, CO: Lynne Rienner, 1995); Robert D. Kaplan, *The Ends of the Earth: A Journey at the Dawn of the Twenty-First Century* (New York: Random House, 1996); Kaplan, "Coming Anarchy."

30. Kaplan, "Coming Anarchy."

31. Francis Fukuyama, *The End of History and the Last Man* (New York: Free Press, 1992).

32. Bruce M. Russett, *Grasping the Democratic Peace: Principles for a Post–Cold War World* (Princeton, NJ: Princeton University Press, 1993).

33. Max Singer and Aaron Wildavsky, *The Real World Order: Zones of Peace, Zones of Turmoil* (Chatham, NJ: Chatham House, 1993). Also see Robert H. Jackson and Alan James, eds., *States in a Changing World* (Oxford: Clarendon Press, 1993).

34. United Nations Development Program, *Human Development Report* (New York: Oxford University Press, 1996, 1997).

35. Kemichi Ohmae, *The End of the Nation State* (New York: Free Press, 1995); Jean-Marie Guehenno, *The End of the Nation-State*, trans. Victoria Elliot (Minneapolis: University of Minnesota Press, 1995); Friedman, *Lexus and Olive Tree;* World Bank, "The State in a Changing World," *World Development Report* (New York: Oxford University Press, 1997).

36. Maley, "Dynamics of Regime Transition."

37. See Roy's *Afghanistan* and *Islam and Resistance*, 1990.

Glossary

Abdur Rahman. Known as the "Iron Amir," he ruled Afghanistan from 1880 to 1901 and was chiefly responsible for transforming it into a state.

Afridi. A Pushtun tribe located in eastern Afghanistan and near Peshawar, Pakistan. Its territory includes the Khyber Pass.

Ahmadzai. An important clan of the Ghilzai Pushtuns.

Aimaq. Also known as Chahar Aimaq, this seminomadic ethnic group lives in northwestern Afghanistan.

Amanullah. King of Afghanistan during 1919–1929. He initiated the Third Anglo-Afghan War in 1919 that led to Afghanistan's independence.

amir. Commander, prince, ruler.

Amir ul-Moemineen. Commander of the Faithful, the title adopted by Mullah Omar of the Taliban in 1996. If acknowledged, this title would make him the leader of all Muslims around the world.

arbab. Chief.

Ariaspians. Tribal forerunners to present-day Pushtuns or Baluch whose tribal council system impressed Alexander the Great enough that he allowed them to continue self-rule.

Aurangzeb. Last of the great Moghul emperors, he ruled in Delhi from 1658 to 1707.

Babur. Founder of the Moghul empire, Babur was a descendent of both Genghis Khan and Tamerlane. He initiated his successful conquest of India from Kabul. He ruled in Delhi only briefly, from 1526 to 1530.

badal. Blood revenge (a theme of Pushtunwali).

baksheesh. Bribe, tip.

Baluch. An ethnic group located in southwestern Afghanistan, in eastern Iran, and, especially, in Baluchistan province of Pakistan.

Barakzai. A major subtribe of the Durrani Pushtuns, the Barakzai have provided Afghanistan's kings since 1835.

basmachi. Outlaw, bandit. The Basmachi rebellion against the USSR occurred in Soviet Central Asia in the 1920s and early 1930s. The Russians called the Central Asian resistance fighters of that time basmachis, or *budmashes,* to try to convince people that they were no more than criminals. The word was also used by the Afghan government and its Soviet advisors during the 1980s to refer to the mujahideen.

Brahui. An ethnic minority living in southwestern Afghanistan and Baluchistan.

burqa. A head-to-toe form of veiling that has a cloth mesh covering the eyes. It is commonly worn by Pushtun women.

buzkashi. The national sport of Afghanistan; it originated on the northern Turkestan plains and in Central Asia. The game involves teams of horsemen competing to lift the carcass of a calf and ride with it to a designated spot while the other riders attempt to stop them.

Chishtiyya. A Sufi order founded in western Afghanistan.

Dari. An Afghan dialect of the Persian language, spoken throughout Afghanistan, especially by Tajiks, Aimaq, and Qizilbash.

Durrani. A major Pushtun tribe based in southwestern Afghanistan. Since

Ahmed Shah Durrani founded Afghanistan in the 1740s, Afghanistan's kings have come from either the Saddozai or Barakzai branch of the Durrani tribe. Some important Taliban leaders are Durrani tribesmen.

Farsiwan. An ethnic group based in western Afghanistan. Its members speak Dari and are primarily Shia Muslims.

Gandamak, Treaty of. A treaty signed in 1879 between the Afghans and the British, meant to conclude the Second Anglo-Afghan War. Under its terms, the British gained substantial Afghan territory and control over Afghanistan's foreign affairs. Afghans viewed it as a national humiliation.

ghayrat. Defense of property and honor (a theme of Pushtunwali).

Ghazni. A strategic town and province between Kabul and Kandahar that was the scene of much fighting in the first two Anglo-Afghan Wars.

Ghilzai. A major Pushtun tribe of eastern and northern Afghanistan.

Gujjar. A tiny ethnic group in eastern Nuristan known for cattle herding. Its members are found in larger numbers in Pakistan.

Hanafi. One of the four major schools of Sunni Islamic law; it is dominant in Afghanistan.

hasht nafari. A system under Abdur Rahman in which one man in every eight was selected for military service on a rotating basis.

Hazara. A major ethnic group of central Afghanistan. The Hazara people are generally Shia, speak Hazaragi, and have Mongoloid racial features.

Hindu Kush. The central mountain range of Afghanistan that splits the northern from the southern part of the country. The name traditionally has been translated as "Hindu Killer," which reflects the fact that the range is viewed as the dividing line between South and Central Asia.

hudud. Penalties prescribed under Islamic law, such as amputations for robbery and stoning for adultery.

Hun. Nomadic, conquering people of ancient Central Asia. Mongoloid in appearance, they may have been ancestors of some present-day ethnic groups of Central Asia.

Imami Shia. Also known as "Twelver" or "Jafari" Shia, this is one of the three major sects of Shiism, the heterodox denomination of Islam that holds that Imam Ali and his descendants should be the leaders of the Islamic community. Most of Afghanistan's Imami Shia are Hazara, Farsiwan, and Qizilbash.

imandari. Righteousness (a theme of Pushtunwali).

Indus. A major river of Pakistan. The Indus delineates the border between the North-West Frontier Province and Punjab Province of Pakistan.

Ismaili Shia. Also known as "Sevener" Shia, this is one of the three major sects of Shiism, the heterodox denomination of Islam that holds that Imam Ali and his descendants should be the leaders of the Islamic community. Most of Afghanistan's small Ismaili Shia population is from tiny northeastern ethnic groups such as the Wakhi and Pamiri people, along with the Hazara.

'isteqamat. Persistence (a theme of Pushtunwali).

Jadidists. Adherents of a liberal Islamic reform movement of Central Asia during the late nineteenth and early twentieth centuries.

Jafari. See **Imami Shia.**

jihad. Holy war.

jirga. A Pushtun council or assembly of elder males; also known as a shura.

Kalashnikovization. Refers to increasing lawlessness, or "Kalashnikov culture," in Pakistan and Afghanistan during the 1980s and 1990s. It is symbolized and was made possible by the ubiquitous availability of the AK-47 assault rifle, or Kalashnikov.

karakul sheep. Fat-tailed sheep whose wool is used to make the distinctive *karakuli* felt caps.

Khalq. Meaning "masses," this was one of the two major factions of the

Afghan communist party, the People's Democratic Party of Afghanistan.
Khalq ruled in 1978–1979.

khan. Landed elite.

khel. Subtribe.

Khilafat (Caliphate). Refers to the leader of the Islamic community.

khol. Extended family group.

Khushal Khan Khattak (1613–1689). The famous Afghan warrior-poet who led
the Pushtuns in revolt against the Moghuls.

Kushan. A Buddhist kingdom that flourished during the first two centuries CE
in areas of present-day Pakistan, Afghanistan, and Central Asia.

Khyber Pass. Historic pass through the present-day Khyber Tribal Agency in
Pakistan to the Afghan border.

kor. Extended family group.

lashkar. War party.

madrasah. Islamic religious school or college.

malik. Local leader, headman.

maulavi. Also an *alim,* this is a madrasah graduate, or religious teacher-
scholar.

mehrmapalineh. Hospitality to guests (a theme of Pushtunwali).

melmastia. Hospitality to guests (a theme of Pushtunwali).

meranah. Manhood (a theme of Pushtunwali).

Moghol. A tiny ethnic group in western Afghanistan that claims to be
descended from the Mongolian soldiers of Genghis Khan. Also, a Muslim
empire in India (1526–1857), founded by Babur.

Mohammadzai. A clan of the Barakzai Durrani that has provided Afghanistan's kings since 1826.

mujahideen. Holy warriors. This was the popular label for the Afghan
resistance fighters during the 1980s and 1990s.

mullah. Local religious leader, priest.

Musahiban. An important family of the Mohammadzai Durrani that
provided Afghanistan's last two kings, Nadir Shah (1929–1933) and Zahir
Shah (1933–1973), as well as two regents in the early years of Zahir Shah's
reign.

namus. Defense of the honor of women (a theme of Pushtunwali).

nanawati. The right of asylum (a theme of Pushtunwali).

Naqshbandiyya. An important Sufi brotherhood in Afghanistan whose present leader is Sibghatullah Mojaddidi, interim president in 1992 and one of
the major mujahideen leaders.

Nuristani. A small ethnic group of eastern Afghanistan whose territory was
called Kafiristan (Land of the Unbelievers) until Abdur Rahman conquered it
and converted the inhabitants to Islam in the 1890s.

Pamiri. A tiny ethnic group in Badakhshan.

Panjdeh Crisis. Russian annexation of an Afghan area in present-day
Turkmenistan in 1885.

Parcham. Meaning "banner," this was one of the two major factions of the
Afghan communist party, the People's Democratic Party of Afghanistan.
Babrak Karmal (1979–1986) and Najibullah (1986–1992) were Parchami rulers
of Afghanistan.

pir. Holy man. This title is usually given to the heads of Sufi orders or to
other religious men with mystical powers.

Pushtun. A major tribal ethnic group living in Afghanistan and the border
areas of Pakistan. The Pushtun speak Pushtu, are primarily Sunni, live by a

tribal code known as Pushtunwali, and have provided virtually all of Afghanistan's rulers since the 1740s.

Pushtunwali. Code of the Pushtuns.

Qadimists. Conservative Islamic rivals to the Jadidists.

Qadiriyya. An important Sufi order in Afghanistan whose present leader is Pir Sayed Ahmed Gailani, one of the major mujahideen leaders of the 1980s.

qarez. Also called *qanat;* an underground aqueduct irrigation system unique to Afghanistan and Iran.

qawm. Communal group.

Qizilbash. A small Shia ethnic minority of Turkic background. Its members live primarily in the major cities.

Rawalpindi, Treaty of. Peace treaty at the end of the Third Anglo-Afghan War of 1919; it established Afghanistan's full independence.

sabat. Steadfastness (a theme of Pushtunwali).

Saddozai. A major subtribe of the Popolzai Durrani Pushtuns. The Saddozai provided Afghanistan's kings from 1747 to 1818.

Safavid. Persian empire (1501–1732) contemporaneous with the Moghul empire of India. The Safavids ruled parts of western Afghanistan.

Saur Revolution. The name given to the PDPA's successful 1978 coup. Also called the April Revolution.

sayyid. In Arabic, the title given to descendants of the Prophet Mohammad. In Afghanistan, it may also be used for holy men and traditional healers.

shabnamah. "Night letters," or antigovernment leaflets distributed clandestinely at night by the mujahideen and more recently by opponents of the Taliban.

sharia. Islamic law; literally, "the path of Allah."

Shia or **Shiism.** A heterodox Islamic sect that believes Ali, son-in-law of the Prophet Mohammad, and Ali's descendents should be the rightful leaders of the Islamic community. About 15 percent of Afghanistan's people are Shia Muslims.

shura. Council or assembly of elder males.

Simla Manifesto. The 1838 declaration of war on Afghanistan by Lord Auckland, governor-general of India. This led directly to the First Anglo-Afghan War of 1838–1842.

Sufism. Islamic mysticism that allows its adherents a more personal experience with Allah. Sufis are organized into *tariqas* (brotherhoods), of which the two most important in Afghanistan today are the Naqshbandiyya and Qadiriyya.

Sunni or **Sunnism.** A major, orthodox Islamic sect that accepts all the early caliphs, or Islamic leaders. Some 80 to 85 percent of Afghanistan's people are Sunni Muslims.

Tajik. A major ethnic group of northeastern Afghanistan; also found in Tajikistan. The Tajiks speak Dari, are both Sunni and Shia, and have provided staunch opposition to the Taliban.

Talibanization. The spread into Pakistan and other countries of the Islamist ideology characteristic of the Taliban movement (for example, no secular entertainment, heavy veiling of women).

tariqa. A Sufi brotherhood.

Timurid. The dynasty founded by Tamerlane and centered on Samarkand and Herat from 1370 to 1506.

Torkham. An Afghan border town at the foot of the Khyber Pass.

tureh. Bravery (a theme of Pushtunwali).

Turkoman. A minor ethnic group of Afghanistan; also found in Turkmenistan.

'ulama. Religious scholars.

Uzbek. A major ethnic group of Afghanistan; also found in Uzbekistan. The Uzbeks speak Turkic dialects, are Sunni, and may have Mongoloid racial features.

Wahhabi. An eighteenth-century conservative Islamic reform movement associated with Saudi Arabia's rulers. Today, a Central Asian Islamist movement is popularly referred to by this name, as were some Arabs serving in Afghanistan with the mujahideen during the 1980s and 1990s.

Wakhi. A minor ethnic group found in the far northeastern Wakhan Corridor.

References Cited

Abdullah, Zaheeruddin. "Taliban Army Hosts Billionaire." *Associated Press,* 5 March 1997.

Abdur Rahman Khan. *The Life of Abdur Rahman, Amir of Afghanistan,* 2 vols. Ed. Mir Munshi Sultan Mahomed Khan. Karachi: Oxford University Press, 1980. First published in 1900.

Adamec, Ludwig. *Afghanistan, 1900–1923.* Berkeley: University of California Press, 1967.

_____. *Afghanistan's Foreign Affairs to the Mid-Twentieth Century.* Tucson: University of Arizona Press, 1974.

_____. *Historical Dictionary of Afghanistan.* Metuchen, NJ: Scarecrow, 1991.

"Afghan Northern Alliance Says Attacked by Pakistan." *Reuters,* 31 July 1998.

"Afghan Taleban Ban Selected Banknotes." *Reuters,* 4 December 1996.

Afghanistan Report. Monthly report by the Crisis and Conflict Analysis Team of the Institute for Strategic Studies, Islamabad, Pakistan. Reports begin in March 1984 (no. 1). Reports up to 1987 (no. 43) were consulted.

Afridi, Rehmat Shah. "Taliban: The Beginning of the End." *Frontier Post,* 11 May 1998.

Ahady, Anwar-ul-Haq. "The Decline of the Pashtuns in Afghanistan." *Asian Survey* 35, no. 7, July 1995, 621–635.

_____. "Saudi Arabia, Iran and the Conflict in Afghanistan." In William Maley, ed., *Fundamentalism Reborn? Afghanistan and the Taliban.* Washington Square, NY: New York University Press, 1998, 117–134.

Ahrari, M. E. "The Dynamics of the New Great Game in Muslim Central Asia." *Central Asian Survey* 13, no. 4, 1994, 525–539.

_____. *The New Great Game in Muslim Central Asia.* Washington, DC: Institute for National Strategic Studies, McNair Paper no. 47, 1996.

Ahtone, Jeral, Altaf-ur-Rahman Khan, Virginia M. Mermel, and Jeanne Betsock Stillman, eds. *Operations Manual for Afghan Refugee Health Programme in Pakistan.* Islamabad: United Nations High Commissioner for Refugees and Chief Commissionerate Afghan Refugees, Government of Pakistan, 1986.

"Alarming Opium Production Rise in Afghanistan Worries UN." *NNI,* 11 September 1999. Found at Afghanistan Online, www.afghan-web.com.

Alexiev, Alexander. *Inside the Soviet Army in Afghanistan.* Santa Monica, CA: RAND Corporation, R-3627-A, May 1988.

_____. "The Soviet Strategy in Afghanistan." *Global Affairs,* Winter 1987.

Ali, Salamat. "A Peace on Paper." *Far Eastern Economic Review,* 18 March 1993, 22.

Alison, Sebastian. "US Firm Unocal Gloomy on Turkmen Pipeline Project." *Reuters,* 11 March 1998.

Allworth, Edward, ed. *Central Asia: 120 Years of Russian Rule.* Durham, NC: Duke University Press, 1989.

Almond, Gabriel A., and James S. Coleman, eds. *The Politics of the Developing Areas.* Princeton, NJ: Princeton University Press, 1960.

Amstutz, J. Bruce. *Afghanistan: The First Five Years of Soviet Occupation.* Washington, DC: National Defense University, 1986.

Anderson, John. *The International Politics of Central Asia.* Manchester, UK: Manchester University Press, 1997.

Arney, George. *Afghanistan.* London: Mandarin, 1990.

Arnold, Anthony. *Afghanistan: The Soviet Invasion in Perspective.* Stanford, CA: Hoover Institution Press, 1981.

_____. *Afghanistan's Two-Party Communism: Parcham and Khalq.* Stanford, CA: Hoover Institution Press, 1983.

Asghar, Raja. "Pakistan Urges World to Recognize Afghan Taleban." *Reuters,* 15 August 1998.

Azhar, Said. *Handbook on Management of Afghan Refugees in Pakistan,* rev. ed. Islamabad: Chief Commissioner for Afghan Refugees, Government of Pakistan, 1984.

_____. "Three Million Uprooted Afghans in Pakistan." Islamabad: Chief Commissionerate for Afghan Refugees, 15 February 1987.

Azoy, G. Whitney. *Buzkashi: Game and Power in Afghanistan.* Philadelphia: University of Pennsylvania Press, 1982.

Bacon, Elizabeth E. *Central Asians under Russian Rule: A Study in Culture Change.* Ithaca, NY: Cornell University Press, 1966, 1980 (paperback).

Banuazizi, Ali, and Myron Weiner, eds. *The New Geopolitics of Central Asia and Its Borderlands.* Bloomington: Indiana University Press, 1994.

_____, eds. *The State, Religion, and Ethnic Politics: Afghanistan, Iran, and Pakistan.* Syracuse, NY: Syracuse University Press, 1986.

Barber, Benjamin R. *Jihad v. McWorld.* New York: Times Books, 1995.

Baxter, Craig, and Charles H. Kennedy, eds. *Pakistan 2000.* New York: Lexington Books, 2000.

Beblawi, Hazem, and Giancomo Luciani, eds. *The Rentier State.* New York: Croom Helm, 1987.

Bennigsen, Alexandre. "The Soviet Union and Muslim Guerrilla Wars, 1920–1981: Lessons for Afghanistan." *Conflict* 4, nos. 2–4, 1983, 301–324.

Bernstein, Carl. "Arms for Afghanistan." *New Republic,* 18 July 1981, 8–10.

Bodansky, Yossef. "Soviet Military Involvement in Afghanistan." In Rosanne Klass, ed., *Afghanistan: The Great Game Revisited.* New York: Freedom House, 1987, 229–285.

Bonner, Arthur. *Among the Afghans.* Durham, NC: Duke University Press, 1987.

Bradsher, Henry S. *Afghanistan and the Soviet Union,* new expanded ed. Durham, NC: Duke University Press, 1985.

Buddenberg, Doris. *Illicit Drugs and Drug Policies in Pakistan.* United Nations Research Institute for Social Development, 1996.

Burke, S. M., and Lawrence Ziring. *Pakistan's Foreign Policy,* 2d ed. Karachi: Oxford University Press, 1990.

Burns, John F. "Afghans: Now They Blame America." *New York Times Magazine,* 4 February 1990, 22 29, 37.

Canfield, Robert L. "Afghanistan: The Trajectory of Internal Alignments." *Middle East Journal* 43, no. 4, Autumn 1989, 635–648.

_____. "Ethnic, Regional, and Sectarian Alignments in Afghanistan." In Ali Banuazizi and Myron Weiner, eds., *The State, Religion, and Ethnic Politics: Afghanistan, Iran, and Pakistan.* Syracuse, NY: Syracuse University Press, 1986, 75–103.

Caroe, Olaf. *The Pathans.* Karachi: Oxford University Press, 1958.

Chaffetz, David. *Afghanistan, Russia's Vietnam?* Special Paper no. 4. New York: Afghanistan Council of the Asia Society, 1979.

Chipaux, Francoise. "The Man behind the Taliban." (*Le Monde*) *World Press Review* 46, no. 2, February 1999.

Collins, Joseph J. *The Soviet Invasion of Afghanistan.* Lexington, MA: Lexington Books, 1985.

Cordovez, Diego, and Selig S. Harrison. *Out of Afghanistan: The Inside Story of the Soviet Withdrawal.* New York: Oxford University Press, 1995.

Cronin, Richard P. "Pakistani Capabilities to Meet the Soviet Threat from

Afghanistan." In Theodore L. Eliot, Jr., and Robert L. Pfaltzgraff, Jr., eds., *The Red Army on Pakistan's Border.* Washington, DC: Pergamon-Brassey's International Defense Publishers, 1986, 19–43.

Davis, Anthony. "How the Taliban Became a Military Force." In William Maley, ed., *Fundamentalism Reborn? Afghanistan and the Taliban.* Washington Square, NY: New York University Press, 1998, 43–71.

_____. "The Not So Hidden Hand." *Asiaweek,* 25 November 1996.

d'Encausse, Hélène Carrère. "Civil War and New Governments." In Edward Allworth, ed., *Central Asia: 120 Years of Russian Rule.* Durham, NC: Duke University Press, 1989, 224–253.

Diller, Daniel C., ed. *Russia and the Independent States.* Washington, DC: Congressional Quarterly, 1993.

Dorronsoro, Gilles, and Chantal Lobato. "The Militia in Afghanistan." *Central Asian Survey* 8, no. 4, 1989.

Dupree, Louis. *Afghanistan.* Princeton, NJ: Princeton University Press, 1973.

_____. *American Universities Field Staff Reports.* Occasional reports in the Asia and South Asia series, 1960–1980.

_____. "Cultural Changes among the Mujahidin and Muhajerin." Paper presented to the seminar "Afghanistan: A Threatened Culture" at the Swedish Institute of International Affairs, Stockholm, December 1985.

_____. "Cultural Changes among the Mujahidin and Muhajerin." In Bo Huldt and Erland Jansson, eds., *The Tragedy of Afghanistan.* London: Croom Helm, 1988, 20–37.

_____. "Post-Withdrawal Afghanistan: Light at the End of the Tunnel." In Amin Saikal and William Maley, eds., *The Soviet Withdrawal from Afghanistan.* Cambridge: Cambridge University Press, 1989, 29–51.

_____. "Soviet Intervention in Afghanistan: A New Ball Game." Paper delivered at the annual meeting of the American Political Science Association, New Orleans, 1985.

Dupree, Louis, and Nancy Hatch Dupree. "Afghan Refugees in Pakistan." In US Committee for Refugees, *World Refugee Survey.* New York: American Council for Nationalities Service, 1988, 18–21.

Edwards, David B. *Heroes of the Age: Moral Fault Lines on the Afghan Frontier.* Berkeley: University of California Press, 1996.

_____. "Marginality and Migration: Cultural Dimensions of the Afghan Refugee Problem." *International Migration Review* 20, no. 2, Summer 1986, 313–325.

Edwards, Mike. "When the Moguls Ruled." *National Geographic* 167, no. 4, April 1985, 462–493.

Eliot, Theodore L., Jr. "Afghanistan in 1990." *Asian Survey* 31, no. 2, February 1991, 125–133.

Emadi, Hafizullah. "The End of *Taqiyya:* Reaffirming the Religious Identity of Ismailis in Shughnan, Badakhshan—Political Implications for Afghanistan." *Middle East Studies* 34, no. 3, July 1998, 103–120.

_____. "The State and Rural-Based Rebellion in Afghanistan." *Central Asian Survey* 15, no. 2, 1996, 201–211.

Esty, Daniel C., et al. *State Failure Task Force Report: Phase 2 Findings.* McLean, VA: Science Applications International Corporation, 31 July 1998.

_____, et al. *Working Papers: State Failure Task Force Report.* McLean, VA: Science Applications International Corporation, 30 November 1995.

Eyre, Vincent. *Journal of an Afghanistan Prisoner.* London: Routledge and Kegan Paul, 1976. First published London, 1843.

Fänge, Anders. "Afghanistan after April 1992: A Struggle for State and Ethnicity." *Central Asian Survey* 14, no. 1, 1995, 17–24.

Farr, Grant M., and John G. Merriam, eds. *Afghan Resistance: The Politics of Survival.* Boulder, CO: Westview, 1987.

Fazal ur Rahim, Khan Marwat. *The Basmachi Movement in Soviet Central Asia.* Peshawar, Pakistan: Emjay Book International, 1985.

Fisher, W. B. "Afghanistan: Physical and Social Geography." *Middle East and North Africa Yearbook 1990.* London: Europa Publications, 1990

Fishlock, Trevor. "Fire of the Taliban Threatens to Ignite Oil Region." *Electronic Telegraph,* Issue 1178, 16 August 1998.

Foreign Broadcast Information Service, Near East Section, vol. 93, transcript no. 135, 16 July 1993.

Fraser-Tytler, W. K. *Afghanistan: A Study of Political Developments in Central and Southern Asia,* 3d ed. London: Oxford University Press, 1967.

Friedman, Thomas L. *The Lexus and the Olive Tree.* New York: Farrar Strauss Giroux, 1999.

Fukuyama, Francis. *The End of History and the Last Man.* New York: Free Press, 1992.

Fuller, Graham E. *Islamic Fundamentalism in Afghanistan: Its Character and Prospects.* Santa Monica, CA: RAND Corporation, 1991.

Galeotti, Mark. *Afghanistan: The Soviet Union's Last War.* London: Frank Cass, 1995.

Gall, Sandy. *Afghanistan: Agony of a Nation.* London: Bodley Head, 1988.

_____. *Behind Russian Lines.* London: Sidgwick and Jackson, 1983.

Gamer, Robert E. *The Developing Nations: A Comparative Perspective,* 2d ed. Dubuque, IA: Wm. C. Brown, 1988.

Gannon, Kathy. "Religious Extremist Threatens to Murder Lawmakers." *Associated Press.* 19 September 1999. Found at Afghanistan Online, www.afghanweb.com.

Garfinkle, Adam. "Why Afghanistan Matters to Everyone." *Orbis* 43, no. 3, Summer 1999, 405–418.

Getler, Michael. "US Stingers Boost Afghan Rebels' Performance and Morale." *Washington Post,* 14 October 1987.

Ghani, Ashraf. "Islam and State-Building in a Tribal Society: Afghanistan, 1880–1901." *Modern Asian Studies* 12, no. 2, 1978, 269–284.

Ghaus, Abdul Samad. *The Fall of Afghanistan.* Washington, DC: Pergamon-Brassey's International Defense Publishers, 1988.

Girardet, Edward. "Afghan Fighters Slowly Erode Soviet Control." *Christian Science Monitor,* 13 December 1987, 7–8.

_____. *Afghanistan: The Soviet War.* New York: St. Martin's, 1985.

_____. "Corrupt Officials Reap Spoils of Afghan War." *Christian Science Monitor,* 7 September 1988.

_____. "Migratory Genocide." *New Republic,* 4 March 1985, 13–18.

_____. "US Humanitarian Aid under Fire." *Christian Science Monitor,* 8 December 1987.

Giustozzi, Antonio. *War, Politics and Society in Afghanistan, 1978–1992.* Washington, DC: Georgetown University Press, 2000.

Glatzer, Bernt. "Is Afghanistan on the Brink of Ethnic and Tribal Disintegration?" In William Maley, ed., *Fundamentalism Reborn? Afghanistan and the Taliban.* Washington Square, NY: New York University Press, 1998, 167–181.

Gleason, Gregory. *The Central Asian States.* Boulder, CO: Westview, 1997.

Goodson, Larry. "Afghan War Spillover into Pakistan." *Frontier Review* 1, no. 4, Spring 1988, 14–16.

_____. "Afghanistan." *Collier's Encyclopedia.* In Russian. Moscow: Open Society Institute, 1999.

_____. "Afghanistan." *Jane's Sentinel Security Assessment, South Asia.* Coulsdon, UK: Jane's Information Group, 1999, 1–47.

_____. "Afghanistan." *Jane's Sentinel Security Assessment, South Asia.* Coulsdon, UK: Jane's Information Group, 2000.

_____. *Afghanistan Culturgram.* Provo, UT: Brigham Young University Press, 1995.

_____. "Clash of Communities in Afghanistan: The Taliban and Their Impact on National Unity." Paper presented at the 32d annual meeting of the Middle East Studies Association, Chicago, December 1998.

_____. "The Culture of Fragmentation in Afghanistan." *Alif: Journal of Comparative Poetics* 18, Spring 1998, 269–289.

_____. "Foreign Policy Gone Awry: The Kalashnikovization and Talibanization of Pakistan." In Craig Baxter and Charles H. Kennedy, eds., *Pakistan 2000.* New York: Lexington Books, 2000, 107–28.

_____. "The Future of Afghanistan in the Changing World Order: Civil War and National Fragmentation as Obstacles to Nation-Building in the 1990s." Paper presented at the annual meeting of the Southern Political Science Association, Tampa, FL, November 1991.

_____. "The Future of the State: Creating an Index of State Fragmentation Likelihood." *Proceedings of the Fifth Annual American University in Cairo Research Conference,* Summer 1998, 310–325.

_____. "The Impact of Arms Proliferation on the Resolution of Regional Conflict: The Drug Culture and 'Kalashnikovization' of Afghanistan." Paper presented at the annual meeting of the American Political Science Association, Chicago, September 1992.

_____. "Jallaluddin Haqqani: Portrait of a Mujahideen Commander." *Free Afghanistan Report,* Special Edition January–February 1988, 4–5.

_____. "Mustaqbal Afghanistan Bayn Al Siraa' Al Erqi Wal Tafattut Al Siyasi" [The Future of Afghanistan: Ethnic Conflict and Political Fragmentation], in Ibrahim Arafat, ed., *Al Qadiyah Al Afghaniyah Wa Inikasatiha Al Iqlimiyah Wal Dawliyah* [The Case of Afghanistan: Its Regional and International Implications]. Center for Asian Studies, Cairo University, 1999, 301–318.

_____. "Periodicity and Intensity in the Afghan War." *Central Asian Survey* 17, no. 3, 1998, 471–488.

_____. "Perverting Islam: Taliban Social Policy Toward Women." Paper presented at the 34th Annual Meeting of the Middle East Studies Association, Orlando, FL, November 2000.

_____. "Refugee-Based Insurgency: The Afghan Case." Ph.D. dissertation, University of North Carolina, 1990.

_____. "Scenarios for the Future of the Afghan State." *Middle East Affairs Journal* 2, no. 1, Spring–Summer 1994, 32–48.

Goodwin, Jan. *Caught in the Crossfire.* New York: E. Dutton, 1987.

Gregorian, Vartan. *The Emergence of Modern Afghanistan.* Stanford, CA: Stanford University Press, 1969.

Guehenno, Jean-Marie. *The End of the Nation-State.* Trans. Victoria Elliot. Minneapolis: University of Minnesota Press, 1995.

Gunston, John. "Special Report: Afghanistan War." *Aviation Week and Space Technology* 121, no. 18, 29 October 1984, 38–44.

Gurt, Marat. "Afghan News: Oil, Gas, and Others." *Reuters,* 25 October 1997 (title incorrect, story provided by Zieba Shorish-Shamley in personal communication).

Habberton, W. *Anglo-Russian Relations concerning Afghanistan: 1837–1907.* Urbana: University of Illinois Press, 1937.

Hagerty, Devin T. "Kashmir and the Nuclear Question." In Charles H. Kennedy and Rasul Baksh Rais, eds., *Pakistan 1995*. Boulder, CO: Westview, 1995, 159–192.

Haghayeghi, Mehrdad. *Islam and Politics in Central Asia*. New York: St. Martin's, 1995.

Hammond, Thomas T. *Red Flag over Afghanistan*. Boulder, CO: Westview, 1984.

Haq, Ikramul. "Pak-Afghan Drug Trade in Historical Perspective." *Asian Survey* 36, no. 10, October 1996, 945–963.

Harpviken, Kristian Berg. "Transcending Traditionalism: The Emergence of Non-State Military Formations in Afghanistan." *Journal of Peace Research* 34, no. 3, 1997, 271–287.

Harrison, Selig S. "Inside the Afghan Talks." *Foreign Policy* 72, Fall 1988, 31–60.

Hauner, Milan, and Robert L. Canfield, eds. *Afghanistan and the Soviet Union: Collision and Transformation*. Boulder, CO: Westview, 1989.

Heathcote, T. A. *The Afghan Wars*. London: Osprey, 1980.

Hodson, Peregrine. *Under a Sickle Moon: A Journey through Afghanistan*. London: Hutchinson, 1986.

Holt, Frank L. *Alexander the Great and Bactria*. Leiden: E. J. Brill, 1988.

Howell, Evelyn. *Mizh*. Karachi: Oxford University Press, 1979.

Huldt, Bo, and Erland Jansson, eds. *The Tragedy of Afghanistan*. London: Croom Helm, 1988.

Human Rights Watch. *Afghanistan: The Massacre in Mazar-i Sharif* 10, no. 7, November 1998, www.hrw.org.

Huntington, Samuel. *The Clash of Civilizations and the Remaking of World Order*. New York: Simon and Schuster, 1996.

Hyman, Anthony. *Afghanistan under Soviet Domination, 1964–1983*. London: Macmillan, 1984.

———. "Russia, Central Asia and the Taliban." In William Maley, ed., *Fundamentalism Reborn? Afghanistan and the Taliban*. Washington Square, NY: New York University Press, 1998, 104–116.

Isby, David. "Flares over Afghanistan." *Soldier of Fortune*, November 1987, 40.

———. *Russia's War in Afghanistan*. London: Osprey, 1986.

Jackson, Robert H., and Alan James, eds. *States in a Changing World*. Oxford: Clarendon Press, 1993.

Johnston, Tim. "Taliban Fire Civil Servants." *Reuters*, 4 November 1997.

Jones, Allen K. *Afghan Refugees: Five Years Later*. US Committee for Refugees Issue Paper, American Council for Nationalities Service, January 1985.

"Kabul's Past." *Los Angeles Times*, 14 November 1996.

Kakar, Hasan Kawun. *Government and Society in Afghanistan*. Austin: University of Texas Press, 1979.

Kakar, M. Hassan. *Afghanistan: The Soviet Invasion and the Afghan Response, 1979–1982*. Berkeley: University of Califonria Press, 1995.

Kamrany, Nake M. *The Six Stages in the Sovietization of Afghanistan*. Boulder, CO: Economic Institute for Research and Education, 1983.

Kaplan, Robert D. "Afghanistan: Postmortem." *Atlantic Monthly*, April 1989, 26–29.

_____. "The Coming Anarchy." *Atlantic Monthly*, February 1994, 44–76.

_____. *The Ends of the Earth: A Journey at the Dawn of the Twenty-First Century*. New York: Random House, 1996.

_____. *Soldiers of God*. Boston: Houghton Mifflin, 1990.

Kennedy, Charles H., and Rasul Baksh Rais, eds. *Pakistan 1995*. Boulder, CO: Westview, 1995.

Khalidi, Noor Ahmed. "Afghanistan: Demographic Consequences of War, 1978–1987." *Central Asian Survey* 10, no. 3, 1991, 101–126.

Khalilzad, Zalmay. "Anarchy in Afghanistan." *Journal of International Affairs* 51, no. 1, Summer 1997, 37–56.

Khan, Aimal. "Dacoities on Rise in Taliban-Ruled Areas." *Frontier Post*, 5 October 1999.

Khan, Riaz M. *Untying the Afghan Knot*. Durham, NC: Duke University Press, 1991.

Kipling, Rudyard. *Kim*. Hertfordshire, UK: Wordworth, 1993. First published 1901.

Klass, Rosanne. "Afghanistan: The Accords." *Foreign Affairs* 66, no. 5, Summer 1988, 922–945.

_____, ed. *Afghanistan: The Great Game Revisited*. New York: Freedom House, 1987.

_____. "The Great Game Revisited." In Rosanne Klass, ed., *Afghanistan: The Great Game Revisited*. New York: Freedom House, 1987, 1–29.

_____. "Who's Who in the Afghanistan Resistance." In Rosanne Klass, ed., *Afghanistan: The Great Game Revisited*, 1987, 427–437.

_____. "Who's Who in the DRA and the PDPA: A Selected List." In Rosanne Klass, ed., *Afghanistan: The Great Game Revisited*, 1987, 439–484.

Langford, Tonya. "Things Fall Apart: State Failure and the Politics of Intervention." *International Studies Review* 1, no. 1, Spring 1999, 59–79.

Lee, J. L. *The 'Ancient Supremacy': Bukhara, Afghanistan and the Battle for Balkh, 1731–1901*. Leiden: E. J. Brill, 1996.

Lessing, Doris. *The Wind Blows Away Our Words*. London: Pan Books, 1987.

"A Letter from a Soviet Ambassador." In Rosanne Klass, ed., *Afghanistan: The Great Game Revisited*. New York: Freedom House, 1987, 31–34.

Mackenzie, Richard. "Afghan Rebels Never Say Die." *Insight*, three-part story, 25 January 1988, 8–21.

_____. "The United States and the Taliban." In William Maley, ed., *Fundamentalism Reborn? Afghanistan and the Taliban.* Washington Square, NY: New York University Press, 1998, 90–103.

Macrory, Patrick. *Signal Catastrophe.* London: Hodder and Stoughton, 1966.

Magnus, Ralph H. "Afghanistan in 1996: Year of the Taliban." *Asian Survey* 37, no. 2, February 1997, 111–117.

Magnus, Ralph H., and Eden Naby. *Afghanistan: Mullah, Marx, and Mujahid.* Boulder, CO: Westview, 1998.

Majrooh, S. B., and S. M. Y. Elmi. *The Sovietization of Afghanistan.* Peshawar, Pakistan: Frontier Limited, 1986.

Maley, William. "The Dynamics of Regime Transition in Afghanistan." *Central Asian Survey* 16, no. 2, 1997, 167–184.

_____, ed. *Fundamentalism Reborn? Afghanistan and the Taliban.* Washington Square, NY: New York University Press, 1998.

_____. "The Geneva Accords of April 1988." In Amin Saikal and William Maley, eds., *The Soviet Withdrawal from Afghanistan.* Cambridge: Cambridge University Press, 1989, 12–28.

_____. "Introduction: Interpreting the Taliban." In William Maley, ed., *Fundamentalism Reborn? Afghanistan and the Taliban.* Washington Square, NY: New York University Press, 1998, 16–23.

_____. "The Perils of Pipelines." *The World Today,* August–September 1998, 231–232.

_____. "Taliban Triumphant?" *The World Today,* November 1996, 275–276.

_____. "The UN in Afghanistan: 'Doing Its Best' or 'Failure of a Mission'?" In William Maley, ed., *Fundamentalism Reborn? Afghanistan and the Taliban.* Washington Square, NY: New York University Press, 1998, 182–198.

Marsden, Peter. *The Taliban: War, Religion, and the New Order in Afghanistan.* London: Zed Books, 1998.

Martin, Mike. *Afghanistan: Inside a Rebel Stronghold.* Poole, Dorset, UK: Blandford Press, 1984.

Mataxis, Theodore. "Perestroika and Glasnost—Not in Afghanistan." *Free Afghanistan Report,* February 1990, 3.

McChesney, Robert D. *Kabul under Siege: Fayz Muhammad's Account of the 1929 Uprising.* Princeton, NJ: Markus Wiener, 1999.

Mecham, Michael. "US Credits Afghan Resistance with Thwarting Soviet Air Power." *Aviation Week and Space Technology,* 13 July 1987, 26–27.

Merriam, John G. "Arms Shipments to the Afghan Resistance." In Grant M. Farr and John G. Merriam, eds., *Afghan Resistance: The Politics of Survival.* Boulder, CO: Westview, 1987, 71–102.

Metcalf, Barbara D. *Islamic Revival in British India: Deoband, 1860–1900.* Princeton, NJ: Princeton University Press, 1982.

Migdal, Joel S. *Strong Societies and Weak States.* Princeton, NJ: Princeton University Press, 1988.

The Military Balance 1989–1990. London: International Institute for Strategic Studies, 1989.

Moorhouse, Geoffrey. *To The Frontier.* New York: Holt, Rinehart and Winston, 1984.

Moshref, Rameen. *The Taliban.* Occasional Paper no. 335. New York: Afghanistan Forum, 1997.

Nathan Associates, Inc.–Louis Berger International, Inc. "Afghanistan Studies Project: Report of the Opium Subsector Survey." Unpublished manuscript, August 1992.

Newell, Richard S., and Nancy Peabody Newell. *The Struggle for Afghanistan.* Ithaca, NY: Cornell University Press, 1981.

Noorzoy, M. Siddieq. "Long-Term Soviet Economic Interests and Policies in Afghanistan." In Rosanne Klass, ed., *Afghanistan: The Great Game Revisited.* New York: Freedom House, 1987, 71–95.

––––––. "Some Observations on and Assessment of the Population Losses in Afghanistan." *WUFA, Journal of the Writers Union of Free Afghanistan* 3, no. 3, 1988, 6–14.

Norris, J. A. *The First Afghan War, 1838–1842.* Cambridge: Cambridge University Press, 1967.

Nyrop, Richard F., ed. *Pakistan: A Country Study.* Washington, DC: Foreign Area Studies, American University, 1984.

Nyrop, Richard F., and Donald M. Seekins, eds. *Afghanistan: A Country Study.* Washington, DC: Foreign Area Studies, American University, 1986.

Ohmae, Kenichi. *The End of the Nation State.* New York: Free Press, 1995.

Olesen, Asta. *Islam and Politics in Afghanistan.* Surrey, UK: Curzon Press, 1995.

O'Rourke, P. J. "Bizarre Bazaar." *Rolling Stone,* 20 April 1989, 87–92, 109.

Ottaway, David B. "Soviets, Afghan Rebels Pressure US on Arms." *Washington Post,* 2 October 1988.

––––––. "US Widens Arms Shipments to Bolster Afghan Guerrillas." *Washington Post,* 21 September 1987.

Pakistan, Chief Commissioner for Afghan Refugees. *Handbook on Management of Afghan Refugees in Pakistan,* (revised) edition. Islamabad: States and Frontier Regions Division, 1984.

––––––. *Humanitarian Assistance Programme for Afghan Refugees in Pakistan.* Islamabad: Chief Commissionerate for Afghan Refugees, July 1984.

Pakistan, Chief and Provincial Commissionerates for Afghan Refugees. Unpublished primary data including monthly refugee totals, memoranda, maps, and other documents.

"Pakistan TV: Government Dismissed." *Associated Press,* 12 October 1999. Found at Afghanistan Online, www.afghan-web.com.

"Pakistani Army Moves against Prime Minister after Military Chief Sacked." *CNN,* 12 October 1999. Found at Afghanistan Online, www.afghanweb.com.

Palmer, Caitriona. "The Taliban's War on Women." *Lancet* 352, no. 9129, 29 August 1998, 734–735.

Palmer, Monte. *Dilemmas of Political Development,* 4th ed. Itasca, IL: F. E. Peacock, 1989.

Payind, Alam. "Evolving Alternative Views on the Future of Afghanistan." *Asian Survey* 33, no. 9, September 1993, 923–931.

———. "Soviet-Afghan Relations from Cooperation to Occupation." *International Journal of Middle Eastern Studies* 21, 1989, 107–128.

Pear, Robert. "Arming Afghan Guerrillas: A Huge Effort Led by US." *New York Times,* 18 April 1988.

Physicians for Human Rights. *The Taliban's War on Women: A Health and Human Rights Crisis in Afghanistan.* Boston: Physicians for Human Rights, 1998.

Pierce, Richard A. *Russian Central Asia 1867–1917: A Study in Colonial Rule.* Berkeley: University of California Press, 1960.

Poladi, Hassan. *The Hazaras.* Stockton, CA: Moghul Press, 1989.

Polonskaya, Ludmilla, and Alexei Malashenko. *Islam in Central Asia.* Reading, UK: Ithaca Press, 1994.

Porter, Bruce D. *The USSR in Third World Conflicts.* Cambridge: Cambridge University Press, 1984.

Poullada, Leon B. *Reform and Rebellion in Afghanistan, 1919–1929.* Ithaca, NY: Cornell University Press, 1973.

———. "The Road to Crisis, 1919–1980." In Rosanne Klass, ed., *Afghanistan: The Great Game Revisited.* New York: Freedom House, 1987, 37–69.

Quddus, Syed Abdul. *The Pathans.* Lahore, Pakistan: Ferozsons, 1987.

Rais, Rasul Baksh. *War without Winners.* Karachi: Oxford, 1994.

Rashid, Abdur. "The Afghan Resistance: Its Background, Its Nature, and the Problem of Unity." In Rosanne Klass, ed., *Afghanistan: The Great Game Revisited.* New York: Freedom House, 1987, 203–227.

Rashid, Ahmed. "Back with a Vengeance: Proxy War in Afghanistan." *The World Today,* March 1996, 60–63.

———. "Crime of the Century." *Far Eastern Economic Review,* 21 September 1995, 60–62.

_____. "Divisions Multiply." *Far Eastern Economic Review*, 31 July 1997, 20–21.

_____. "Massive Arms Supplies Reach All Afghan Factions." *The Nation*, 15 March 1998.

_____. "Pakistan and the Taliban." *The Nation*, four-part article, April 1998.

_____. "Pakistan and the Taliban." in William Maley, ed., *Fundamentalism Reborn? Afghanistan and the Taliban*. Washington Square, NY: New York University Press, 1998, 72–89.

_____. *The Resurgence of Central Asia*. Karachi: Oxford University Press, 1994.

_____. "The Taliban: Exporting Extremism." *Foreign Affairs* 78, no. 6, November–December 1999, 22–35.

_____. *Taliban: Militant Islam, Oil, and Fundamentalism in Central Asia*. New Haven, CT: Yale University Press, 2000.

Reeves, Richard. *Passage to Peshawar*. New York: Simon and Schuster, 1984.

Rizvi, Hasan-Askari. "Afghan Refugees in Pakistan: Influx, Humanitarian Assistance, and Implications." *Pakistan Horizon* 37, no. 1, Spring 1984, 40–61.

Rogers, Tom. *The Soviet Withdrawal from Afghanistan: Analysis and Chronology*. Westport, CT: Greenwood, 1992.

Roy, Olivier. *Afghanistan: From Holy War to Civil War*. Princeton, NJ: Darwin Press, 1995.

_____. *The Failure of Political Islam*. Cambridge: Harvard University Press, 1994.

_____. "Has Islamism a Future in Afghanistan?" In William Maley, ed., *Fundamentalism Reborn? Afghanistan and the Taliban*. Washington Square, NY: New York University Press, 1998, 199–211.

_____. *Islam and Resistance in Afghanistan*. Cambridge: Cambridge University Press, 1986.

_____. *Islam and Resistance in Afghanistan*, 2d ed. Cambridge: Cambridge University Press, 1990.

_____. "The New Political Elite of Afghanistan." In Myron Weiner and Ali Banuazizi, eds., *The Politics of Social Transformation in Afghanistan, Iran, and Pakistan*. Syracuse, NY: Syracuse University Press, 1994, 72–100.

Roy, Ranjan. "Afghans Want Entertainment." *Associated Press*, 7 December 1996.

_____. "City Crackdown." *Associated Press*, 9 December 1996.

Rubin, Barnett R. "Afghanistan: Back to Feudalism." *Current History* 88, no. 542, December 1989, 421–424, 444–446.

_____. "Afghanistan: Persistent Crisis Challenges the UN System." *REFWORLD, WRITENET Country Papers*, August 1998. www.unhcr.ch/refworld.country/writenet/wriafgo3.htm.

_____. "Afghanistan in 1993: Abandoned but Surviving." *Asian Survey* 34, no. 2, February 1994.

_____. "Afghanistan under the Taliban." *Current History* 98, no. 625, February 1999, 79–91.

_____. "The Fragmentation of Afghanistan." *Foreign Affairs* 68, no. 5, Winter 1989–1990, 150–168.

_____. *The Fragmentation of Afghanistan.* New Haven, CT: Yale University Press, 1995.

_____. "The Political Economy of War and Peace in Afghanistan." Online Center for Afghan Studies, www.afghan-politics.org, 21 June 1999.

_____. "Political Elites in Afghanistan: Rentier State Building, Rentier State Wrecking." *International Journal of Middle East Studies* 24, no. 1, February 1992, 77–99.

_____. *The Search for Peace in Afghanistan.* New Haven, CT: Yale University Press, 1995.

_____. "Testimony on the Situation in Afghanistan." United States Senate, Committee on Foreign Relations, 8 October 1998. Found at Online Center for Afghan Studies, www.afghan-politics.org.

Rupert, James. "Afghanistan: The New Battlefields." *Washington Post,* five-part series, 12–16 January 1986.

Russett, Bruce M. *Grasping the Democratic Peace: Principles for a Post–Cold War World.* Princeton, NJ: Princeton University Press, 1993.

Ryan, Nigel. *A Hitch or Two in Afghanistan: A Journey behind Russian Lines.* London: Weidenfeld and Nicolson, 1983.

Saikal, Amin. "Afghanistan's Ethnic Conflict." *Survival* 40, no. 2, Summer 1998, 114–126.

Saikal, Amin, and William Maley, eds. *The Soviet Withdrawal from Afghanistan.* Cambridge: Cambridge University Press, 1989.

Salahuddin, Sayed. "Afghan Rivals Said to Agree on Gas Pipeline Plan." *Reuters,* 22 May 1998.

_____. "Aid Agencies' Exit Means Hardship for Kabul." *Reuters,* 23 July 1998.

Sale, Lady Florentia. *A Journal of the Disasters in Affghanistan, 1841–1842.* London: John Murray, 1843.

Shahrani, M. Nazif. "The Future of the State and the Structure of Community Governance in Afghanistan." In William Maley, ed., *Fundamentalism Reborn? Afghanistan and the Taliban.* Washington Square, NY: New York University Press, 1998, 212–242.

Shahrani, M. Nazif, and Robert L. Canfield, eds. *Revolutions and Rebellions in Afghanistan.* Berkeley: University of California, Institute of International Studies, 1984.

"Shame." *Friday Times* (Pakistan), 13–19 August 1999. Found at Afghanistan Online, www.afghan-web.com.

Sierakowska-Dyndo, Jolanta. "The State in Afghanistan's Political and Economic System on the Eve of the April 1978 Coup." *Central Asian Survey* 9, no. 4, 1990, 85–97.

Sikorski, Radek. "Afghanistan Revisited." *National Review,* August 23, 1993, 40–42.

Singer, Andre. *Guardians of the North-West Frontier.* Amsterdam: Time-Life Books, 1982.

Singer, Max, and Aaron Wildavsky. *The Real World Order: Zones of Peace, Zones of Turmoil.* Chatham, NJ: Chatham House, 1993.

Sliwinski, Marek. "Afghanistan: The Decimation of a People." *Orbis* 33, no. 1, 1989, 39–56.

Smith, Vincent A. *The Oxford History of India,* 4th ed. Ed. Percival Spear. Karachi: Oxford University Press, 1983.

Spain, J. W. *The Way of the Pathans.* London: Robert Hale, 1962.

Spanier, John. *American Foreign Policy since World War II,* 12th ed. Washington, DC: Congressional Quarterly, 1991.

Sykes, Sir Percy. *History of Afghanistan,* 2 vols. London: Macmillan, 1940.

"Taleban Say 225 Women Punished for Improper Dress." *Reuters,* 5 December 1996.

"Taliban Arrest Dozens of Alleged Coup Plotters." *AFP,* 23 October 1998.

"Taliban Denounce Mediatory Efforts." *Dawn,* 11 January 1999.

"Taliban Make Bonfire of Hindi Movies." *AFP,* 8 December 1996.

"Taliban Smash Televisions in Kabul." *Associated Press,* 1 August 1998.

"Taliban Tightens Grip on Northern Afghanistan." *AFP,* 11 August 1998.

"The Talibanisation of Chitral." *Frontier Post,* 7 September 1999. Found at Afghanistan Online, www.afghan-web.com.

Tarzi, Shah M. "Afghanistan in 1992." *Asian Survey* 33, no. 2, February 1993, 165–174.

———. "Politics of the Afghan Resistance Movement." *Asian Survey* 31, no. 6, June 1991, 479–495.

Thomas, Christopher. "Lost Forever: A Nation's Heritage Looted by Its Own People." *London Times,* 22 October 1996.

Tilly, Charles. *Coercion, Capital, and European States, A D 990–1990.* Cambridge, MA: Blackwell, 1990.

Todaro, Michael. *Economic Development in the Third World,* 4th ed. London: Longman, 1993.

Tomsen, Peter. "A Chance for Peace in Afghanistan." *Foreign Affairs* 79, no. 1, January–February 2000, 179–182.

"Turkmen Gas Pipe Might Help Afghan Peace." *Reuters,* 6 April 1998.

Twining, David E. *The New Eurasia.* Westport, CT: Praeger, 1993.

"UN: 120 Per Cent Increase in Production of Raw Opium in Afghanistan for

1999." *M2 Communications,* 13 September 1999. Found at Afghanistan Online, www.afghan-web.com.

"UN Chief Urges Afghanistan's Neighbours to Stay Out of Fight." *AFP,* 6 August 1999.

United Nations. *The Geneva Accords: Agreements on the Settlement of the Situation relating to Afghanistan.* New York: UN Department of Public Information, July 1988.

United Nations Children's Fund. "Statistics." At www.unicef.org/statis/, updated 1 December 1999.

United Nations Co-Ordinator for Humanitarian and Economic Assistance Programmes Relating to Afghanistan (UNCHEAP). *First Consolidated Report.* Geneva, September 1988.

United Nations Development Program. *Human Development Report.* New York: Oxford University Press, 1996, 1997.

United Nations General Assembly. *Situation of Human Rights in Afghanistan.* New York: Report of the Economic and Social Council, 31 October 1986.

United Nations General Assembly. *Situation of Human Rights in Afghanistan.* New York: Report of the Economic and Social Council, A/53/539, 26 October 1998.

United Nations High Commissioner for Refugees. *Report on UNHCR Assistance Activities in 1983–84 and Proposed Voluntary Funds, Programmes and Budget for 1985.* Geneva, 1984, 378–391.

United Nations High Commissioner for Refugees. "Fact Sheet: Iran," vol. 2, no. 2, October 1988.

United Nations High Commissioner for Refugees. "Fact Sheet: Pakistan," vol. 2, no. 2, October 1988.

United Nations High Commissioner for Refugees. *Refugees,* various issues, 1986–1999.

United Nations Security Council. *Resolution 1267 on the Situation in Afghanistan.* Adopted 15 October 1999.

_____. *Resolution 1333 on the Situation in Afghanistan.* Adopted 19 December 2000.

United States Committee for Refugees. *World Refugee Survey.* New York: American Council for Nationalities Service, 1981–1999 (annually).

United States Department of State. Special Reports, nos. 86 and 79 (1981), 106 (1982), 112 (1983), 120 (1984), 135 (*Afghanistan: Six Years of Soviet Occupation,* 1985), 155 (1986), and 173 (*Afghanistan: Eight Years of Soviet Occupation,* December 1987). Washington, DC: Bureau of Public Affairs.

United States Department of State. *Afghanistan: Human Rights Practices.* Washington, DC: Bureau of Democracy, Human Rights, and Labor, 1995–1999 (annually).

United States Department of State. *International Narcotics Control Strategy Report*. Washington, DC: Bureau of Public Affairs, 1990–1999 (annually).

Urban, Mark. *War in Afghanistan*. New York: St. Martin's, 1988.

_____. *War in Afghanistan*, 2d ed. New York: St. Martin's, 1991.

USSR Academy of Sciences, Institute of Oriental Studies, Afghanistan Section of the Middle and Near East Department. *Afghanistan: Past and Present*. Moscow: Social Sciences Today, 1981.

Waller, John H. *Beyond the Khyber Pass*. Austin: University of Texas Press, 1990.

Weinbaum, Marvin G. "Pakistan and Afghanistan: The Strategic Relationship." *Asian Survey* 31, no. 6, June 1991, 496–511.

_____. "The Politics of Afghan Resettlement and Rehabilitation." *Asian Survey* 29, no. 3, March 1989, 287–307.

_____. "War and Peace in Afghanistan: The Pakistani Role." *Middle East Journal* 45, no. 1, Winter 1991, 71–85.

Weiner, Myron, and Ali Banuazizi, eds. *The Politics of Social Transformation in Afghanistan, Iran, and Pakistan*. Syracuse, NY: Syracuse University Press, 1994.

Weiner, Tim. "Blowback from the Afghan Battlefield." *New York Times Magazine*, 13 March 1994, 52–55.

_____. "Leaks in Afghan Arms Pipeline Cost CIA Millions." *News and Observer*, 28 February 1988.

Wilber, Donald N. *Afghanistan*, 2d ed. New Haven, CT: Yale University Press, 1962.

Wilkinson, David. "Unipolarity without Hegemony." *International Studies Review* 1, no. 2, Summer 1999, 141–172.

Wimbush, S. Enders, and Alex Alexiev. "Soviet Central Asian Soldiers in Afghanistan." *Conflict* 4, nos. 2–4, 1983, 325–338.

World Bank. *World Development Report*. New York: Oxford University Press, 1980, 1984–1999 (annually).

Wren, Christopher S. "Afghanistan's Opium Output Drops Sharply, UN Survey Shows." *New York Times*, 27 September 1998, 11.

Yousaf, Mohammad. *Silent Soldier: The Man behind the Afghan Jehad*. Lahore, Pakistan: Jang Publishers, 1991.

Yousaf, Mohammad, and Mark Atkin. *The Bear Trap*. Lahore, Pakistan: Jang Publishers, 1992.

Yusufzai, Rahimullah. "Pakistani Taliban at Work." *The News*. December 21, 1998.

Zahid, Mohammed. "Taliban: Ring of Leadership." *Frontier Post*, 24 February 1995.

Zaman, Shah, comp. and ed. *Humanitarian Assistance Programme for Afghan Refugees in North West Frontier Province, Pakistan*. Peshawar, Pakistan: Afghan Refugee Commissionerate, January 1987, December 1985.

Zartman, I. William, ed. *Collapsed States*. Boulder, CO: Lynne Rienner, 1995.

Index